Detroit Monographs in Musicology

* * *

The Operas and Operatic Style

of

John Frederick Lampe

by

Dennis R. Martin

DETROIT MONOGRAPHS IN MUSICOLOGY   NUMBER 8
INFORMATION COORDINATORS   1985   DETROIT

Printed and bound in the United States of America
Published by
Information Coordinators, Inc.
1435-37 Randolph Street
Detroit, Michigan 48226

Editing by J. Bunker Clark
Book design by † Vincent Kibildis, Nicholas Jakubiak
Photocomposition by Joy Hick, Elaine Gorzelski

Library of Congress Cataloging in Publication Data
Martin, Dennis.
   The operas and operatic style of John Frederick Lampe.
   (Detroit monographs in musicology ; no. 8)
   "Lampe's books and treatises, extant operatic music,
and song collections": p.
   Includes index.
   1. Lampe, John Frederick, 1703?-1751. Operas.
2. Opera. I. Title. II. Series.
ML410.L2457M4   1985   782.1'092'4   85-14496
ISBN 0-89990-024-0

50,925

C ONTENTS

PART I
LAMPE'S LIFE AND CAREER

PART II
LAMPE'S MUSICAL STYLE

ILLUSTRATIONS

TABLES

Music Examples

PREFACE

IN THE EARLY EIGHTEENTH CENTURY, London was a major musical center of Europe. The high salaries and excellent musical establishments of the city attracted musical celebrities like Handel and Farinelli, as well as many of their less-renowned countrymen. Among these lesser-known musicians was the young John Frederick Lampe, who came to London in the middle 1720s to play bassoon in Handel's orchestra, and who soon established a considerable reputation throughout the British Isles.

Most studies of foreign musicians in the British capital during the early eighteenth century have dealt with exceptional individuals, such as Handel. Little published material exists, however, concerning Handel's less well-known contemporaries in London, such as Johann Christoph Pepusch, John Christopher Smith, John Frederick Lampe, and Johann Ernst Galliard, or their British counterparts including William Boyce, Maurice Greene, and Henry Carey. Even Thomas Arne, composer of "Rule, Britannia" and perhaps the best-known British musician of the age, is represented in the literature by a mere handful of outdated, Victorian biographies. Roger Fiske's admirable *English Theatre Music of the Eighteenth Century* (London, 1973), one of the few recent works on early eighteenth-century London music not directly related to Handel, unfortunately remains a general study of music and musical trends throughout the entire eighteenth century and includes little about composers' lives or individual musical styles. Such lacunae exist concerning the above men in spite of their having constituted the mainstay of much of London's musical life for more than a quarter of a century.

This study of John Frederick Lampe helps to fill some of these gaps in knowledge about him and his music, as well as provides a better understanding of some of his contemporaries and their works, for Lampe represents the best among the noncelebrity London musicians of his time. Handel esteemed Lampe so highly as a performer that the master commissioned a double bassoon, the first ever seen in Britain, to be built for Lampe to play. Lampe's *The Dragon of Wantley* (1737) became the most successful eighteenth-century English opera ever written in the opera seria style, being performed sixty-nine times during its first season and surpassing the previous record first season-run in London by *The Beggar's Opera* almost a decade earlier. Lampe's other stage works were highly acclaimed as well, so that throughout parts of the 1730s and 1740s one could find as many as three different Lampe works being performed in London theaters during the same week. He became popular as an editor, composer, and compiler of vocal and instrumental collections, and was in demand as a teacher. A scholar as well as a practical musician, Lampe also wrote a treatise on thoroughbass and a book on music aesthetics, both of which gained the respect of his day. Lampe, therefore, enjoyed success in most musical endeavors open to a foreign musician in early eighteenth-century London.

Lampe possessed considerable creative and innovative ability, and produced works that were highly esteemed by his contemporaries. This study proposes to improve understanding of Lampe's music and the music and attitudes of his time, provide a clearer glimpse of some additional and fascinating details in the broad picture of music history, and arouse increased interest in the rich and relatively unknown literature and musicians of eighteenth-century Britain.

This study is divided into two sections: a biographical survey of Lampe's life and career, followed by a detailed investigation of his music and musical style. In the first section, data concerning performance dates and places, performers, and some other comments often are taken from *The London Stage, 1660-1800* (1960-68). This monumental five-part collection includes information on all varieties of London theater, transcribed from newspapers and advertisements, playbills, diaries, journals, pamphlets, and other original sources of the time. In the following pages, when no other source is given for a performance date, a performer, or such, the information is from *The London Stage*, although whenever possible items have been checked against the original sources. Analogous collections exist for the Dublin and Edinburgh theaters, where Lampe also was active, and these works have been utilized in a similar manner; they are Esther K. Sheldon's *Thomas Sheridan of Smock-Alley . . . Including a Smock-Alley Calendar for Years of His Management* (1967) and James Dibdin's *The Annals of the Edinburgh Stage* (1888). Additional information of the same sort, often taken from sources now lost and thus of considerable supplementary value, appears in Allardyce Nicoll's *A History of Early Eighteenth Century Drama* (1925), and especially in John Genest's great ten-volume *Some Account of the English Stage* (1832), herein abbreviated as Nicoll and Genest.

The musical section of this study has relied almost totally on extant original sources of Lampe's music, since none of his works exist in modern published editions. Thus, numerous music examples have been included both to illustrate Lampe's particular techniques and to contrast them with those of his contemporaries. Those works of other composers mentioned usually are available in modern editions.

Many friends and colleagues have generously given their help during the course of this project. Professors Albert T. Luper, Sven H. Hansell, Frederick B. Crane, Walter T. Atcherson, Robert W. Eckert, and David S. Chamberlain of the University of Iowa read parts of this study as a dissertation, long before a book was imagined, and offered valuable suggestions. The late Dr. Rita Benton and Dr. Avery T. Sharp of the University of Iowa Music Library, Professor Ardis C. Sawyer of the Minnesota Bible College Library, and others helped me obtain photocopies and microfilms from many European and American libraries, without which my work would have been impossible and for which I am most grateful. I have enjoyed corresponding with Stanley Sadie, Roger Fiske, and Watkins Shaw in Great Britain, and appreciate their many valuable comments and their encouragement. Dr. Helmut Rösing of the RISM manuscript cataloging project in Kassel was kind enough to send me photocopies of their Lampe manuscript file, which greatly expedited my locating copies of Lampe's music. Dr. Manfred R. W. Garzmann of the Braunschweig Stadtarchiv und Stadtbibliothek, Dr. Rudolf Meier of the Niedersächsische Staatarchiv in Wolfenbüttel, and Herr Rolf Volkmann, Leiter der Ehemalige Universitätsbibliothek, Helmstedt, all graciously assisted me and answered numerous questions concerning their collections, which I was unable to visit personally. Finally, I must thank my wife, Mary, who typed the entire manuscript several times, who is to a large extent responsible for its neatness and accuracy, and who patiently suffered and unfailingly encouraged throughout it all.

DENNIS R. MARTIN

Minnesota Bible College
Rochester
December 1981

PART I LAMPE'S LIFE AND CAREER

Early Life and Brunswick

Although John Frederick Lampe and his music were well known in Great Britain during the mid-eighteenth century, few facts are available concerning his early life. According to the epitaph on his tombstone, he was born in late 1702 or early 1703 and died on July 25, 1751, in Edinburgh. The exact date and place of his birth, however, remain unknown.[1] Because the title page of Lampe's thoroughbass treatise states that he was "Sometime Student at HELMSTAD in SAXONY," some scholars have speculated that he was born in Helmstedt, but no records of his birth exist in Helmstedt churches or archives.[2] Burney, who probably knew Lampe, and Hawkins both state that Lampe was Saxon, and they apparently are the earliest sources to mention the general geographic area of his birth.[3] Neither author offers any other facts concerning Lampe's origin, however, nor their sources of information, and the terms "Saxon" or "Saxony" are, unfortunately, far from precise. Having been applied at various times to widely differing peoples, areas, duchies, electorates, kingdoms, provinces, and states, the words "Saxony" or "Saxon" seem to have been used by eighteenth-century Englishmen as general expressions for anything in, from, or related to central Germany. Even Lampe, a native of the area, followed such a practice when writing in Britain for British readers, since Helmstedt, which he characterizes on his thoroughbass treatise title page as being in "Saxony," actually was part of the duchy of Brunswick-Wolfenbüttel.

Another city in "Saxony," or rather Brunswick-Wolfenbüttel, with which Lampe was associated is the duchy's capital city of Brunswick, about twenty miles west of Helmstedt. It seems that there was once "a record that connects him with St. Catherine's School, Brunswick," but regrettably all records from the school were destroyed during World War II, so that the exact nature or time of his relationship with the school remain uncertain.[4] As was the case with Helmstedt, no church registries or civic archives exist in Brunswick that can prove Lampe was born in that city, although since he seems to have lived in or near

---

[1] Lampe's approximate birthdate has been calculated from his tombstone, which states that he died "in the forty-eighth year of his age." The entire tombstone epitaph is quoted in Chapter 5 below.

[2] See, e.g., David Fraser Harris, *Saint Cecilia's Hall in the Niddry Wynd* (Edinburgh & London: Oliphant, Anderson, & Ferrier, 1899), 265; and James Love, *Scottish Church Music: Its Composers and Sources* (Edinburgh & London: William Blackwood & Sons, 1891), 188-89.

[3] Charles Burney, *A General History of Music* (London, 1776-89), new ed. in 2 vols. with critical and historical notes by Frank Mercer (New York: Harcourt, 1935; reprint, New York: Dover, 1957), 2:1001; Sir John Hawkins, *A General History of the Science and Practice of Music* (London, 1776), reprint of the 1853 Novello ed. in 2 vols. with a new introduction by Charles Cudworth (New York: Dover, 1963), 2:828, 895.

[4] The document is mentioned in the articles on Lampe in both *Grove's*, 5th ed. (but, unexplicably, not in *New Grove*) and *Die Musik in Geschichte und Gegenwart*, which unfortunately tell nothing of its contents. Dr. Manfred R. W. Garzmann and the staff of the Braunschweig Stadtbibliothek und Stadtarchiv graciously assisted me in my work by answering questions about this particular document, the Brunswick schools and churches, and Lampes in Brunswick. My comments concerning Brunswick civic records and archives are based on information supplied by them.

Helmstedt and Brunswick until about 1720, he likely was born and grew up in their vicinity. Possibly he was christened in a small country church nearby, or the records of his birth have been lost or destroyed during the intervening centuries, wars, and natural catastrophes.

As with the exact date and place of his birth, it also is impossible to determine anything certain about Lampe's family or parents. His later study of law at the famous university in Helmstedt implies that he would have come from among the upper middle class or even the lower nobility, and easily could have been the son of a Lutheran pastor.[5] The name Lampe had been an important one among German Protestant theologians for generations, and Lampes had been closely associated with the churches and cloisters in and around Brunswick since the Middle Ages.[6] Extant records contain several Lampes of approximately the right age to have been Johann Friedrich's father, but unfortunately no family relationship between J. F. Lampe and any of them can be documented.

In spite of so few facts being available about Lampe, it nevertheless is possible to reconstruct and provide a good picture of much of his early life and education. His later proficiency in performance, composition, and music theory suggests that his musical education began quite early. Not known to have come from a famous musical family as did the Bachs, or to have studied with a distinguished teacher as Handel did with Zachow, Lampe probably received his early musical education at one of the many church and cathedral schools in Germany. St. Catherine's School of Brunswick is the most plausible site, in light of Lampe's known connection with the institution. It is quite unlikely that Lampe's relationship with St. Catherine's would have been that of a teacher, for a law graduate seldom even briefly entered the public teaching profession, which in many places in the eighteenth century hardly qualified as a profession at all. On the other hand, Lampe's having studied the exceptionally broad humanistic curriculum of St. Catherine's, with its much greater emphasis on music than the public Latin schools of the time, would help to explain many of his later skills and interests.

The school of St. Catherine was part of a long educational and musical tradition in Brunswick. Schools had been affiliated with the Brunswick churches and cloister from at least the twelfth century, and music was an important area of study, with many of the school boys expected to play and sing at services in return for free room and board.[7] Composition for the Brunswick churches also flourished quite early, and by the beginning of the fourteenth century music and drama were being combined in liturgical dramas, possibly involving the children. St. Catherine's School, along with another in Brunswick, St. Martin's, was given a charter by the Council of Constance in 1415, and the institution opened its doors in 1419. Music remained a significant part of the boys' studies, and included both theoretical and practical instruction as well as public performances. The two schools and Brunswick grew to be respected centers of learning in the Renaissance, and with such musicians as Auctor Lampadius, Michael Praetorius, and Heinrich Schütz in residence, Brunswick's proud musical

---

5 Walter Horace Bruford, *Germany in the Eighteenth Century* (Cambridge: Cambridge University Press, 1935), 247-48, 260-61.

6 Hermann Dürre, *Geschichte der Stadt Braunschweig im Mittelalter* (Braunschweig: Grüneberg, 1861), 517ff.; Christian Gottlieb Jöcher, *Allgemeines Gelehrten-Lexicon*, Supplement, 6 vols. (Leipzig: Johann Friedrich Gleditschen, 1784-87; Delmenhorst: Georg Jönssen, 1810-13; Bremen: Johann Georg Hense, 1816-19), 3:1118-21; Carl Hessenmüller, *Heinrich Lampe, der erste evangelische Prediger in der Stadt Braunschweig* (Braunschweig: Fr. Otto, 1852).

7 Richard Elster, ed., *Gymnasium Martino-Katharineum Braunschweig: Festschrift zur 500-Jahr-feier am 17. und 18. März 1926* (Braunschweig: Friedr. Vieweg & Sohn, 1929), 2-3; hereafter designated as *Braunschweig Festschrift*. Heinrich Sievers, "Braunschweig," *Die Musik in Geschichte und Gegenwart*, vol. 2, col. 229.

tradition continued into the Baroque. As a member of St. Catherine's School and a resident of Brunswick, Lampe would have shared in this rich musical heritage, which helped to shape his future, even while he may have been preparing for a nonmusical career.

In Lampe's day the students of St. Catherine received a broad liberal arts education, which included Greek, Latin, French, Italian, and English, as well as history, geography, mathematics, science, and sometimes even art and dancing, in addition to a continued emphasis on music. Such a humanistic variety of subjects was quite uncommon in German secondary schools of the time, where students studied mostly Latin grammar and rhetoric, a little Greek, and perhaps a bit of mathematics, philosophy, or logic. Modern languages or historical and scientific disciplines hardly ever were considered. In his later treatise *The Art of Music* (1740), however, Lampe demonstrates a good reading knowledge of all the modern languages named above, as well as considerable preoccupation with the history of theory, mathematics, science, and philosophy, which significantly strengthens the case for his having studied at St. Catherine's.

The early eighteenth-century musical instruction at St. Catherine resembled that of the more familiar St. Thomas in Leipzig, although unfortunately there was no Bach serving as cantor. The boys were taught to sing, read, and if they showed some aptitude, to play keyboard and other instruments. A possible incentive would have been St. Catherine Church's fine 26-rank organ built by Gottfried Fritzsche in 1621-23. As the boys grew older and more proficient, they would have assisted in accompanying, copying, rehearsing, arranging, performing, and even composing. Nor were their performances confined to the churches. Brunswick was the capital city, with the ducal residence in Wolfenbüttel, a few miles to the south, and civic musicians and others often were called upon to assist with music on special court occasions.

Perhaps more interesting, in light of Lampe's later activity, were the so-called *actus oratorii dramatici* of St. Catherine's, which by the eighteenth century had replaced the earlier Latin *Schuldramen*.[8] Often written entirely by the boys of the school, who also were the performers, these sacred and secular vernacular works frequently included considerable music. The musical plays enjoyed substantial popularity, not only in Brunswick but also at the Wolfenbüttel court, where they frequently were performed. Lampe's first contact with combined music and drama likely occurred through these school plays, and like Telemann at nearby Hildesheim, Lampe probably composed his first dramatic music for them. Even greater opportunities existed, however, for becoming acquainted with more sophisticated music and drama in the new Brunswick opera house.

The Brunswick opera house had opened in 1690 and soon grew into one of the important operatic centers of Germany. For the first half of the eighteenth century the house was dominated by the composer Georg Caspar Schürmann, Kapellmeister at the court of Brunswick-Wolfenbüttel and mentor of J. A. Hasse, C. H. Graun, and others.[9] Lampe must have been familiar with Schürmann's works, for the imprint of many of Schürmann's personal and exceptional techniques on Lampe's later operatic style is often quite striking in his libretto subjects, use of ensembles and choruses, treatment of arias, choice of the vernacular for his texts, and in many other areas. Such a stylistic resemblance cannot be merely coincidental, for many of the traits involved were uncommon in most other German operatic centers of the time, such as Vienna, Dresden, Munich, Düsseldorf, and Bonn, where Italian serious opera

---

[8] *Braunschweig Festschrift,* 34.

[9] The most thorough discussion of Schürmann and his music is in Gustave Friedrich Schmidt, *Die frühdeutsche Oper und die musikdramatische Kunst Georg Casper Schürmanns,* 2 vols. (Regensburg: Gustav Bosse, 1933).

dominated and where young German composers like C. H. Graun became Italianate out of necessity. Lampe's acquaintance with Schürmann's music, whether only as a listener or occasionally as a performer, certainly proved providential and fortunate, however, for it provided some of the best elements of Lampe's personal and distinctive dramatic musical style of the future.

Helmstedt and After

After completing his education at Brunswick, Lampe journeyed to nearby Helmstedt to enroll in the famous university there, and a May 2, 1718, entry in the university records lists "Johannes Fridericus Lampe, Brunsvicensis," among newly matriculating students.[10] The Helmstedt university had been founded in 1576 by Duke Julius of Brunswick-Wolfenbüttel as one of the earliest institutions established to help train leaders for Protestant Reformation Germany. The school was organized into the four faculties of theology, law, medicine, and philosophy (or arts), according to educational traditions dating back to the Middle Ages, and it grew rapidly.[11] By the early seventeenth century, the Helmstedt university had become widely known as a leading institution in free thinking, with it and its faculty being responsible for advances in medicine, chemistry, and German law, and with law becoming especially important. In spite of the fact that Brunswick was a major battlefield during the Thirty Years War, by 1624 — in the middle of the conflict — the enrollment at Helmstedt had reached the then unheard of total of 2000 students,[12] and as early as the middle of the seventeenth century the university's library had become famous, containing many rare prints and manuscripts now in the Herzog August Bibliothek in Wolfenbüttel. The second half of the seventeenth century and the beginning of the eighteenth was the greatest period for the university, when it developed a considerable reputation as a center for the study of Roman and natural law and expanded its curriculum in many directions, including such luxuries as a Professor of Oriental Languages.

The German universities began to suffer from hard times during the middle and later eighteenth century, and frequently were criticized for their archaic curricula and teaching methods and their lack of contact with the real problems of society. An especially difficult blow for Helmstedt was the founding in 1737 of the University of Göttingen, with a curriculum based on new educational theories and tailored to contemporary interests. Göttingen soon usurped Helmstedt's position as the leading university in central Germany, and the older university's fortunes gradually deteriorated until it, like a number of other German universities

---

[10] I wish to thank Dr. Rudolf Meier of the Niedersächsische Staatarchiv, Wolfenbüttel, for kind and willing assistance in locating Lampe's matriculation date and answering other questions concerning Lampe and Helmstedt University. At my request Dr. Meier and staff searched their entire archive file of extant Helmstedt University material, but found no other surviving documents that mentioned Lampe. The matriculation data also is included in *Die Matrikel der Universität Helmstedt 1685-1810*, ed. Herbert Mundhenke, Veröffentlichungen der Historische Kommission für Niedersachsen und Bremen IX, Abt. 1, Bd. III (Hildesheim, 1979), p. 113, no. 4822. Of particular interest, especially in light of the lack of concrete information about Lampe's birthplace and early education, is the inclusion of "Brunsvicensis" in his entry. Mundhenke explains in his preface (p. ix) that such city names are "not always identical with the birthplace" of the matriculant, but "also can signify the father's place of residence at the time of matriculation." Nevertheless, the entry provides significant additional evidence supporting the likelihood of Lampe's early education in Brunswick, and of his birth in or near the city.

[11] The original university charter and statutes have been edited, with introduction and commentary, as *Die Statuten der Universität Helmstedt 1685-1810*, ed. Peter Baumgart and Ernst Pitz (Göttingen: Vanderhoeck & Ruprecht, 1963).

[12] Richard Graf du Moulin-Eckard, *Geschichte der deutschen Universitäten* (Stuttgart: Ferdinand Enke, 1929), 228.

Engraving of Helmstedt University, which Lampe attended. From vol. I of Zacharias Konrad von Uffenbach's *Mehrwurdige Reisen durch Niedersachsen, Holland, und Engelland.* 3 vols. (Frankfurt and Leipzig, 1753).

of its time, was finally closed by an edict of 1810. When Lampe attended Helmstedt, however, near the beginning of the eighteenth century, the decline had not yet begun, and the institution, its faculty, and its students were still at their height of prestige.

In the early eighteenth century young men went to German universities to prepare for the professions in one of the "higher" faculties of law, theology, or medicine; the "lower" faculty of philosophy or arts served merely a preparatory function. A student entered the university at about the age of fifteen, and after two or three semesters studying Latin and Greek grammar, dialectic and rhetoric, basic mathematics, foundations of astronomy, and world history, he took an examination for the baccalaureate degree in arts. He then could proceed into the two-year program in ethics, geometry, astronomy, physics, and Aristotelian philosophy, which led to the Master of (Liberal) Arts degree. If a student completed the lower-level courses, he could progress into one of the three "higher" faculties for specialized study, although students of exceptional educational background sometimes were permitted to enter the higher faculties directly, or with only brief study in the arts.[13] Such seems to have been the case with Lampe, since the printed edition of his law dissertation is dated March 1720, less than two years after he had entered the university.

It may be noted that most of the above subjects mentioned as being in the lower-level curriculum were members of the traditional medieval trivium and quadrivium, with their emphasis on Latin, dialectic, and Aristotle, although music, an important element of the quadrivium, apparently was absent. According to university statutes music was supposed to

---

[13] Bruford, *Germany,* 239-40.

be taught at Helmstedt as part of the arts program,[14] but the university never had a chair nor offered an emphasis in the area, which makes Hawkins's assertion that Lampe went to Helmstedt to study music highly questionable.[15] It should not be thought, however, that Helmstedt and its university were entirely devoid of musical opportunities. University students under the direction of a cantor participated in church festivals and other celebrations, and from 1717, about the time Lampe entered, there was a collegium musicum.[16] Also, Brunswick and Wolfenbüttel, with their churches, court, opera, and Lampe's previous musical acquaintances, each were only about twenty miles away, so that he easily could have been involved in the musical life of all three cities while pursuing his university education. Apparently, though, Lampe went to Helmstedt solely intending to study law and having little if any thought of music as a career.

Most students in the higher faculties of German eighteenth-century universities were studying either law or theology. Law was the more important and prestigious of the two, partly because its students usually came from the better classes of society and were preparing for lucrative positions as government civil servants. The theological students generally were from the lower middle class and peasantry and planned to enter the Lutheran ministry, not always an especially rewarding occupation financially nor one that carried the highest social standing.[17] Thus, Lampe's entrance into the juristic faculty may be seen as an attempt to move up in the world and better his lot in life. Young men of such inclination constituted the majority of university students in early eighteenth-century Germany, and academic historians sometimes describe them as:

> . . . the subclass of "movers and doers," those who left the fixed place in life guaranteed and decreed by the German towns to join the comparatively "rootless" class of professionals, civil or ecclesiastical, who belonged to another world wherever they lived. Rather than being fixed in the carefully heirarchical world of the German towns and cities, this branch of the bourgeoisie placed itself at the disposal of the expanding professions and, above all, the new territorial bureaucratic states. In training, language, clothing, life expectations, life-style, and function, the academic "bourgeoisie" was far removed from the traditional world of the German *Bürger*, as the frequent clashes between urban "philistines" and university students or professors might indicate.[18]

Lampe continued to be a "mover and doer" throughout his life, and his desire to better his position likely prompted his leaving Lower Saxony, his journey to London, his various theatrical and musical enterprises, and his eventual leaving London in search of new opportunities.

Helmstedt boasted a fine and ancient reputation in law. The law faculty members were the best faculty at the school and the law students were the best students—and some of the

---

14 Baumgart and Pitz, *Statuten,* 42-43.

15 Hawkins, *History,* 2:895.

16 Heinrich Sievers, "Helmstedt," *Die Musik in Geschichte und Gegenwart,* vol. 6, col. 133; Arthur Behse, "Das Collegium musicum an der Helmstedter Universität," *Zeitschrift Alt-Helmstedt* 1 (1915): 10.

17 Bruford, *Germany,* 247-48.

18 Charles E. McClelland, *State, Society, and University in Germany 1700-1914* (Cambridge: Cambridge University Press, 1980), 32.

proudest. Because of their generally high birth status and their preparation for influential and lucrative public positions, the law students frequently imitated court manners, dress, and affectations, and even wore swords. The curriculum they sought to master was based on a thorough understanding of Roman law, plus more modern German practices in personal and contract law, heredity and succession, civil suits and similar actions, and trial and feudal law.[19] All teaching was done in Latin, the living language of scholarship and law until the end of the eighteenth century, and the students were expected to use it solely in discussion, debate, and declamation. The final requirement for graduation was the preparation of a thesis or dissertation followed by a public debate upon its contents, where the candidate had to defend his thesis and respond to questions from students and faculty alike. Such dissertations usually were printed, and copies of Lampe's "Dissertatio Academica" still exist.[20]

Lampe's dissertation, *De jure augustissimae et augustae domus Brunsvicensis in comitatum peinensem* (The Criminal Court of the Most Esteemed Court of Justice and Noble House of Brunswick), is a historical study of the Brunswick penal system, and a work of considerable scholarship for an eighteen-year old, having numerous footnotes, lengthy quotations, and careful organization (see pages 10-11). The defense of the thesis took place in March 1720, and was presided over by Johann Wilhelm Goebel, the Dean of the Law Faculty and a respected jurist. Goebel had been appointed to the Law Faculty at Helmstedt in 1717, possibly at the suggestion of his friend Leibnitz whom he had assisted in preparing the edition of *Scriptores rerum Brunsvicensium* (3 vols., 1707-11) and other works. Goebel spent the rest of his life on the Helmstedt faculty, serving as Dean of the Law Faculty and Rector, and publishing numerous treatises of his own. Like many professors of his time, Goebel also remained involved in court and civic affairs while continuing to teach. In 1727 he became the supervisor of the Helmstedt prison system, and in 1720 was named by Duke August Wilhelm of Brunswick as a Counselor at Court and Assistant Judge of the Brunswick Court of Justice. Also in 1730 Emperor Charles VI elevated Goebel to the nobility.[21]

Additional positions, such as those held by Goebel, were necessary for eighteenth-century professors not only because the jobs provided needed additional income — university teaching being then as now often poorly remunerated — but also because such offices established the connections and prestige essential in obtaining the best possible posts for one's students. Famous professors often were asked to recommend students for positions, and trained jurists were in great demand in eighteenth-century Germany. The political ideal of benevolent despotism necessitated a burgeoning bureaucracy that exceeded almost anything imaginable today. Besides the three hundred independent German "territories," there were five times as many semi-independent fiefs, counties, manors, and estates, each with its own set of officials to collect taxes, maintain order, dispense justice, and serve as counselors, treasurers, recorders, and so forth. And if a graduate, either legal or theological, could not find a position immediately after leaving the university, he could become a private tutor with a well-to-do family for a few years in order to make a living. Many famous men of the eighteenth and

---

19 Baumgart and Pitz, *Statuten*, 36, 104-105.

20 U. S. copies can be found in the Harvard and Yale Law Libraries.

21 *Allgemeine deutsche Biographie*, 56 vols. (Bayern: Königl. Akademie der Wissenschaft, 1875-1912; reprint, Berlin: Dunker & Humblot, 1967-71), s.v. "Göbel, Johann Wilhelm von"; Christian Gottlieb Jöcher, *Allgemeines Gelehrten-Lexicon*, 4 vols. (Leipzig: Johann Friedrich Gleditschen, 1750-51), s.v. "Goebel, Johann Wilhelm"; *Biographie universelle*, ed. Machaud, 45 vols. (Paris: Desplaces, 1843-65), s.v. "Goebel, Jean-Guillaume de"; *Nouvelle biographie generale*, ed. Hoefer, 46 vols. (Paris: Didot Frères, 1853-66; reprint, Copenhagen: Rosenkilde & Bagger, 1963-69), s.v. "Goebel, Jean-Guillaume de."

Title page of Lampe's dissertation, written at Helmstedt University, 1720.

DISSERTATIO ACADEMICA

DE

JVRE AVGVSTISSIMÆ ET AVGVSTÆ DOMVS BRVNSVICENSIS

IN COMITATVM PEINENSEM

PRÆSIDE

JO. WILHELMO GOEBEL

J. V. D. EJVSDEMQVE IN REGIO-DVCALI
JVLIA P. P. O.

PVBLICE ERVDITORVM DISQVISITIONI
SVBMITTET

A. ET R.

IOHANNES FRIDERICVS LAMPE

BRVNSVICENSIS.

AD DIEM   MARTII MDCCXX.

HELMSTADII,
TYPIS HERMANNI DANIELIS HAMMII,
ACAD. TYPOGR.

CAPVT I.

DE COMITATV ET COMITIBVS
PEINENSIBVS.

§. I.

Germania in varios olim pagos id est tractus, (a) quorum alii majores, alii minores erant, distinguebatur. Varii eorum compilarunt catalogos, (b) qui

A 2   tamen

(a) *Marculfus formul. lib, 1. c. 8. p. 380. apud Baluzium. Bignonius ad c. 28. formul. Marculfi p. 916. apud Baluzium. Lindenbrogus, Spelmannus & du Cange in gloss. in vocabul. pagus. Meib. sub initium tract. de pagis veteris Saxoniæ Lehmanni chronic. Spirense. p. 72.*

(b) *Marquard. Freherus in origin: palat. c. 5. p. 57. seq. Meibom. t. 3. Rer. Germ. p. 96. seq. Paulinē Syntagm. Rer. Germ. p. 2. p. 574. seq. Vid. Autor. vitæ Meinwerci & Scriptores R. Brunsvic. passim: Winckelmanni notitia Histor. Politica veteris Westph. lib. 2. p. 256. seq.*

nineteenth centuries served as tutors, at least briefly, among them Jean Paul, Kant, Hölderin, Hegel, and Schleiermacher.

Thus, after concluding his studies in law at Helmstedt, two possibilities would have been open to Lampe: to seek a civil service position, and if that effort failed to try to obtain employment for a time as a private tutor. In either case, he likely returned to Brunswick, where both he and Goebel had some connections and friends, and which, as the capital and nearest large city, would have offered the most opportunity of employment.

The life of a civil servant, although attractive and potentially quite profitable, however, was not always an especially easy one in eighteenth-century Germany. The petty rulers often treated their officials with a complete lack of consideration and respect, and constantly interfered in their personal lives. Corruption ran rampant, and positions were bought and sold as a matter of course. A young man fresh out of the university, if he were fortunate enough to find a job, frequently would have to work for a year or two with little or no salary. Only by personally ingratiating himself to the local potentate or through actual dishonesty could he generally hope for much advancement. Lucrative positions certainly existed, but they often remained out of reach of many aspirants. It goes without saying that in such a system security or tenure of office was an ideal virtually unknown.[22]

Whether Lampe found a minor appointment as a court or civic official, or whether he supported himself by tutoring or some other means, his new life seems to have been less than he had hoped. Perhaps his honest and serious character recoiled from the fawning unscrupulousness of much of court life, perhaps the legendary financial rewards of government service failed to meet his expectations, or he may have found his work unappealing and uninteresting. As he became less satisfied with government service, Lampe's interest in music, formerly an avocation, apparently increased. He likely had continued performing some through his university years, and additional performance opportunities would have awaited him upon his return to Brunswick. As a government official or fellow musician, he may have met Schürmann, in the service of the Brunswick court as Kapellmeister, and the two may even have worked together. At first Lampe probably had no thought of abandoning a legal career for music, only of enjoying music as a hobby or perhaps of combining music and government work. As time passed, however, he likely became aware of and attracted to unique opportunities that existed nearby, where careers incorporating both music and civil service were not only considered but were practiced and encouraged. Thus it seems almost certain that within a few short years after graduating from Helmstedt, Lampe left his homeland of central Germany forever to seek his fortune in one of Germany's greatest free cities: the *Hansastadt* of Hamburg.

Hamburg

Hamburg was a city of considerable musical and political importance in the early eighteenth century. As one of the chief ports of northern Europe, it commanded much of the commerce to and from northern and central Germany, and with the accession of the house of Hanover to the British throne it became a vital and strategic communications link between England and the German interior. Its rapid economic and political growth during the seventeenth century had resulted in a cosmopolitan and extravagant atmosphere in which the

---

[22] Bruford, *Germany*, 262-65.

arts came to be regarded highly. Both sacred and secular music flourished, creating a musical reputation that drew such musicians as Handel, Telemann, Keiser, and Mattheson to the city.[23] Mattheson serves as a good example of the frequent mixing of politics and music in Hamburg. Although he is known to musicians as a composer, theorist, and writer, his major occupation was chief secretary to the British envoy of the city. Nor was he alone in combining politics and music, for even the nobility exercised their amateur musical talents in composition and performance. For example, Sir Cyril Wich, the British Envoy and Mattheson's employer, contributed seven arias of his own to a performance of Handel's *Tamerlano* at the Hamburg opera, September 27, 1725.[24]

Lampe likely would have found such possibilities of blending government service and music appealing. Also, he could not have been insensitive to the fact that the free cities of Germany generally did not demean or meddle with the lives of their civil servants as did the petty princedoms, and that such cities frequently awarded important positions to men of merit and knowledge, not merely to those of high birth. In addition, as Lampe's interests in opera increased, the famous Hamburg opera, the oldest opera house in Germany, would have become more attractive.

The Hamburg and Brunswick operas had many similarities and several direct connections. The famous Hamburg operatic composers Johann S. Kusser and Reinhart Keiser and the great scenographer Johann Oswald Harms all had worked in Brunswick before coming to Hamburg. Schürmann's works were much admired in Hamburg as well, and from the summer of 1719 through the fall of 1722 at least twelve productions of Schürmann operas appeared in Hamburg's Goosemarket Theater, involving over a hundred performances.[25] Perhaps Lampe first became aware of the opportunities of Hamburg during this period of Schürmann's popularity there, and he may have taken advantage of Schürmann's success and acquaintances to gain some introductions or maybe even a position in the *Hansastadt*. Mattheson, a leader in the opera house, seems often to have been willing to befriend young musicians, and the fact that Lampe also was a jurist would have been additional recommendation.

In any case, Lampe almost certainly passed through Hamburg sometime on his way to London. As mentioned above, Hamburg provided the most direct route from central Germany to the sea, and hence to Britain. Also, experience at Hamburg best explains Lampe's acquaintance with Handel and his music, which seems to have been the main reason for Lampe's going to London. Handel's operas seldom were seen in Brunswick or the German interior, but they were so popular in Hamburg during the early 1720s that one may justifiably speak of that time as a Handel period at the Goosemarket Theater.[26] The Hamburg opera of the 1720s, in fact, had many British connections. Sir Cyril Wich, the British Envoy and Mattheson's employer, was the proprietor of the house, and another of his secretaries, Thomas Lediard, became its director and manager about 1724. Lediard, a British career diplomat, also designed scenery, wrote and translated librettos (among which was the first German

---

[23] Also among the musicians attracted by the opportunities of Hamburg in the 1720s was J. S. Bach, who applied for the position of organist at St. James's Church, but decided not to accept it, possibly because the successful applicant seems to have been expected to make a sizeable contribution to the church treasury.

[24] Otto Erich Deutsch, *Handel, A Documentary Biography* (New York: Norton, 1955), 187.

[25] Schmidt, *Frühdeutsche Oper*, 1:136-63.

[26] Mattheson, in his article on Handel in the *Ehren-Pforte* (Hamburg: Mattheson, 1740), 93-101, lists all of Handel's operas performed in Hamburg.

translation of Handel's *Giulio Cesare*), and prepared masque-like productions for the opera house. Lediard's work is especially interesting because after leaving Hamburg he wrote a similar masque-like production for London in 1732—and asked Lampe to compose the music for it! Lediard's choosing the virtually unknown Lampe over many other famous London composers can best, and perhaps only, be explained by the two men having met and perhaps even worked together in Hamburg.[27] Such an acquaintance easily could have occurred, either through musical or governmental circles, and Lediard, Mattheson, and others may have assisted Lampe in his decision to begin preparations for travel to London. Sir Cyril Wich, because of his position and family, certainly would have had some influence with the noble sponsors of the Opera of the Nobility, with his relatives and Handel's close friends the Granvilles, and possibly even with Handel himself, who had been Wich's harpsichord teacher. Thus Wich could have, perhaps at the suggestion of his secretaries Mattheson and Lediard, helped Lampe gain a position in the opera house orchestra in London, just as Wich's father probably had aided Handel in his first venture to the British capital.[28]

The case for Lampe having spent time in Hamburg would be incomplete without mention of musical corroboration, for many elements of Lampe's operas such as the presence of the double da capo and strophic variation forms, the variety and kinds of overture forms, and some elements of orchestration, also point to Hamburg influence. Hamburg's operas received only occasional performances outside the city, and such productions were mostly pasticcio adaptations and were too infrequent to account for the resemblances between Hamburg operatic style and Lampe's music. Moreover, the techniques involved were uncommon or unknown elsewhere in Germany, so that, like his knowledge of Handel, Lampe's familiarity with Hamburg operatic styles and techniques almost certainly implies direct and personal contact with the opera there.

It seems, then, that as a boy Lampe probably attended St. Catherine's School in Brunswick, where he received his earliest training in music, languages, and the arts. After earning his degree from the nearby Helmstedt university in 1720, he likely sought a civil service position in or around Brunswick, the area's capital. Gradually, however, he grew disenchanted with the possibilities of a government career and was attracted more and more toward music, especially opera. He became familiar with the music and musical styles of the opera houses of Brunswick and Hamburg, elements of which would appear later in his own operatic works, and he probably met one of his future librettists, Thomas Lediard. By 1725 Lampe had become sufficiently confident of his ability and future as a musician to leave Germany, again the "mover and doer," for the opportunities of London and the prospect of working under and learning from the great master George Frideric Handel.

London and Harry Carey

In the 1720s London was a musical Mecca of Europe. Musicians flocked to the city from all over the continent, attracted by the varied and numerous musical opportunities available, the higher-than-average salaries, the prospects of performing in Handel's renowned

---

[27] Lediard and his works are discussed in detail in a series of articles in the *Theatre Notebook* 2 (April-June 1948), and in Dennis R. Martin, "*Eine Collection curieuser Vorstellungen* (1730) and Thomas Lediard, an Early Eighteenth-Century Scenographer," *Current Musicology* 26 (1978): 83-98.

[28] For information on Sir John Wick's possible role in Handel's decision to go to London, see Paul Henry Lang, *George Frideric Handel* (New York: Norton, 1966), 32, 37, 110-11.

Lampe's close friend and librettist Henry Carey. Engraving from the 1853 Novello edition of Sir John Hawkins'
A General History of the Science and Practice of Music (London, 1776).

orchestra, or the chance to work with, study from, or simply see the master himself. Perhaps all of these thoughts influenced Lampe's decision to seek his fortune in the British capital. Whatever the reason, by the mid-1720s Lampe could be found playing bassoon for Handel in London's King's Theatre. And it was in the London theater that the young musician was to spend most of the rest of his life.

Burney and Hawkins are the earliest known sources for the date of Lampe's arrival in London. Hawkins says "about the year 1725," and Burney gives "about the year 1726."[29] Lampe certainly was in London by early 1726, however, and probably before, for in that year a poem dedicated to him was written by a popular London playwright and theater musician, Henry (Harry) Carey.[30] Carey included the quatrain in his *Poems on Several Occasions* (1729), in a section containing poems about outstanding London musicians. The Lampe poem also appeared as part of Carey's dedication in the libretto of Lampe's *The Dragon of Wantley* (1737), which dates the verse as being from 1726. The 1729 published version of the poem is as follows:

---

[29] Hawkins, *History*, 2:895; Burney, *History*, 2:1001.

[30] Three good dissertations exist on Henry (Harry) Carey (1687-1743): Henry James Dane, "The Life and Works of Henry Carey" (Ph.D. dissertation, English Literature, University of Pennsylvania, 1967); Edward Leonard Oldfield, "The Achievement of Henry Carey (1687-1743)" (Ph.D. dissertation, English Literature, University of Washington, 1969); and Jack Trevithick, "The Dramatic Work of Henry Carey" (Ph.D. dissertation, Yale University, 1939). A born humorist and ardent patriot, Carey used his wit and pen in poetry, plays, and music to champion British authors, British theater, and British music. Although more significant as a writer than a musician, by the 1720s Carey was in demand as a teacher, playwright, and theater composer, with a number of successful songs, plays, and poems to his credit. Carey seems to have become Lampe's closest friend in London and probably was of considerable influence on the young composer.

To

My Studious FRIEND

Mr. *John-Frederick Lamp*

Call not my LAMP obscure, because unknown,
He shines in secret (now) to Friends alone;
Light him but up! let him in publick blaze,
He will delight not only but amaze.[31]

The *Dragon* version of the poem uses the correct spelling "Lampe," as do all other known occurrences of the composer's name; Carey's spelling is interesting, however, since the pun possibly implies that Lampe's name took on an English pronunciation in London. Lampe and Carey must already have been more than mere acquaintances in 1726 for such a verse to have been written then, since the tone of Carey's poem on Lampe suggests a close personal relationship between the poet and his subject, much closer than between Carey and the other men eulogized in the musicians' section of his *Poems on Several Occasions*. Lampe also is the only one of the musicians in the anthology described by Carey as being his friend, although at the time Lampe was by far the least well-known of the group, which included Handel, Pepusch, and others.

Perhaps Lampe and Carey had met at the opera house, where Lampe played in the orchestra and where Carey frequently went to admire Handel's music and to enjoy the company of other musicians. Lampe and Carey could have been attracted by their similar interests in opera, song, and theater music, and judging from their many subsequent collaborations the two soon became fast friends. Carey admired the younger man's talent so much that, according to Hawkins, he studied with Lampe for a time;[32] but Carey, in his turn, likely reciprocated by aiding the young German in finding students and his first opportunities for composition and publication.

Soon after his arrival in London, Lampe also began to attract the attention of other musicians beside Carey. By 1727 Handel's respect for Lampe's ability was such that the master had a contrabassoon, the first ever seen in the British Isles, built for Lampe to play for the coronation of George II. The instrument was used in the Handel commemoration festival almost sixty years later, and both the bassoon and Lampe's connection with it were described in Burney's account of the concerts:

The DOUBLE BASSOON, which was so conspicuous in the Orchestra and powerful in its effect, is likewise a tube of sixteen feet. It was made with the approbation of Mr. Handel, by Stainsby, the Flute-maker, for the coronation of his late majesty, George the Second. The late ingenious Mr. Lampe, author of the justly admired Music of *The Dragon of Wantley*, was the person intended to perform on it; but, for want of a proper reed, or for some other cause, at present unknown, no use was

---

[31] Henry Carey, *Poems on Several Occasions*, 3rd ed. (London: E. Say, 1729), 115.

[32] Hawkins, *History*, 2:895.

made of it, at the time; nor, indeed, though it has often been attempted, was it ever introduced into any band in England, till now, by the ingenuity and perseverance of Mr. Ashly, of the guards.[33]

Whether the contrabassoon was or was not performed in George II's coronation celebration is uncertain. Burney is the only source to mention it, but since Burney did not come to London until 1744, his information on earlier events is second-hand. At any rate, Handel wrote for the double bassoon again in *L'Allegro* (1740), and it is unlikely that he would have taken the time to write a part for an instrument that he knew would not be played. Probably Lampe, for whom the bassoon had been built, also was the performer in 1740, since no one else is known to have played the instrument until the Handel commemoration concerts, decades later.[34]

During the late 1720s Lampe's reputation as a performer, teacher, and composer seems to have grown. Hawkins states that about 1730 Lampe went to work for John Rich at Covent Garden as a composer of pantomime music. But since Covent Garden did not open until 1732, when Lampe is known to have been at the Little Haymarket Theatre, there is no reason to connect Lampe with Rich or with Covent Garden before 1737, when *The Dragon* was first performed there. More likely, Lampe began his theater composing at Drury Lane, where Carey was a popular and successful pantomime composer and could have recommended his young friend's work. Lampe's first known theater music certainly was perfomed at Drury Lane, not in Covent Garden or in Rich's previous theater, Lincoln's Inn Fields.

Earliest Theater Music and Publications

The earliest theater compositions definitely attributable to Lampe are pantomimes, which like Lampe's operas and most ballad operas, generally were programmed as "afterpieces" in the London playhouses. A typical evening's program consisted of a half-hour instrumental concert, usually involving three short concertos, overtures, or early symphonies; the "mainpiece," a spoken drama, comedy or tragedy, of three to five acts; an "afterpiece," often musical; plus entr'actes of singing, dancing, and other entertainments. The entire evening's program could last from 6:00 or 6:30 until 10:00.[35]

Lampe's pantomimes were members of a genre unique in theater history.[36] The British pantomime of the eighteenth century was much less closely related to the old *commedia dell'arte* than were the pantomime traditions of other countries, even though some of the characters

---

[33] Charles Burney, *An Account of the Musical Performances in Westminster-Abbey, and the Pantheon, May 26th, 27th, 29th; and June the 3d, and 5th, 1784. In Commemoration of Handel* (London: The Musical Fund, 1785), Introduction, 7.

[34] Other descriptions of the double bassoon used in the Handel commemoration are in Abraham Rees, *The Cyclopaedia; or, Universal Dictionary of Arts, Sciences and Literature . . . First American Ed.*, 41 vols. and 6 vols. of plates (Philadelphia: Robert Carr, 1810-17?), s.v. "Solo"; and William T. Parke, *Musical Memoirs*, 2 vols. (London: H. Colburn & R. Bentley, 1830), 1:42.

[35] *The London Stage, 1660-1800*, 5 parts (Carbondale: Southern Illinois University Press, 1960-68), 3:clvii, clxxxi-clxxxiv; Mary F. Klinger, "Music and Theater in Hogarth," *Musical Quarterly* 57 (July 1971): 409-10; Roger Fiske, *English Theatre Music in the Eighteenth Century* (London: Oxford University Press, 1973), 259-60.

[36] More information on pantomime can be found in the following works: Fiske, *English Theatre Music*, 67-93, 160-69; R. J. Broadbent, *A History of Pantomime* (London: Simkin, Marshall, Kent, & Co., 1901); Albert Edward

had similar names. The genre was extremely popular, with London audiences flocking to the playhouses to see the pantomime spectacles, which generally included fantastically elaborate scenery, magic tricks, and rather coarse humor. Serious authors, on the other hand, condemned the frivolous form as lessening the dignity of the stage and interest in serious drama (their own works). Fielding, one such injured author, described pantomimes in his *Tom Jones* (1749):

> This Entertainment consisted of two Parts, which the Inventor distinguished by the Names of *the Serious* and *the Comic.* The *Serious* exhibited a certain Number of Heathen Gods and Heroes, who were certainly the worst and dullest Company into which an Audience was ever introduced; and (which was a Secret known to few) were actually intended so to be, in order to contrast the *Comic* Part of the Entertainment, and to display the Tricks of Harlequin to the better Advantage.
>
> This was, perhaps, no very civil Use of such Personages; but the Contrivance was nevertheless ingenious enough, and had its Effect. And this will now plainly appear, if instead of *Serious* and *Comic,* we supply the Words *Duller* and *Dullest*; for the *Comic* was certainly duller than anything before shewn on the Stage, and could be set off only by that superlative Degree of Dulness, which composed the *Serious.* So intolerably serious, indeed, were these Gods and Heroes, that Harlequin (tho' the *English* Gentleman of that Name is not at all related to the *French* Family, for he is of a much more serious Disposition) was always welcome on the Stage, as he relieved the Audience from worse Company.[37]

In such a work, music played an inconspicuous role, being relegated to dance and background accompaniments and simple songs. An entrepreneur, therefore, could have been persuaded to trust the writing of such elementary music to a young and untried composer, such as Lampe. Although the task might not have been an inspiring one for the musician, it at least would have provided the opportunity to compose some theater music for public performance and would have helped to make his works and talents known.

Diana and Acteon, Lampe's earliest known theater work and a pantomime, was performed on April 23, 1730, for the benefit night of one Mons. Roger, who had written the libretto and choreographed the work. Neither music nor text survives. Roger was dancing master at Drury Lane at least during the 1729-30 season and possibly other times as well.[38] He also may have had some connection with Carey, since he and Carey shared a benefit at Drury Lane on May 21, 1730. Allardyce Nicoll lists Lampe as the composer of *Diana and Acteon*,[39] although his name does not seem to have appeared in any contemporary advertisements. The absence is not extraordinary, however, for composers of pantomimes

---

Wilson, *King Panto, the Story of Pantomime* (New York: E. P. Dutton, 1935); Maurice Sand, *The History of the Harlequinade*, 2 vols. (Philadelphia: J. B. Lippincott, 1915); T. Earl Pardoe, *Pantomimes for Stage and Study* (New York: D. Appleton-Century, 1931); Winifred Smith, *The Commedia dell'arte* (New York: Columbia University Press, 1912); David Mayer III, *Harlequin in His Element* (Cambridge, Mass.: Harvard University Press, 1969); Allardyce Nicoll, *The World of Harlequin* (Cambridge: Cambridge University Press, 1963). Good eighteenth-century descriptions of the genre are to be found in Alois M. Nagler, *A Source Book in Theatrical History* (New York: Dover, 1959), 344-51.

[37] Henry Fielding, *The History of Tom Jones*, Wesleyan Edition of the Works of Henry Fielding, introduction and commentary by Martin C. Battestein, ed. Fredson Bowers (Oxford: Clarendon Press, 1974), 213-14.

[38] *The London Stage*, 3:clxxix.

[39] Allardyce Nicoll, *A History of Early Eighteenth Century Drama* (Cambridge: Cambridge University Press, 1925), 370.

often were not listed in newspapers, and thus Lampe could have written other early pantomime scores for Drury Lane as well.

Diana and Acteon was performed only once at Drury Lane, and probably was a special production for Roger's benefit night. Two performances of a work having the same title were given at Goodman's Fields in April and May of 1734, but it is uncertain whether Lampe or Roger were connected with the productions. An additional performance of a *Diana and Acteon* is listed in Nicoll (but not in *The London Stage*) as having occurred in September 1746 at N. W. Clerkenwell, but again any relationship between it and Lampe remains speculative. All in all, Lampe appears to have had little enduring interest in pantomimes, and seems rather to have preferred the greater musical opportunities of operas and plays. *Diana and Acteon* remains significant, however, as Lampe's first attempt at writing for the theater.

In 1731 Lampe's *Wit Musically Embellish'd*, an anthology of forty original English ballads, was published; the earliest advertisement mentioning the collection seems to be in the *Grub Street Journal* of August 5. Besides being the first of his music to appear in print, the work provides some indication of Lampe's expanding professional activity as a teacher and composer during the late 1720s, when he was still playing bassoon for Handel and just beginning to become involved writing theater music. In his preface to the collection, Lampe relates that most of the songs had been written for his patrons and students, many of whom are listed as subscribers. The subscriber list includes diplomats, government officials, nobility, gentlemen and ladies, actors, authors, and musicians, who form an impressive cross section of London's artistic community, and with whom Lampe had, it appears, gained sufficient recognition and favor to warrant a publication of his works. Lampe's preface also defends ballads and his writing of them against critics who "will despise them merely upon Account of the Name they are distinguished by." His language and reasoning are similar to that of Carey's prefaces to his *Six Songs for Conversations* (1728) and *Six Ballads on the Humors of the Town* (1728), as well as to Mattheson's *Der vollkommene Capellmeister,*[40] thus indicating two possible sources of influence on Lampe's ballad writing.

The publication of his first works also marks the end of his student period and the beginning of his life as a composer. Having studied the scores of the best masters available, as he stated later in *The Art of Musick,*[41] his experiences in the opera houses of London, and perhaps Brunswick and Hamburg as well, solidified his musical style and proficiency. In London he had become respected as a performer and teacher and had made impressive attempts at composition. He was ready to try his hand at a major operatic work, and he soon found the opportunity, as part of an elaborate effort at an English opera revival.

---

[40] Henry Carey, *Six Songs for Conversation* (London, 1728), and *Six Ballads on the Humours of the Town* (London, 1728); Johann Mattheson, *Der vollkommene Capellmeister* (Hamburg: Christian Herold, 1739), 73.

[41] John Frederick Lampe, *The Art of Musick* (London: C. Corbett, 1740), 17.

CHAPTER 2
THE EARLY OPERAS

The English Opera Revival and the Question of Lampe's Piracy

The years of 1732 and 1733 were notable in the history of English opera, for during them there was an attempt by Lampe, Carey, Thomas Arne, Jr., J. C. Smith, Jr., and others to establish a strong, English, serious opera, such as had not existed since the time of Purcell. Lampe's earliest operas were written for this English opera revival, which included eight different works (listed in Table 2, page 88), and he participated in the project in a number of other ways as well. Carey, the oldest and most experienced member of the group and already a popular theater composer, was possibly the project's leader and organizer.

The aim of the English opera company seems not so much to have been to break with opera seria as to anglicize it, by producing new operas written in English for English performers but retaining Italian forms and styles. Carey, ever the ardent patriot, admired Handel's music greatly, but despised the vain and greedy Italian musicians, who often were rumored to have returned home carrying chests of gold after a few years in London while British musicians starved. Carey's sentiments, at least in milder tones, were common among many London artists, so that the efforts of the English opera company often fell upon sympathetic ears, and likely inspired Aaron Hill's famous letter of December 5, 1732, to Handel on English vernacular opera:

> Having this occasion of troubling you with a letter, I cannot forbear to tell you the earnestness of my wishes, that as you have made such considerable steps towards it, already, you would let us owe to your inimitable genius, the establishment of *musick*, upon a foundation of good poetry; where the excellence of the *sound* should be no longer dishonour'd, by the poorness of the *sense* it is chain'd to.
>
> My meaning is, that you would be resolute enough, to deliver us from our *Italian bondage*; and demonstrate, that *English* is soft enough for Opera, when compos'd by poets, who know how to distinguish the *sweetness* of our tongue, from the *strength* of it, where the last is less necessary.
>
> I am of opinion, that male and female voices may be found in this kingdom, capable of every thing, that is requisite; and, I am sure, a species of dramatic Opera might be invented, that, by reconciling reason and dignity, with musick and fine machinery, would charm the *ear*, and hold fast the *heart*, together.
>
> Such an improvement must, at once, be lasting, and profitable, to a very great degree; and would, infallibly, attract an universal regard, and encouragement.
>
> I am so much a stranger to the nature of your present engagements, that, if what I have said, should not happen to be so practicable, as I conceive it, you will have the goodness to impute it only to the zeal, with which I wish to at the head of a design, as solid, and unperishable, as your musick and memory. . . .[1]

---

[1] Otto Erich Deutsch, *Handel: A Documentary Biography* (New York: Norton, 1955), 299.

Hill's opinion must have been of some interest to Handel, since Hill had written the libretto for Handel's first London opera, *Rinaldo* (1711). Handel's reply to Hill's letter, if any, is unknown. Handel certainly did not switch immediately to composing English opera, although the success of the English opera company and other circumstances seem to have encouraged his interest in oratorios.

The first offering of the English opera revival and Lampe's first known operatic collaboration with Carey was entitled *Amelia*, and the work was quite well received. In a day when half a dozen performances of a new play or Handel opera were thought to constitute a rousing success, *Amelia* was presented on four subscription nights as well as six additional evenings, plus twice the following year. The libretto was published in 1732 and was included in Carey's *Dramatick Works* (1743), but two printed arias are all of the music that survive.[2] In subject and form Carey's story resembles the heroic operas made popular by Handel in the 1720s and 1730s, and Lampe's music demonstrates a thorough understanding of the Italian style and conventions. Advertisements described the work as "A New English Opera (after the Italian Method)." The cast were all new British singers, and presumably Lampe followed the custom of conducting his work from the harpsichord.

About three weeks after the final performance of *Amelia* the English opera company presented Handel's *Acis and Galatea*, a work he had written more than ten years before for the Duke of Chandos's palace at Cannons, and the only work of the English opera revival not composed by a member of the English opera company. Because Lampe and the English opera company twice performed Handel's *Acis*, and Handel revived the work in a revised format about a month later, writers sometimes have suggested that the English company stole the work from Handel for a pirate performance and that Handel's own production was a retaliatory blow intended to crush his adversaries.[3] In spite of the fact that piracy of composers' and authors' works by both unscrupulous performers and publishers was not uncommon in eighteenth-century London (Carey especially had suffered from such treatment),[4] there is almost no evidence to support the theory that Lampe and the English opera company "stole" Handel's work, and actually much evidence to suggest the contrary.

Many of the members of the English opera company were Handel's friends and associates. Lampe had been and possibly continued to be his bassoonist and student; J. C. Smith, Jr. was Handel's student and his musical assistant and amanuensis when the master's sight failed. Two of the company's performers, Susanna Arne (the future Mrs. Cibber) and Gustave Waltz, came to be among Handel's favorite singers, and Waltz also may be remembered as Handel's "cook" in the probably apocryphal anecdote concerning Gluck's counterpoint.[5] Carey had great respect for Handel, and Handel subscribed to some of Carey's publications, although nothing is known of their personal relationship. If these individuals of the English opera company had "stolen" from Handel, the later close and apparently friendly

---

2 Two broadside prints are the only surviving music of *Amelia*: Casimir's "Ah, traitress! wicked and impure" and Amelia's "Amelia wishes when she dies." There is no reason to believe that any more of the opera ever was printed.

3 See Herbert Weinstock, *Handel* (New York: Alfred A. Knopf, 1946), 165; Paul Henry Lang, *George Frideric Handel* (New York: Norton, 1966), 240.

4 For an example see Henry Carey's preface to his *The Musical Century*, 2 vols. (London: Carey, 1737-40, facsimile ed., New York: Broude Brothers, 1976); also the preface to the Gilliver ed. of Carey's *The Honest Yorkshireman* (London: L. Gilliver, 1736; facsimile ed., New York: Garland, 1974).

5 An interesting and informative discussion of the question of Waltz's "cookship" may be found in William C. Smith, *Concerning Handel* (London: Cassel, 1948), chapter 6, 165-94, "Gustavus Waltz: Was He Handel's Cook?"

relationship between many of them and the great composer becomes difficult to explain.

Accounting for the source of the music used for the English opera company performances also is problematic when one relies on the piracy theory. William C. Smith points out that since the only available published score of *Acis* did not include the choruses, "some of the music must have been obtained from manuscripts probably in Handel's possession."[6] It seems unlikely that Handel's young friends and employees would have stolen the score from him—for fear of reprisal, if for no other reason—and a much more believable theory is that Handel allowed them to use a work for which he, then occupied with Italian opera, had no use at the time.

Other points and authors add to the confusion surrounding the *Acis* performances. Burney writes:

> It seems as if the elder Arne, the Upholsterer, in King's-Street, Covent-garden, mentioned in the Spectator, and father of Dr. Arne and Mrs. Cibber, had been the principal projector and manager of these performances of Handel's compositions to English words; as it is said in one of the advertisements, that subscriptions for English operas "are only taken in by *Mr. Arne*, at the Crown and Cushion, King's Street, Covent-garden." J. C. Smith, J. F. Lampe, and Harry Carey, as well as his son young Arne, were adventurers in this undertaking; and Miss Arne and Miss Cecilia Young, afterwards Mrs. Arne, were the principal female singers.[7]

Since Thomas Arne, Sr. is not known to have had any sort of relationship with Handel, and hence no reason to fear either artistic reprisal or loss of friendship and employment, it has been argued that he, as the leader of the English group, could have instigated the piracy with impunity.

An examination of the London newspaper advertisements for the company's *Acis* and for their earlier productions of Lampe's *Amelia*, however, seems to indicate that Burney is mistaken in the quotation he relates and in his subsequent inferences from it. The newspapers never include Arne senior's name, but rather list the source of the *Acis* tickets as a Mr. Fribourg, "Maker of Rappee Snuff, at the Playhouse Gate,"[8] who likely was one of the financial backers of the project. The earlier *Amelia* advertisements give Fribourg and Carey as ticket salesmen.[9] The first mention of Arne senior's name instead of Fribourg's is in the advertisements for Thomas Arne, Jr.'s production of J. C. Smith's *Teraminta* at Lincoln's Inn Fields during the following November, a performance which the elder Arne probably did sponsor. Other errors also exist in the Burney passage; e.g., the Arne mentioned in *The Spectator* actually was Dr. Arne's grandfather, not his father.

The evidence, therefore, fails to support the theory of a pirate conspiracy by Lampe and his friends, and the explanation that Handel allowed them to perform *Acis* is more plausible. In 1732 Handel was still firmly committed to and very successful in Italian opera, and he had little concern or use for his earlier English works which his Italian singers could

---

6 Smith, *Handel*, 215.

7 Charles Burney, *A General History of Music* (London, 1776-89), new ed. in 2 vols. with critical and historical notes by Frank Mercer (New York: Harcourt, 1935; reprint, New York: Dover, 1957), 2:776.

8 *The Daily Post*, May 17, 1732.

9 See, e.g., *The Daily Post*, February 26, 1732.

not perform.[10] Perhaps the general interest in and good support for the English opera company's vernacular productions, including *Acis*, and public enthusiasm for a similar work, *Esther*, presented by Handel and others a few months earlier, prompted Handel to capitalize on the new musical tastes through his own revival of *Acis*. Although Handel undeniably rewrote *Acis* for his presentation, perhaps to accommodate his Italian singers whose English pronunciation in *Esther* had been ridiculed,[11] there exists no evidence that he felt any ill will toward anyone in the English opera company. In fact, Lampe could have continued to perform in Handel's orchestra throughout 1732-33, since only once was there a performance of a Lampe opera on the same night as a Handel work.

The Later English Opera Revival

By late 1732 Lampe seems to have been in charge of the enterprise at the Little Theatre, as he possibly had been from the beginning, for throughout the English opera revival, with the exception of Handel's *Acis and Galatea*, the Little Theatre performed only Lampe operas. In contrast, the operas of Smith and Arne were given solely at Lincoln's Inn Fields. Carey's works were performed at both theaters.

Lampe's first new work for the 1732-33 season was *Britannia*, with a libretto by Thomas Lediard, a British diplomat who had served as director and scenographer of the Hamburg opera house during the 1720s. Since *Britannia* was to be the first presentation of their first full season, and Lediard's first production in London, Lampe and the English opera company seem to have worked to make the event as impressive as possible. The Little Theatre was completely redecorated, and Lediard devised elaborate transparent scenery, his personal scenographic innovation which he intended to introduce to the London public. A lavish libretto was prepared, with a large, folding, engraved frontispiece depicting Lediard's opening set (see pages 24-25), and including a long prefatory explanation of the techniques and symbolism involved. *Britannia* was presented in a public rehearsal on November 14, 1732 and later in four subscription performances. Reviews praised both Lampe and Cecilia Young, who had replaced Susanna Arne as the company's principal female singer.[12]

Britannia is unlike any other Lampe opera, for it is more similar to the elaborate, allegorical, and masque-like operatic prologues and epilogues that Lediard had produced for Hamburg's Goosemarket Theater than it is to Italian and English works. *Britannia's* lavish libretto, with its large folding plate of the scenery and its detailed commentary, also resembled Hamburg practices, as did the great number of mythological characters, the classical and allegorical elements in the transparent scenery, and the plot glorifying the king and the state.[13]

---

[10] *Giulio Cesare* had just enjoyed a successful revival and a new opera, *Sosarme*, was quite popular. Viscount Percival wrote in his diary that the work "takes with the town, and that justly, for it is one of the best I ever heard." Quoted in Deutsch, *Handel*, 285; see the preceding pages of Deutsch for information on Handel's *Ezio* and the revival of *Giulio Cesare*.

[11] For the history of the *Esther* revivals, see Winton Dean, *Handel's Dramatic Oratorios and Masques* (London: Oxford University Press, 1959), 203-07; see also Deutsch, *Handel*, 300-01, for a pamphlet describing the oratorio performances and the English opera.

[12] See *The Daily Post*, November 15, 1732. Fribourg also was listed in newspaper advertisements as the sole ticket agent for this production; see, e.g., *The Daily Advertiser*, November 14, 1732.

[13] The preface and plate of Thomas Lediard's *Britannia, an English Opera* libretto (London: J. Watts, 1732) might be compared with the descriptions and pictures in his *Eine Collection curieuser Vorstellungen* (Hamburg: Philipp

Plate from *Britannia* libretto, showing Thomas Lediard's lavish scenery, constructed especially for the event.

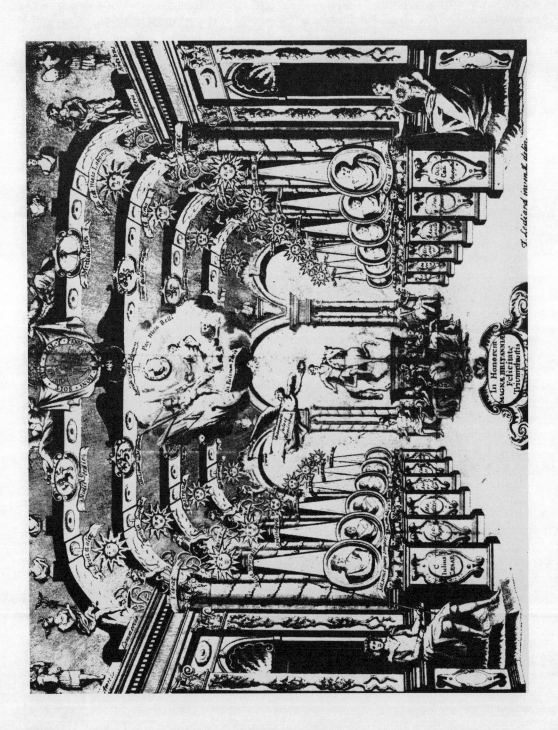

Title page of libretto of *Britannia*, 1732.

BRITANNIA

AN

ENGLISH OPERA.

As it is Perform'd at the

NEW THEATRE

IN THE

HAY-MARKET.

With the Repreſentation and Deſcription of a

TRANSPARENT THEATRE,

Illuminated, and adorn'd with a great Number of *Emblems*, *Mottoes*, *Devices* and *Inſcriptions*, and embelliſh'd with Machines, in a manner entirely *New*.

By Mr. *LEDIARD*.

Late Secretary to His MAJESTY's Envoy Extraordinary in *Hamburg*, and many Years Director of the ſamous Opera Houſe in that City.

First Edition

The Muſick compos'd after the *Italian* Manner,

By Mr. *LAMPE*.

LONDON,

Printed for J. WATTS at the Printing-Office in *Wild-Court* near *Lincoln's-Inn Fields*. MDCCXXXII.

[Price One Shilling and Six Pence.]

Britannia failed to meet the tastes of the London public, however, and although it enjoyed four performances, a moderate success for its day, it was never revived. Lampe never wrote another similar work, and he and Lediard did not collaborate again. Perhaps Lediard was disappointed that his efforts had not attracted as much interest and support from the nobility as had been hoped. At any rate, *Britannia* seems to have been Lediard's last connection with the stage, and he spent the rest of his life in London occupied as an author, architect, and jurist.

Lampe did not forget *Britannia*, however. He reworked one aria, "Furies of Orcus," for inclusion in *The Dragon of Wantley*, one of his few examples of borrowing and an indication of his own high opinion of *Britannia*'s music. Ten arias from the opera, along with arias from Lampe's *Dione*, exist in full score in a manuscript in the British Library, copied by John Christopher Smith.[14] The manuscript rearranges the order of the arias to produce shortened versions of the operas, and the collection appears to have been prepared for concerts by Cecilia Young and her sister Isabella. An advertisement for an August 10, 1734 concert by Cecilia Young and others includes "Welcome, Mars," a *Britannia* aria, as well as arias by Handel and other composers. Perhaps the shortened versions of the operas were sung with a narrator assisting in the story; no recitatives are included in the manuscript.

Less is known about Lampe's next opera, *Dione*, which received three performances at the Little Theatre, the first on February 23, 1733.[15] During December 1732, *Amelia* had been revived for two performances, and Cecilia Young had sung the part of Amelia, earlier played by Miss Arne. Although a libretto of *Dione* was printed,[16] no copy seems to have survived. The only performer known is Cecilia Young, listed in the advertisements in *The Daily Advertiser* of February 26 and 27 and March 14 and 16 as singing Dione. Someone, possibly Carey, reworked Gay's earlier five-act tragedy of the same title, shortening it, creating arias and recitatives, and perhaps adding a *lieto fine*, in order to produce Lampe's libretto. Gay's plot had been based on the Marcella tale in *Don Quixote* and presumably Lampe's opera retained it, although one cannot really tell from the eight *Dione* arias contained in the partial manuscript score mentioned above, none of which contain any of Gay's text. The music of some of the pieces however, can be both moving and beautiful, and works such as Dione's death aria "Cease complaining" foreshadow the great dramatic sensitivity that helped to make *The Dragon* and other of Lampe's later operas so successful.

Sometime before November 1732, a split seems to have occurred in the English opera company, with some members of the group leaving Lampe and the Little Theatre to set up their own operation at Lincoln's Inn Fields, recently deserted by its owner, John Rich, for his new building at Covent Garden. Thomas Arne, Jr. appears to have been one of the leaders of the splinter group, and from Burney to the present many writers have spoken of a strong rivalry between Lampe and Arne.[17] The rivalry theory has little foundation, however, for

---

Ludwig Stromer, 1730), discussed with reproductions of plates and text in Dennis R. Martin, *"Eine Collection curieuser Vorstellungen* (1730) and Thomas Lediard, An Early Eighteenth-Century Operatic Scenographer," *Current Musicology* 26 (1978): 83-98.

14 *GB* Lbm Add. MS 39816; *Britannia* is on ff. 1-45v. and *Dione* on ff. 46-79v.

15 Again Fribourg was the sole ticket agent; see *The Daily Advertiser*, February 21, 22, 23, 1733.

16 Allardyce Nicoll, *A History of Early Eighteenth Century Drama* (Cambridge: Cambridge University Press, 1925), 370; David Erskine Baker, *Biographia Dramatica; or, A Companion to the Playhouse*, 3rd ed. in 3 vols., ed. Isaac Reed and Stephen Jones (London: Longman, Hurst, Rees, Orme, Brown, 1812), 2:163; H. J. Eldredge, *The Stage Cyclopaedia* (London, "The Stage," 1909; facsimile reprint, New York: Lenox Hill, 1970), 114.

17 See, e.g., Phillip Lord, "The English-Italian Opera Companies 1732-33," *Music & Letters* 45 (July 1964): 239-51; Burney, *History*, 2:1001.

Folios 1 and 46 from British Library Add. Ms. 39816, which contains arias from Lampe's *Britannia*, 1732, and *Dione*, 1733. The two pages show the beginning of the arias "Happy Britain, darling state," *Britannia*, and "Fly me, Love, thou headstrong boy," *Dione*. Ms. probably dates from 1733-34, copied by Lampe's friend John Christopher Smith, better known as Handel's amanuensis late in life.

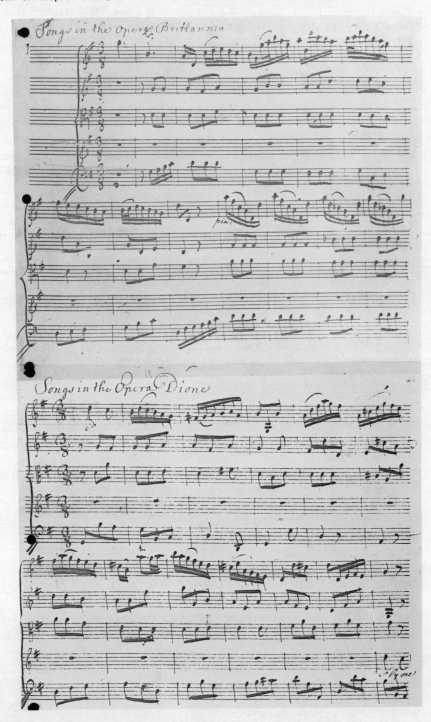

throughout their careers Lampe and Arne often seem to have worked together. They married sisters (Cecilia and Isabella Young), and after Lampe's death Arne not only appears to have cared for Lampe's widow but assisted in the posthumous publication of his works. Rather than strong rivalry between the two young men, the split more likely resulted from Arne's ambitious father's desire to show off his talented children, to try his own hand as an impresario, and to cash in on the potential theater profits. Burney lends credence to this alternative theory when he declares that the impetus for Arne's first opera, *Rosamond*, was the success of Lampe's *Amelia* and of his sister, Susanna Arne, as Lampe's leading lady.[18]

The first production of the new company was not an opera by Arne, however, but *Teraminta*, with music by John Christopher Smith and libretto by Harry Carey. Performed three times, *Teraminta* was the first work of the English opera revival to name the senior Arne as ticket agent, and therefore the first work of either group with which a financial connection to the Arnes can be documented. *Teraminta*, because of it being by Smith and Carey, casts further doubt on the rivalry theory, at least for this production, since there is never any evidence of bad feelings between Lampe and either Smith or Carey. Smith possibly presented his opera in Lincoln's Inn Fields with Arne so that the work could be performed sooner than might have been possible at the Little Theatre (*Teraminta* ran simultaneously with Lampe's *Britannia*) or to take advantage of a larger house.[19] Whether Carey was involved with the actual production of *Teraminta* is unknown.

The splinter company's next opera and young Arne's first and only complete operatic contribution to the English opera revival was not ready for almost four more months. *Rosamond*, first performed on March 7, 1733, was a moderate success that earned seven performances, but only one song, "Was ever a nymph like Rosamond," survived for long after the work's first short season. The advertisements for *Rosamond* are the first of any in the English opera revival to mention Thomas Arne, Jr., so that this work possibly marks his first real involvement with the opera revival. The elder Arne was again listed as the sole ticket agent outside the theater.

The last English opera company production at Lincoln's Inn Fields was a single performance of Smith's *Ulysses*, given on April 16, 1733. The libretto had come from Samuel Humphreys, better known as the librettist of Handel's oratorios *Deborah* and *Athalia* as well as of several Handel opera librettos and translations. Members of Lampe's company, such as Waltz and Cecilia Young, sang, and Lampe may have participated. The reason his company performed at Lincoln's Inn Fields rather than at the Little Theatre, however, remains a mystery. Nothing exists to connect any of the Arnes with this production.

The Opera of Operas *and the End of the Opera Revival*

The final offering of the English opera revival was *The Opera of Operas*, which like other works of the opera revival has sometimes been surrounded by confusion. Burney writes:

Having succeeded so well in a serious opera [*Rosamond*], our young musician [Arne] tried his powers at a burletta, and fixed upon Fielding's *Tom Thumb* for that

---

[18] Burney, *History*, 2:1001-02.

[19] According to *The London Stage, 1660-1800*, 5 parts (Carbondale: Southern Illinois University Press, 1960-68), 3:clxi, the Little Theatre held about 800 people, while Lincoln's Inn Fields could seat 1400.

purpose, which under the title of the *Tragedy of Tragedies* having met with great success, in 1731, he now got it transformed into the *Opera of Operas*, and setting it to Music, "after the Italian manner," had it performed May 31st, at the new theatre in the Hay-market; the part of Tom Thumb by Master Arne, his brother.[20]

There are indications, however, that Burney's account, probably based on information from his teacher Arne, may again be inaccurate. *The Opera of Operas* was produced at Lampe's theater, not Arne's, and most of the performers were either members of Lampe's company or were new singers. Of the thirteen roles, only two were sung by members of Arne's group, Master Arne (his brother) and a Miss Jones. Susanna Arne did not sing. If Arne had written the original version of *The Opera of Operas*, he almost certainly would have used his own singers, and especially would have included an important part for his sister, as he had in *Rosamond*.

Neither the name of Thomas Arne, Jr. nor his father is ever mentioned in advertisements or contemporary accounts of performances of *The Opera of Operas*; instead, notices carried the phrase "Places to be taken and tickets to be had at Mr. Fribourg's, Maker of Rappee-Snuff under the theatre,"[21] the Fribourg who had sponsored and sold tickets for *Amelia*, *Acis and Galatea*, and all other previous Lampe productions. As far as can be determined, Fribourg never had any connection with the Arnes, who always were sole ticket salesmen for their own productions.

Much of the music of *The Opera of Operas* was published by Benjamin Cole in a continuo-vocal score entitled *The Most Celebrated Aires in the Opera of Tom Thumb*, printed about 1733. Although the print lists no composer on its title page, it gives the names of both the character and singer for each aria, and the cast exactly matches that of the original Little Theatre version of *The Opera of Operas*. One known Arne setting of an *Opera of Operas* song text exists. "In that dear hope" appears in *The British Musical Miscellany*, vol. 3, with the heading "A SONG set by Mr. Arne," but this setting is much different from the setting of the same text in the Cole publication mentioned above. Stylistically the Cole version of this song and others is more consistent with Lampe's writing than with Arne's, especially in terms of melodic and phrase structure, harmonic technique and vocabulary, and text setting. From the published evidence, then, it appears that the original version of *The Opera of Operas* almost certainly was by Lampe, and Arne's connection with it, if any, was slight.[22]

The original version of *The Opera of Operas* enjoyed eleven performances its first season, the most successful first season of any offering of the entire English opera revival. It was attended night after night by ambassadors, princesses, dukes, earls, and other royalty, and contemporary newspapers tell of the "vast Concourse of the Nobility and Gentry" in the audience.[23] The production probably would have continued even longer, but the heat of the

---

[20] Burney, *History*, 2:1002.

[21] See *The Daily Post* and *The Daily Advertiser* of May 29, 30, and 31, 1733.

[22] Julian Herbage, "The Vocal Style of Thomas Augustine Arne," *Proceedings of the Royal Musical Association* 78 (1951-52): 83-96; see also Stephen Thomas Farish, Jr., "The Vauxhall Songs of Thomas Augustine Arne" (D.M.A. thesis, University of Illinois, 1962).

[23] See *The Daily Advertiser* of June 5, 7, 9, and 12, 1733, for listings of members of the nobility present and other descriptions of the "vast concourse." The issue of June 7, 1733 is the source of the above quotation. See also John Percival Egmont, *Diary of Viscount Percival, Afterwards First Earl of Egmont*, 3 vols. (London: H. M. Stationery Office, 1920-23), 1:384.

summer finally forced performances to stop,[24] and ended the English opera revival.

Although the work of Lampe and the English opera revival frequently is dismissed in modern sources or categorized as a failure (*The London Stage* calls it "an immediate failure"[25]), the venture actually did achieve many of its goals. A number of new works of both substantial literary and musical quality were produced. A group of new English vocalists, including Gustave Waltz, Susanna Arne (the future Mrs. Cibber), Cecilia Young (the future Mrs. Arne), and others all made their debuts and went on to become famous singers in oratorios and opera. The English opera revival also demonstrated that English opera could pay its own way, while its Italian counterpart failed financially again and again, even though heavily subsidized. Also, the circumstances surrounding the performance of Handel's *Acis* suggest that the success of Lampe's group may have helped to encourage Handel to begin to explore the possibilities of oratorio.

Lampe emerges as the major figure of the English opera revival and as being largely responsible for the early and enduring prosperity of the endeavor. The only one of the composers and librettists to remain at the Little Theatre throughout the opera revival,[26] he was by far the most prolific and successful member of the company. Of the ten new operatic works presented in all London theaters from March 1732 through May 1733, four were by Lampe, one by Handel, two by Smith, one by Arne, and two were anonymous ballad operas. Of the forty-three operatic performances by the two English opera companies during the opera revival, thirty were of Lampe works—more than twice as many performances as had the works of all the other composers combined. The records demonstrate, therefore, that in less than two years Lampe had become a notable figure in English theater music, and the opera revival and his work with it possibly would have continued had he not been offered a singularly great opportunity—the position of composer at one of London's royal patent theaters, Drury Lane.

1733-1734: Drury Lane

London's two patent theaters, whose owners held valuable royal licenses or patents entitling them to present theatrical productions, were the most important dramatic houses in the city, even the kingdom, but the situation in which Lampe found himself in the fall of 1733 had become both perplexing and unstable. Since 1719 Drury Lane had been run by a triumvirate of actor-managers: Barton Booth, Robert Wilks, and Colley Cibber, who had brought stability and prosperity to the theater. But by September 1732, two of the triumvirate were dead. Booth's share of the royal patent was sold to a theatrical amateur, John Highmore, and Wilks's widow appointed another amateur, a painter named Ellis, to administer her husband's share. Old Cibber could not get along with the two dilettantes and assigned his third of the patent to his son Theophilus to manage. The junior Cibber, who is remembered in theatrical history as a particularly nasty and cantankerous character, had even more trouble with the two partners than did his father, and Highmore finally offered Colley Cibber three

---

[24] *The Daily Advertiser*, June 27, 1733.

[25] *The London Stage*, 3:cxli.

[26] Harold Rosenthal, *Two Centuries of Opera at Covent Garden* (London: Putnam, 1958), 12, even asserts that Lampe "became the official composer at the Haymarket," a statement that I have been unable to verify.

thousand guineas for his share of the patent and a chance to be rid of the young nuisance.[27]

Highmore's problems were far from over, however. Young Cibber, unhappy with the change in events, promoted a revolt among the actors, who also were none too pleased with Highmore, and led most of the best talent of Drury Lane away to form a new company at the Little Haymarket Theatre. In the ensuing shuffle and Highmore's attempt to fill the void left by the revolters, Lampe and most of his company were hired at Drury Lane, while the Arnes went with Cibber to the Little Theatre. Lampe's wife-to-be, Isabella Young, sister of Cecilia, also performed at Drury Lane during this season, her first extended theatrical engagement.[28]

For Cibber's company Arne prepared a new version of *The Opera of Operas* cut down to a one-act afterpiece. The only members of the original cast were Master Arne and Miss Jones, and Miss Arne now took the leading role. About a week after the Arne setting of *The Opera of Operas* appeared, Drury Lane presented its own version of the work, in three acts like the earliest performances, and advertised as being by Lampe.

Although Lampe's Drury Lane version of *The Opera of Operas* used most of the original singers and presumably most of the original music, in the 1733-34 season Arne's afterpiece proved to be the more successful, for the full-length version was performed only twice while the afterpiece was given at least eighteen times. Perhaps three acts of Italian burlesque were too much of a good thing, or more likely, in light of its previous success, Highmore may merely have preferred to schedule spoken drama instead of musical works. Arne and young Cibber would have needed to continue to perform anything that might bring them attention and support. *The Opera of Operas* remains important, however, as Lampe's first real connection with burlesque, and particularly with burlesque of Italian opera. In a very real sense it is a predecessor of *The Dragon of Wantley*, which probably would not have been possible without it.

Meanwhile, Highmore evidently wished to capitalize as much as possible on the popularity of Lampe and company. Within six months Lampe had written music for four new works, besides reworking *The Opera of Operas*. Two of the works, John Hewitt's *The Fatal Falshood* [sic] and James Ralph's adaptation of Vanbrugh's *The Cornish Squire*, were merely plays with occasional songs and incidental music, but good music was considered by all to be vital to the success of such works. *The Cornish Squire*, first given on January 23, 1734, was seen on six nights, and *The Fatal Falshood* was performed four times, beginning on February 11, 1734. According to advertisements in *The Daily Post* and *The Daily Advertiser*, the former was to include "a new Grand Dance in Grotesque Characters, proper to the play," in addition to "the Songs new set by John Frederick Lampe." Librettos of the two works were published and are extant, but only one song survives, "Whilst endless tears and sighs" from *The Fatal Falshood* (see page 32).

Only the libretto remains from another Lampe work for Drury Lane. *Aurora's Nuptials*[29] was one of a number of similar pieces assembled by the London theaters to celebrate the wedding that had been arranged by George II between his respected eldest daughter

---

[27] See Nicoll, *History*, 271; Walter James Macqueen-Pope, *Theatre Royal, Drury Lane* (London: W. H. Allen, 1945), 144.

[28] The first advertisement mentioning her name is from the November 26, 1733 issue of *The Daily Advertiser*.

[29] The best discussion of the theatrical events surrounding the royal nuptials is the article by Emmett L. Avery, "A Royal Wedding Royally Confounded," *Western Humanities Review* 10 (1955-56): 153-64, which is the basis for much of the following discussion.

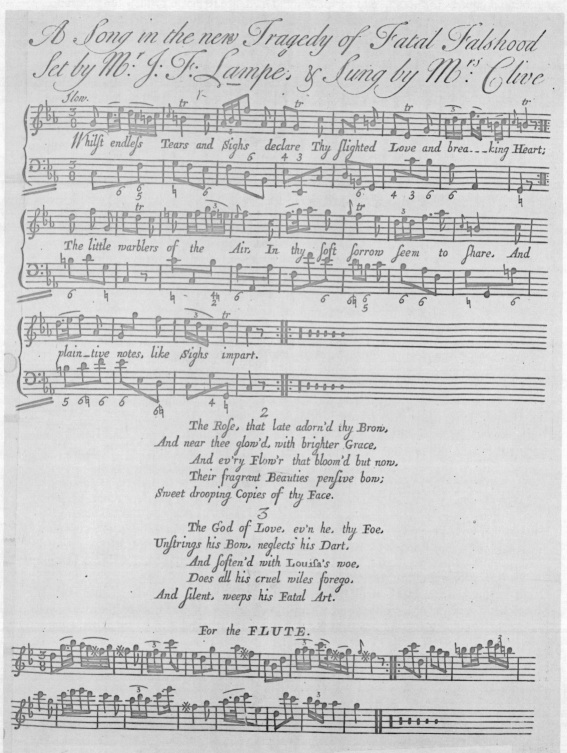

A Song in the new Tragedy of Fatal Falshood
Set by Mr. J. F. Lampe, & Sung by Mrs. Clive

Slow.

Whilst endless Tears and Sighs declare Thy slighted Love and brea___king Heart;

The little warblers of the Air, In thy soft sorrow seem to share. And

plain___tive notes, like Sighs impart.

2
The Rose, that late adorn'd thy Brow,
And near thee glow'd, with brighter Grace,
And ev'ry Flow'r that bloom'd but now,
Their fragrant Beauties pensive bow;
Sweet drooping Copies of thy Face.

3
The God of Love, ev'n he, thy Foe,
Unstrings his Bow, neglects his Dart,
And soften'd with Louisa's woe,
Does all his cruel wiles forego,
And silent, weeps his Fatal Art.

For the FLUTE.

32

Title page of libretto of *Aurora's Nuptials*, 1734.

AURORA's NUPTIALS.

A

DRAMATICK PERFORMANCE:

Occasion'd by the NUPTIALS of his Serene Highness

WILLIAM, PRINCE of *ORANGE*,

With Her Royal Highness

ANNE, PRINCESS-ROYAL of GREAT BRITAIN.

As it is Represented at the

THEATRE-ROYAL in *DRURY-LANE*.

By His MAJESTY's Servants.

First Edition.

The Song Part Set to Musick by

Mr. *JOHN FREDERICK LAMPE*.

Humani Generis Deliciæ.

LONDON:

Printed for JOHN WATTS at the Printing-Office in *Wild-Court* near *Lincoln's-Inn Fields*.

MDCCXXXIV.

Anne and the unknown Prince of Orange, William Charles Henry (see page 33). The politically expedient match had little prospect of being a happy one, and the royal wedding was postponed time and again because of the sickly Prince's recurring bouts with various illnesses. In the surrounding confusion the theaters continually postponed and rescheduled their nuptial celebrations, or in some cases presented them anyway at their scheduled times.

In the second week of November (the wedding was to have been on Monday, November 12, 1733, but was postponed until Thursday because of the Prince's sickness) *The Daily Post* advertised that "a grand Dramatick Masque call'd *Aurora's Nuptials*" would be staged at Drury Lane "immediately after the Nuptials." The royal wedding actually did not take place, however, until March 14, 1734, four months later, so that it is not certain whether the work ever was performed. If it was, the single performance probably occurred on the evening of March 15, 1734, when most of the London theaters presented their nuptial entertainments. No music is extant, but the preface to the anonymous libretto, dated 1734, implies that the work had been written earlier and then postponed until after the wedding actually had taken place. The preface also is notable because it expresses sentiments on English and Italian music similar to those of the English opera revival. The cast list includes many names familiar from Lampe's company of 1732-33.

In addition to his other new works, the 1733-34 season at Drury Lane included Lampe's first great theatrical success, the pantomime *Cupid and Psyche*, also often called *Columbine Courtezan* (see pages 36-37). The work was performed twenty-five times during the first season, beginning on February 5, 1734, and was frequently revived in London theaters through the end of the 1750s. Although Lampe is known to have composed its medley overture, is generally credited with having written the comic tunes and at least a single extant song (see page 37), "Who to win a Woman's Favour," and probably arranged all of the pantomime's music, one song in the work is by Carey. "Crowds of coxcombs thus deluding" appears in Carey's *The Musical Century*, vol. 1, with the caption "Sung by Mrs. Clive in Columbine Courtezan." Because of Carey's song in the pantomime, some scholars have suggested that he wrote the anonymous libretto, thus making *Cupid and Psyche* the first great success of the Lampe-Carey collaboration which produced *Amelia*, *The Dragon of Wantley*, *Margery*, and possibly other works. The close relationship between Lampe and Carey also has prompted other sources to state that Lampe wrote the music for Carey's *Chrononhotonthologos*, first produced February 22, 1733 at the Little Theatre by the dissenting players while Lampe was at Drury Lane. Carey almost certainly wrote what little music is in the piece, however, for the songs all used simple ballad tunes, which he could have set himself as easily as he did in other similar works.

The popularity of *Cupid and Psyche* was a financial godsend for the troubled Highmore, even though critics as usual attacked the pantomime on aesthetic grounds. A particularly offensive point was the presence of a giant, Mynheer Cajanus, who was said to have been over seven feet tall[30] and who attracted great crowds to the theater at the expense of legitimate drama elsewhere. The following complaint in a letter printed in *The Universal Spectator and Weekly Journal* of February 23, 1734 is so typical and amusing that it merits an extended quotation:

---

[30] Egmont, *Diary*, 2:33, an entry for Friday, February 22, 1734, states "In the evening went to the Island Princess [which was the mainpiece performed before *Cupid and Psyche*] . . . where was shown the tallest man of all I have seen. He is seven feet ten inches and a half in height, a German by birth."

. . . The *Taste* for *theatrical* Representations, is at present at a very low Ebb; but what is surprising, every one seems sensible of it; every one complains of the *Depravity* of the *Stage* at the same Time they themselves are contributing to it. Some have urged this *Depravity* is owing to Want of good *Dramatick Writers*; tho' I am rather inclin'd to attribute it to another Cause, when I see *Harlequin's* Sword can draw him a larger Audience than all the *Magick* of *Shakespeare*; his *Grimace* of more Power to captivate than the *softest scenes* of *Otway*, and his Agility more pleasing than the *Wit* of a *Wickerley* or a *Congreve*. . . . Since Monsier *Harlequin* has conjur'd up his *Gargantua* at *Drury-Lane*, the Town have *flock'd* to that *Theatre* they just before *deserted*; and to their Emolument, with Wonder beheld *Mynheer Cajanus* stalk round the Stage with a becoming Dignity. . . . The Gentleman who has lately succeeded in the Propriety and Management of that *Theatre*, seems to have a Mind well turn'd for the present Gout, and will, in all probability, succeed. When the *Tall Man's* time which he is contracted for is expired, I have been inform'd, his Part is to be supplied by a *fat Man*; and that a Treaty is now on the Carpet to bring on the **strong Man** of *Islington*, when *Custards* and *Pokers* are to be demolish'd in great Number, for the *Edification* of his Majesty's liege Subjects.

As I am no Enemy of *Mynheer Gargantua*, farther than he is a *Monster* of the *Stage*, which the Rules of the *Drama* give no Authority for, I would indulge him on the *theatre* till the new Comedy of Mr. *Gay's*, now in *Rehearsal*, is exhibited to the Town; after which, if he *spirits* away any Subject of *Britain* from being improv'd in *manly Sentiments* and *Principles* of *Honesty*, I humbly intreat he may feel the utmost Marks of your *Spectatorial Displeasure*; which will oblige all Lovers of *Sense* and *Old Britain* as well

Your constant Reader,

Middle Temple, Feb. 12   EUCRATES

Columbine Courtezan remained quite popular and successful financially, however, much to the encouragement of the manager and composer, but it was virtually the only major work at Drury Lane to enjoy a long run and consistent full houses. Lampe's other music also was admired, and Drury Lane advertisements often mention that there will be "Selected Pieces between the Acts, Composed by Mr. Lampe." During a series of performances in February 1734 two Lampe works, *The Fatal Falshood* and *Columbine Courtezan*, constituted most of the evening's entertainment. It is fair and accurate, therefore, to say that without Lampe's popular music to bolster the programs Highmore's theatrical fortunes probably would have sunk even more rapidly than they did. Good music, however, could not sustain Highmore's company against the superior acting talents of the revolters. Drury Lane's and Highmore's financial situation continued to worsen throughout the season until finally, around the first of February 1734, he sold his shares of the patent to another wealthy amateur, Charles Fleetwood, who soon negotiated a reconciliation with the rebel company.

On March 12, 1734, the revolters returned in triumph to Drury Lane, and immediately almost all of those who had worked for Highmore either were dismissed outright or relegated to minor roles and positions for the rest of the season.[31] Lampe appears largely to have been replaced by Arne and Richard Charke (young Cibber's brother-in-law), who had served as

---

[31] William W. Appleton, *Charles Macklin* (Cambridge, Mass.: Harvard University Press, 1960), 27.

Title page of libretto of the popular pantomime *Cupid and Psyche*, also called *Columbine Courtezan*, 1734.

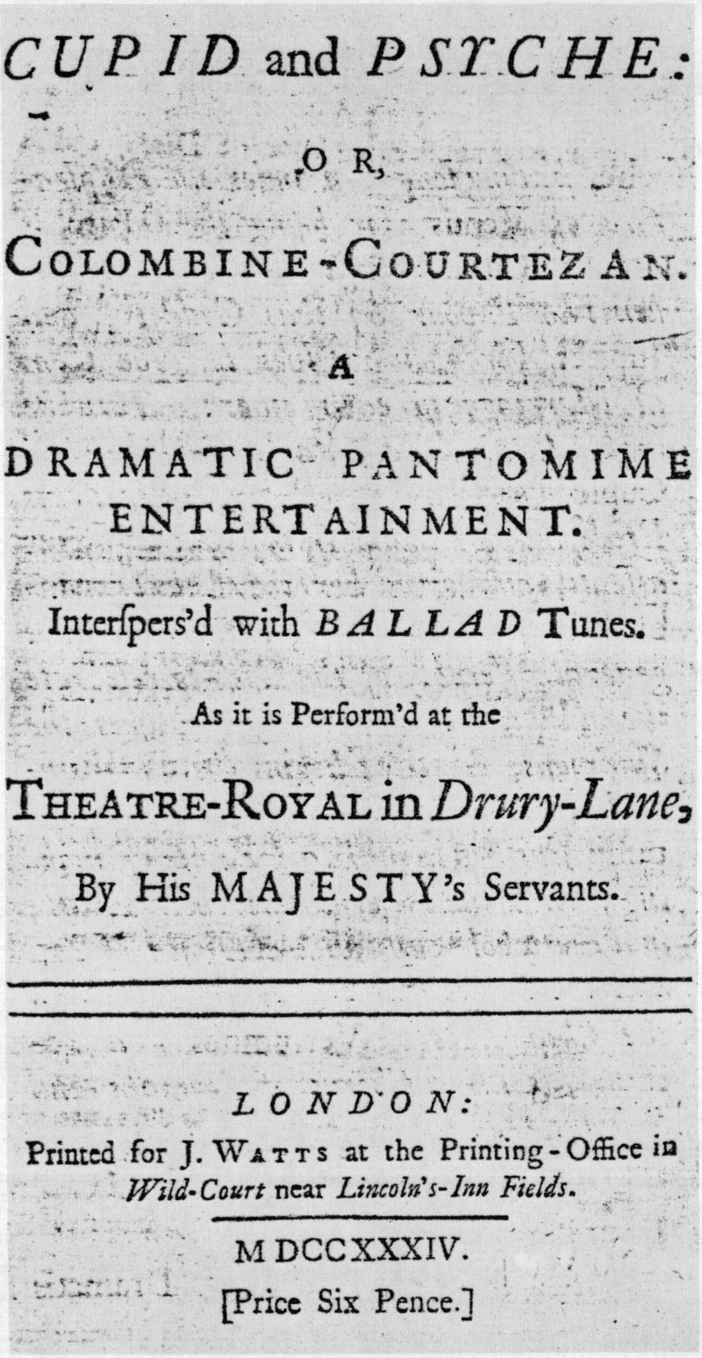

CUPID and PSYCHE:

OR,

COLOMBINE-COURTEZAN.

A

DRAMATIC PANTOMIME ENTERTAINMENT.

Interspers'd with *BALLAD* Tunes.

As it is Perform'd at the

THEATRE-ROYAL in *Drury-Lane*,

By His MAJESTY's Servants.

LONDON:

Printed for J. WATTS at the Printing-Office in *Wild-Court* near *Lincoln's-Inn Fields*.

MDCCXXXIV.

[Price Six Pence.]

A broadside, at the British Library, of a song from *Columbine Courtezan*, 1734.

Sung by M^r. Salway in Colombine Courtezan.
Set for the German Flute.

Who to win a Woman's Favour, Would solicit long in vain?

Who to gain a Moments Pleasure, Would endure an Age of Pain?

Idle toying, ne'er enjoying, Pleas'd with suing, Fond of Ruin, Made y^e

Martyr of Disdain: Made the Martyr of Disdain.

Give me Love the beauteous Rover,
Whom a gen'ral Passion warms;
Fondly blessing ev'ry Lover,
Frankly proff'ring all her Charms:
Never flying,
Still complying,
Train'd to please you,
Glad to ease you,
Circled in her snowy Arms.

Flute.

Cibber's composers for the revolting company. Soon after the return, young Cibber married Arne's sister, Susanna,[32] further cementing his relationship with Arne, so that Lampe was left firmly on the outside. Although *Columbine Courtezan* and its popular medley overture continued to be performed, his other works were ignored, and their composer received no better treatment. Lampe's association with Drury Lane, which had begun so promisingly, was over before the end of his first season because of an unfortunate turn in theatrical politics.[33]

During the rest of the season Lampe participated in various concerts around London. An April 5, 1734 benefit for Charke at Hickford's included a work for four French horns "Compos'd by: Seedo and Lampe." Miss Arne also sang on the program, and Lampe's participation demonstrates his continued good relations with the musicians, if not the management, of Drury Lane. By May, Lampe was at Lincoln's Inn Fields, for an advertisement of May 9, 1734 mentions "Selected Pieces composed by Lampe," and a notice a week later for *The Island Princess* at Lincoln's Inn Fields states that the work will be followed by "A Masque of Pastoral Musick, compos'd by Lampe." Possibly the masque was part of *Cupid and Psyche/Columbine Courtezan*, which frequently had been performed with *The Island Princess* before the return of the rebels to Drury Lane. If, however, Lampe's masque was a new work, no other trace or mention of it has survived.

1734-1737: Interlude

For the next few years Lampe disappeared almost as completely from London theatrical life as had the lost masque. There is no trace of him in the chronicles of *The London Stage* from May 16, 1734 until April 29, 1737, and the latter only lists Lampe's medley overture as being played at Drury Lane. Since, however, the overture already had been published by Walsh in a collection of four medley overtures (first advertised in the *Country Journal, or the Craftsman* on December 25, 1736), its performance is no indication whatsoever of Lampe's own activities. In 1735 Walsh also had printed the *Columbine Courtezan* music in a collection with some of Lampe's other incidental music for Drury Lane (the first advertisement appeared December 10, 1735 in the *London Daily Post, and General Advertiser*), perhaps as an attempt by Lampe to improve his financial situation or to get new theater commissions. But no new compositions by him are known to have been performed during the period.

Lampe probably returned to his activities as a teacher, a writer of songs, and a bassoonist. Perhaps he would have tried to rebuild the English opera company and revival, but the split in London's Italian opera companies drew several of his former leading singers, including Waltz, Stoppelaer, and Cecilia Young, to work for Handel. Possibly Lampe also returned to play in Handel's orchestra. His association with the Youngs and Italian opera certainly continued, for "Welcome, Mars," from his *Britannia*, was advertised as being sung by Cecilia Young at Hickfords on July 10, 1734.

As early as 1726 Harry Carey had remarked that Lampe was a studious fellow,[34] so that Lampe's new activity of theoretical writing during the 1734-37 period is not especially

---

[32] She is first called Mrs. Cibber in an April 29, 1734 advertisement for a Drury Lane performance of Arne's *Britannia: or, Love and Glory*.

[33] A good discussion of the theater revolt is to be found in *The London Stage*, 3:lxxxix-xciii.

[34] See the Carey poem quoted earlier in this chapter, which dates from 1726.

surprising. His resulting thoroughbass treatise, *A Plain and Compendious Method of Teaching Thorough Bass* (see pages 39-41), published by John Wilcox in September 1737,[35] probably had originated as a group of exercises, lessons, and explanations for Lampe's students, and its organization and preparation for publication likely became possible because Lampe no longer had any strenuous theatrical creative responsibilities to consume his time.

A *Plain and Compendious Method* is dedicated to Colonel Blathwayt, a subscriber to Lampe's *Wit Musically Embellished* (1731) and acknowledged as Lampe's patron, an indication that throughout 1734-37 Lampe continued to rely on patrons and students such as those listed in his early song collection. The thoroughbass treatise is divided into two major sections: forty-five pages of text followed by ninety-three plates of lessons and examples. Designed for novices, as were probably most of Lampe's students, the work begins by explaining intervals and figures (see below) and ends with instructions for varying a thoroughbass line. The style is kept quite simple, with the left hand playing the thoroughbass, while the right plays chords in quarter notes. Besides being easier for his inexperienced students, this style likely was related to Lampe's harpsichord experience in the orchestra pit, where such repeated quarter notes provided an important percussive effect that helped to keep the orchestra together.[36] Lampe's orchestra harpsichord playing probably also was responsible

---

[35] A modern facsimile edition of Lampe's treatise has been published (New York: Broude Bros., 1969).

[36] See Charles Avison's description of the function and style of orchestral continuo performance in *An Essay on Musical Expression* (London: C. Davies, 1753), 132-34.

Plate 1 of Lampe's *A Plain and Compendious Method of Teaching Thorough Bass* (London, 1737).

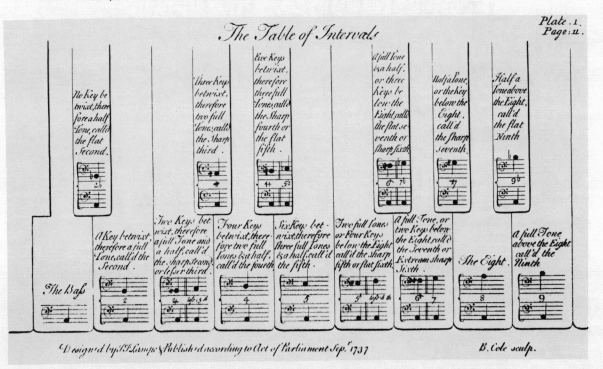

Title page of Lampe's thoroughbass treatise (London, 1737).

A

PLAIN and COMPENDIOUS

METHOD

Of Teaching

THOROUGH BASS,

After the moſt Rational Manner.

WITH

Proper RULES for Practice.

THE

EXAMPLES and LESSONS

Curiouſly Engraved on Copper Plates.

By JOHN FREDERICK LAMPE,

Sometime Student at *HELMSTAD* in *SAXONY*.

LONDON:

Printed for J. WILCOX, at *Virgil*'s Head over-againſt the New Church in the *Strand*.

MDCCXXXVII.

First page of text of Lampe's thoroughbass treatise (London, 1737).

A PLAIN and COMPENDIOUS METHOD, OF Teaching THOROUGH BASS.

THOROUGH BASS is of that Conſequence in *Muſick*, that he who is not well acquainted with it, can only play by *Gueſs*; this being the *Ground-work* upon which all *true Performances* are built, and muſt be the *Regulator* of the *Performer*, if he intends either to do *Juſtice* to himſelf, or the *Piece* he performs; to come to the Knowledge of which the *Scholar* muſt be firſt taught the due *Order of Sounds*; for from their due Order the Beauty of *Harmony* ariſes, each Part having its Stated Courſe, ſtill keeping cloſe to the firſt *Regular Order and Method*. Thorough

B Baſs

for other stylistic peculiarities found in the book, e.g., occasional parallel fifths and octaves and the frequent appearance or disappearance of extra voices, which, although certainly not acceptable in careful four-part writing and not found in Lampe's compositions, would have been covered up by the sound of the instruments in the orchestra pit and therefore of no consequence.

Perhaps the most interesting aspects of *A Plain and Compendious Method* are the instructions and examples of how to vary and play divisions on a given thoroughbass line. Many Baroque as well as modern scholars have regarded the written continuo line with a fair degree of sanctity, preferring to perform the bass line as written while varying the upper voices, or realization. Lampe, however, as a performer of that bass line on both harpsichord and bassoon, seemed to feel the upper voices to be less important. The way to add interest and variety to a work, as well as to demonstrate one's own ingenuity, would not be in the mere realization of the continuo, which anyone should be able to do, but by varying and embellishing the given thoroughbass line itself. Near the end of the treatise, therefore, Lampe includes varied versions of the simple thoroughbasses in many of his preceding lessons. Although such concepts and techniques may be thought today to have been uncommon in the Baroque, Lampe's feelings are in fact shared by some of his contemporaries, particularly Geminiani in his *Rules for Playing in a True Taste* (ca. 1745), which postdates Lampe's treatise and may be indebted to it.

Like Lampe, Carey also had his troubles with the new management of Drury Lane. A new ballad opera by Carey, *The Honest Yorkshireman*, had been kept by Fleetwood all through the 1734-35 season and then returned rather ungraciously.[37] The ballad opera finally was first performed during the summer of 1735 at the Little Theatre by a company headed by young Cibber,[38] and the work soon became quite popular at other London theaters. Possibly Lampe also was at the Little Theatre during the years 1734-37, for plays continued to be given there in spite of the fact that none were ever advertised,[39] and musicians certainly would have been needed. Another indication of Lampe's possible association with the Little Theatre is that it was there, in the spring of 1737, that *The Dragon of Wantley* was first performed. The originator and financer of the production is unknown, but whatever the circumstances, the brief appearance of *The Dragon* near the end of the 1736-37 season was to have far-reaching consequences for Lampe and Carey. Because of this work their theatrical fortunes finally would change for the better, and they would achieve some degree of lasting success and security. *The Dragon* also would mark the highest fulfillment of many of the goals of the earlier English opera revival, and the work would assure Lampe and Carey a place in the history of English theater music. For after its humble beginning near the very end of a season, when it went almost unnoticed, the opera was to return and take musical London by storm as had no work since Gay's *Beggar's Opera*. The next season of 1737-38 was to become "The Year of *The Dragon*."

---

[37] Contemporaries and later writers seem to have shared a generally low opinion of Fleetwood's character; see Benjamin Victor, *The History of the Theatres of London and Dublin*, 3 vols. (London: T. Davies, 1761), 1:63.

[38] Carey's enlightening and spirited account of the earlier performances of the work are given in his preface to the 1736 Gilliver libretto *The Honest Yorkshireman. A Ballad Farce* (London: L. Gilliver, 1736), facsimile ed. in *York Ballad Operas and Yorkshiremen*, selected and arranged by Walter H. Rubsamen (New York: Garland, 1974). See also Arthur H. Scouten, "The First Season of *The Honest Yorkshireman*," *Modern Language Review* 40 (1945): 8-11.

[39] *The London Stage*, 3:cv, cxliii-cxlvii.

CHAPTER 3

THE TALE OF *THE DRAGON*

The year 1737 was rendered memorable at Covent-garden theatre by the success of the burlesque opera of the *Dragon of Wantley*, written by Carey, and set by Lampe, "after the Italian manner." This excellent piece of humour had run twenty-two nights, when it was stopped, with all other public amusements, by the death of her Majesty Queen Caroline, November 20th, but was resumed again on the opening of the theatres in January following, and supported as many representations as the *Beggar's Opera* had done, ten years before. And if Gay's original intention in writing his musical drama was to ridicule the opera, the execution of his plan was not so happy as that of Carey; in which the mock heroic, tuneful monster, recitative, splendid habits, and style of Music, all conspired to remind the audience of what they had seen and heard at the lyric theatre, more effectually than the most vulgar street tunes could do; and much more innocently than the tricks and transactions of the most abandoned thieves and prostitutes. Lampe's Music to this farcical drama, was not only excellent fifty years ago, but is still modern and in good taste.[1]

Thus writes Burney in his *General History*, in a passage that must be considered especially high praise, since it comes from the pen of one who usually championed things Italian at the expense of those of his own countrymen. Burney's praise was certainly justified, however, for *The Dragon* was highly successful as theater. In its first season at Covent Garden it was performed sixty-nine times—eleven more performances than *The Beggar's Opera* had achieved during its first season. And *The Dragon*'s record occurred during a season when the theaters were closed for six weeks because of the death of the queen.

This popular work was not a mere ballad opera, however, but as Burney stated was written "after the Italian manner," made up of florid da capo arias and secco recitatives. Because of Lampe's solid German training and his experience with Handel, he understood and could use well the Italian styles and conventions, so that the burlesque of *The Dragon* became all the more pointed. The opera quickly grew to be the most successful parody of Italian opera of its time, partly because its fine music demonstrated that English vernacular opera could compete on an artistic level with opera seria, and the work became a rallying point and symbol of anti-Italian sentiment. It was said even to have replaced *The Beggar's Opera* in the esteem of the theater-going public.[2]

---

[1] Charles Burney, *A General History of Music* (London, 1776-89), new ed. in 2 vols. with critical and historical notes by Frank Mercer (New York: Harcourt, 1935; reprint, New York: Dover, 1957), 2:1003-04.

[2] Arthur V. Berger, "*The Beggar's Opera*, the Burlesque, and Italian Opera," *Music & Letters* 17 (April 1936): 103.

The Origin of The Dragon

A major element contributing to *The Dragon*'s success, but not noted by Burney, was its amusing, typically British plot. Although the story worked well as a parody of opera seria, it also was the kind of tale that had delighted Englishmen for centuries. Besides being a comedy, the work contained a dragon—and not a Mediterranean or classical beast, but a true British monster in the tradition of those fought by Beowulf and St. George. In addition, the Dragon of Wantley story and ballad seem to have been based on actual events in British history.

The source of the Dragon of Wantley story used by Carey for Lampe's opera libretto was an old ballad popular at the time, although the tale also likely was familiar through oral folklore tradition. The legend is interesting both in its similarities to and differences from general English dragon lore. As in many dragon stories, the populace begs a valiant knight to deliver them from a dragon who is ravishing the countryside; the knight honors their request, vanquishes the dragon, and wins the hand of a fair damsel—but here the similarities end. Moore, Lampe's hero, unlike most dragon killers, is neither saint nor saintly. Rather than arming himself with prayers and the sign of the Cross, he drinks "six Pots of Ale, and a Quart of Aqua Vitae."[3] Nor does Moore kill the dragon out of chivalry or sacred duty, but rather because it seems to be the easiest way to get the reward he asks, "A fair Maid of sixteen, that's brisk." In addition, during the battle neither Moore's nor the dragon's tactics reflect exactly exemplary character. One can possibly understand, however, how this tale with its rather rough humor would have appealed to eighteenth-century Englishmen, for whom cockfighting, bearbaiting, and public executions were enjoyable pastimes.

While part of the appeal of Moore and the dragon was the inconsistency of its characters with the types usually inhabiting dragon stories, some of the more bizarre elements of the tale, such as the spiked armor, are not in fact unique within dragon lore. Spiked armor also was used to defeat dragons in the legends of the Lambton Worm, the Dragon of Loschy Hill, and the Worm of Nunnington. Also, wells, deep pools, or their vicinity were commonly thought to be inhabited by dragons or other monsters, such as in the legends of local British Knuckers or the Longwitton Dragon, or even the ancient Greek Cadmus myth. The monsters that did not live in wells often had insatiable thirsts, so that they frequently went to the wells to drink.[4] Thus, Moore's hiding in the well to wait for the dragon is not surprising, although it must be admitted that his other tactics were unusual. Likewise unparalleled in all dragon lore is the Dragon of Wantley's demise, which also must have contributed to the popularity of the story and opera. Of all the dragons in history only he was killed by a kick to the "back-side" (Carey's term used in the opera).[5]

In spite of its mythical nature, however, the Dragon of Wantley legend also seems to have had some foundation in historical fact. There is a place named Wantley, or Wharncliffe, in southwest Yorkshire, about six miles northwest of Sheffield, and a Moore (or More, or Moor) Hall exists close by. Local tradition calls a nearby cave "The Dragon's Den," and a

---

[3] This quotation and the following one are from the text of the Dragon ballad as it appeared in the 1737 libretto of the opera.

[4] Lewis Spense, *The Minor Traditions of British Mythology* (London: Rider, 1948), 122.

[5] Ernest W. Baughman, *Type and Motif-Index of the Folk-Tales of England and North America* (The Hague: Mouton, 1966), 80; Stith Thompson, *Motif-Index of Folk-Literature*, rev. and enl. ed., 6 vols. (Bloomington: Indiana University Press, 1955-58), 1:355.

"Dragon's Well" also is found in the vicinity.[6] Whether the local legend actually antedates the ballad is uncertain, however, since a detailed description of Wantley from 1639, written by John Taylor the water poet, includes the cave but fails to mention its connection with the dragon.[7] The conflicting explanations of the source of the Dragon of Wantley story that appear in eighteenth-century ballad collections seem to indicate that by then the factual origin of the legend had been forgotten and the story had become a part of well-known folk tradition. There have been numerous other attempts to determine the exact historical foundation of the tale, but none have been completely convincing.[8]

The earliest known printed version of the dragon ballad is from 1685, on a broadside that included both text and music.[9] In addition to appearing on various other different broadsides, the ballad was popular enough to have been included in many editions of the famous D'Urfey ballad collection *Wit and Mirth: or, Pills to Purge Melancholy*, as early as 1699. The tune in *Pills*, as the collection usually is known, is different from the tune on the earliest known broadside,[10] but the later tune seems to have been the one generally associated with the ballad, possibly because of the great popularity of *Pills*. Rather than *Pills*, however, Carey probably used the textual version of the ballad found in *A Collection of Old Ballads* (1723), edited by Ambrose Phillips, around whose poetic neck Carey had hung the literary albatross of "Namby Pamby," for Carey took the "Critical Remark" in his libretto directly from that of Phillips's collection.

Carey may have heard of the Dragon of Wantley story during his youth, for some scholars believe Carey to have been born in Yorkshire, perhaps in or near Sheffield and the legendary home of the Wantley Dragon.[11] The idea of using the Dragon of Wantley as an opera plot may not have been original with Carey, however, for James Ralph in *The Touchstone* includes the dragon story in a list of well-known British "fables" that he believed should be considered as material for English operas and translated into Italian if necessary. Ralph's discussion is one long, amusing burlesque of Italian singers and practices, and suggests as opera plots "Whittington and his Cat," "St. George" (which recommends that the famous castrato Farinelli sing the part of St. George's horse with Senesino, another castrato, on his

6 Llewellynn Jewitt, "The Dragon of Wantley & the Family of Moore," *The Reliquary* 18 (April 1878): 200.

7 Much of Taylor's account is quoted in the Rev. Joseph Hunter's *South Yorkshire*, 2 vols. (London: J. B. Nichols & Son, 1828-31), 2:331. This section also discusses the Dragon legend.

8 See, e.g., *A Collection of Old Ballads* [ed. Ambrose Phillips?], 3 vols. (London: J. Butherton, 1723), 1:36-42; Thomas Percy, *Reliques of Ancient English Poetry* (London, 1765); editions of Percy after the 3rd (1775) include a description of the origin of the ballad, supposedly given to Percy in 1767. See also the 5th ed., 3 vols. (London: F. C. & J. Riberton, 1812), 3:364-67, as well as the additional notes and commentary on the description included in the 1886 ed., ed. Henry B. Wheatley, 3 vols. (reprint, New York: Dover, 1966), 3:179-83. In addition to these two ballad collections, more information can be found in Matthew Gregson, *Portfolio of Fragments Relative to the History and Antiques, Topography and Geneologies of the County Palatine and Duchy of Lancashire*, 3rd ed., ed. John Harland (London: John Routledge & Sons, 1869), 151-53; Jewitt, "Dragon," 192-202; Hunter, *South Yorkshire*, 2:329-32; Frederick Ross, *Legendary Yorkshire* (Hull: William Andrews, 1892), 168-75; and John Harland and T. T. Wilkinson, *Lancashire Legends* (London: John Heywood, 1882), 264-70.

9 See Claude M. Simpson, *The British Broadside Ballad* (New Brunswick, N. J.: Rutgers University Press, 1966), 196-97; Gregson, *Fragments*, 152-53; and Jewitt, "Dragon," 192-202.

10 Simpson, *Broadside Ballad*, 196; and Thomas D'Urfey, ed., *Wit and Mirth: or, Pills to Purge Melancholy*, 6 vols. (London: W. Pearson & J. Tonson, 1719), 3:10-15.

11 See Edward Leonard Oldfield, "The Achievement of Henry Carey (1687-1743)" (Ph.D. dissertation in English Literature, University of Washington, 1969), 264-84, which is the most recent biographical study of Carey.

back), "Robin Hood and Little John," "Tom Thumb" (Cuzzoni, Handel's rotund soprano, was proposed to play Thumb in breeches), and of course "The Dragon of Wantley."[12] Ralph's section on *The Dragon* is longer than that for any other opera and is perhaps even more entertaining:

> Most of our Countrymen, who are deeply read in the old *Brittish* Ballads, (which have been so curiously and carefully collected lately by a judicious Antiquary, with learned Observations and Annotations, by which means many remarkable Transactions are preserv'd in those Singsong *Annals*, which History has neglected) will readily imagine that I hint at the noted Combat betwixt *Moor* of *Moor-hall*, and the Dragon of *Wantcliff*; which for the Beauty of Fable, Variety of Incidents, a Quantity of the Marvellous, and a glorious Catastophe, may vie with any Story, ancient or modern.
>
> Indeed this *Dramma* will admit but of two principal Characters; *viz.* 'Squire *Moor* and the *Dragon:* But here is the most proper Occasion imaginable of introducing a magnificent Chorus in every Act; a Stage-Decoration so esteem'd by all the Ancients and Learned Moderns, that they thought all Theatrical Entertainments imperfect without one; as I shall farther explain in a separate *Essay*.
>
> In the first Act you have a Chorus of Men, Women, and Children, whose Bread and Butter, Milk-Pottage or Relations the Dragon had devour'd, accompany'd by a suitable Noise of Sobs, Sighs and Groans on proper Instruments; which must have a fine Effect, as to moving Pity. These Lamentations rousing up the dormant Spirit of *Moor*, he declares for the Combat, which naturally ushers in the second Act a Chorus of warlike Instruments on his Part, preparative to the Battle, join'd to a compleat Roar on the Part of the Dragon, which must exhibit Terror to a vast Degree: Then the third Act beginning with the Combat, concludes nobly with the Dragon's Death, and a grand Chorus of the whole Country; where Sounds of Triumph and Joy, mix'd with Bells, Bon-fires and Country-Dances, perform'd by Country-Squires, Shepherds, Milk-Maids, and a Saint or two introduc'd by a Machine; one suppos'd to have given *Moor* a Breast-Plate and Head-Piece, another more than humane Courage, to atchieve so wonderful an Exploit: Thus the Whole ends agreeably, and sends every Person of the Audience Home well pleased: In this little Story all the Passions are finely express'd.[13]

Although Ralph's suggestions often are obviously posed in jest, the number of ideas incorporated by Carey into his final version of *The Dragon*'s libretto is striking. Also of interest, because of its connection with Lampe, Carey, and the English opera revival, is Ralph's proposal of "Tom Thumb" as an opera plot, which possibly provided the impetus for Fielding's play, and through it Lampe's setting of the same story.

The dragon ballad had created some interest in London literary circles even before Ralph, for in 1721 *Mist's Weekly Journal* included a burlesque article comparing the ballad with Homer, Ovid, and Virgil. The article ends by saying, "But since it [the Dragon of Wantley ballad] has been so shamefully neglected, I beg this Criticism of it may in some Measure,

---

[12] James Ralph, *The Touchstone* (London, 1728), 21-31; suggestions of this sort were not original with Ralph, but also had appeared in *The Spectator*, nos. 70 and 74, written by Addison.

[13] Ralph, *Touchstone*, 24-25.

by being admitted into your Paper, shew the World some of its Beauties."[14] Lampe and Carey therefore were working with a subject both well known and enjoyed by the London public of their day.

The Dragon *in London*

Lampe can justifiably be named alongside Carey as sharing responsibility for *The Dragon*'s existence, textual as well as musical. In his dedication to the libretto Carey implies that Lampe contributed the idea of using the dragon story and pushed to bring the work to completion, and that he and Carey shared in the composition of the text. The dedication also states that their work (the plural pronoun is significantly conspicuous throughout the section) had been kept several years by Fleetwood, the manager at Drury Lane, without its being performed. As Fleetwood also had rejected Carey's *The Honest Yorkshireman* after holding it for the entire 1734-35 season, there is little reason not to accept Carey's statement, which also means that *The Dragon* could have been written as early as 1734-35, perhaps as an attempt by Carey and Lampe to regain favor at Drury Lane. The reason Fleetwood rejected the opera is unknown, but as a result of his action the first performance of *The Dragon* occurred not in one of the patent houses but in the Little Haymarket Theatre, probably given by Lampe and Carey themselves in what may have been intended to be the beginning of another English opera revival.

The work was not successful at first, however. It received only four performances during the third week of May, and was given no more during the rest of the 1736-37 season. Success really could not have been expected from a work beginning so late in the year, for by May the London theatrical season was for all practical purposes finished. In addition, the Licensing Act, passed in June 1737, threatened to close the Little Theatre for good,[15] and must have caused some concern if Lampe and Carey actually were planning a second opera revival.

Unexpected encouragement for *The Dragon* and its creators came from John Rich, the owner and manager of Covent Garden, who invited them to his theater for the fall. Rich did not, however, take over the opera merely because "the entire production of *The Dragon* could be had, fully rehearsed, for the asking," as sometimes is reported.[16] Extensive revisions were made in the work during the summer of 1737 and throughout much of the fall as well, for the advertisements of May 1737, list the opera as having two acts, while the Covent Garden version was in three acts from the beginning. Early Covent Garden librettos even contain differences among themselves, until the form of the work became standardized in early 1738. It therefore appears that Rich, an astute businessman and judge of his theatrical public, saw in *The Dragon* a work well worth sponsoring, which would appeal to Londoners weary of supporting two lavish, rival Italian opera companies. And he was not mistaken, for *The Dragon* was more popular in its first season than had been Rich's earlier similar success and the foundation of his fortune, *The Beggar's Opera*.

London received *The Dragon* enthusiastically, from the lowest commoners to the highest nobility. The King himself was fascinated by the opera and continually talked about it, even

---

[14] *The Weekly Journal or Saturday's Post*, September 2, 1721.

[15] See the section on the Licensing Act in *The London Stage, 1660-1800*, 5 parts (Carbondale: Southern Illinois University Press, 1960-68), 3:xlviii-lx.

[16] Roger Fiske, *English Theatre Music in the Eighteenth Century* (London: Oxford University Press, 1973), 150.

when he should have been worrying about his very ill queen. Lord Hervey, a high official in George II's court, records in his *Memoirs*:

> On Wednesday, the 9th of November [1737], the Queen was taken ill in the morning. . . . When the clock struck two, and the King proposed sending Lord Grantham to dismiss the company, and declare there would be no drawing-room, she, according to the custom of the family, not caring to own, or at least to have it generally known, how ill she was, told the King that she was much better, that she would get up and see the company as usual. As soon as she came into the drawing-room she came up to Lord Hervey. . . . Lord Hervey asked her what she had taken, and when she told him he replied: "For God's sake, Madam, go to your own room; what have you to do here?" She then went and talked a little to the rest of the company, and coming back to Lord Hervey, said: "I am not able to entertain people." "Would to God," replied Lord Hervey, "the King would have done talking of the Dragon of Wantley, and release you." (This was a new silly farce which everybody at this time went to see.) At last the King went away, telling the Queen as he went by that she had overlooked the Duchess of Norfolk. The Queen made her excuse for having done so to the Duchess of Norfolk, the last person she ever spoke to in public, and then retired, going immediately into bed, where she grew worse every moment.[17]

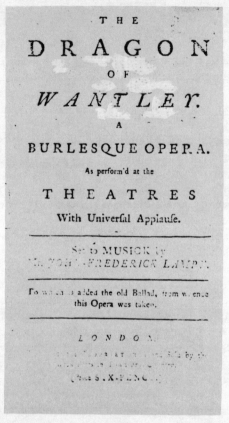

Eleven days later the Queen was dead, and the theaters were closed from Monday, November 21, 1737 to Monday, January 2, 1738 for a period of mourning. When the theaters reopened, though, enthusiasm for *The Dragon* continued unabated, often at the expense of Italian opera. On January 16, 1738, the young Lord Wentworth wrote to the Earl of Stafford:

> We was at Covent Garden Play House last night, my mother was so good as to treat us with it, and the Dragon of Wantcliff was the farce. I like it vastly and the music is excessively pretty, and tho' it is a burlesque on the operas yet Mr. Handel

---

17 Lord John Hervey, *Some Material towards Memoirs of the Reign of King George II*, ed. Romney Sedgwick, 3 vols. (London: Eyre & Spottiswoode, 1931), 3:877-78.

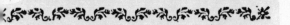

Dramatis Perſonæ.

ℭe DRAGON.

ꟿOORE *of* Moore-Hall, *a Valiant Knight in Love with* MARGERY.

Ɡaffer GUBBINS, *Father to* MARGERY.

ꟿARGERY, *in Love with* MOORE.

ꟿAUXALINDA, *his Caſt off Miſtreſs.*

CHORUS *of Nymphs and Swains.*

ꟲCENE, *that Part of* Yorkſhire, *next* Rotheram,

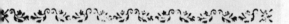

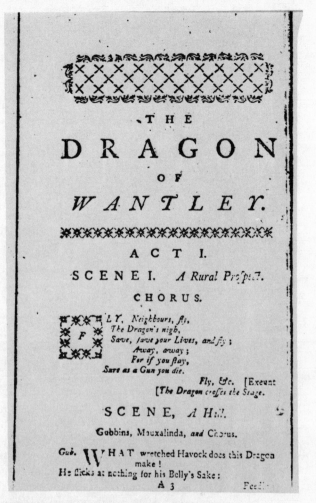

Opposite and above. Pages from a 1737-38 London libretto of *The Dragon of Wantley.*

owns he thinks the tunes very well composed. I conclude your lordship will go to it as soon as you come to town, for every body generally commends it and it has been acted 36 times already and they are always pretty full. The poor operas I doubt go on but badly, for tho' everybody praises Cafferielli [in Handel's *Faramondo*] and the opera yet it has never been full, and if it is not now at first it will be very empty towards the latter end of the winter.[18]

This letter is the sole source of any Handelian comment or opinion about *The Dragon,* which was to undermine the foundation and popularity of Italian opera so greatly. There is no cause to doubt the story, however — young Wentworth would have had no reason to lie — so that the letter may be the best account of eighteenth-century professional assessment of the musical quality of *The Dragon.* Handel's praise was nevertheless magnanimous, for the successful and popular burlesque of opera seria in *The Dragon* undoubtedly helped to destroy Italian opera in London as Handel knew it. Commentators, in fact, have called *The*

---

[18] James J. Cartwright, ed., *The Wentworth Papers, 1705-1739* (London: Wyman & Sons, 1883), 539.

Dragon "the death-blow of Italian opera,"[19] and although such a claim may seem extreme, one must note that after the triumphant first season of *The Dragon* no Italian operas were performed in the King's Theatre opera house for three years, and that after it Handel never had another operatic success in London.

The Dragon's popularity was such that it enjoyed the distinct tribute of being pirated by the rival house, Drury Lane, for a performance late in the 1737-38 season by "Lilliputians," or child actors. One of the Hallams also used the Drury Lane Lilliputian company for *Dragon* performances at his booth at Bartholemew Fair, August 23-26, 1738, and probably at Welsh Fair, August 28. Also at Bartholemew Fair and later that year at Mile End Fair, on October 3, 1738, *The Dragon* was performed by Yeats Jr. and Sr. using puppets. In the London playhouses *The Dragon* was revived repeatedly, and even ten years after its debut it continued to be used to prop up serious spoken drama. The opera appeared not only throughout the British provinces but in the major centers of Dublin and Edinburgh, and popular demand for it endured into the 1780s.

The Dragon *as Burlesque*

Besides its English plot and vernacular text, probably the most significant element contributing to *The Dragon*'s appeal was its burlesque of Italian opera. Literary and dramatic burlesque, the aim of which was to excite laughter through caricature of the manner, spirit, or subject of serious works, had become quite popular in the early eighteenth century. Burlesque differs subtly from satire by being more amiable and fun-loving in its criticism, as the author of *The Burlesque Tradition in the English Theater after 1660* explains:

> Like satire, burlesque employs laughter as criticism and reflects truth rather than the artifical or the ideal; but in every other purpose and method the two arts are entirely different . . . satire [is] violent and angry: but burlesque is never angry, because its criticism is directed not against faults of virtue, but against faults of style and of humour. It wants to destroy nothing—not even sententiousness, its dearest enemy: for if sententiousness were dead there would be one less joke in the world to laugh at. Burlesque serves truth, not with the bitterness of its tongue, but with the irreverence and deliberate impropriety of its laughter. Satire is the schoolmaster attacking dishonesty with a whip. Burlesque is the rude boy attacking pomposity with a pea-shooter. Satire holds up the multiple mirror of the tailor's shop, pitilessly revealing shameful idiosyncrasies. Burlesque holds up the concave mirror and shows the world, not how contemptible it is, but how funny. Satire must laugh not to weep. Burlesque must laugh not to burst—and best of all it likes to laugh among friends, for burlesque discovers laughter not in the objects of its hatred but rather in the objects of its affection: and that is the abiding difference between the two arts.[20]

Keeping such distinctions in mind, the subtle differences in practice and intent between the parody of *The Dragon* and works like *The Beggar's Opera* become clearer, for while

---

[19] Percy M. Young, *Handel* (New York: E. P. Dutton, 1947), 63.

[20] Victor C. Clinton-Baddeley, *The Burlesque Tradition in English Theatre after 1660* (London: Methuen, 1952), 1-2.

Moore's Engagement to Margery.

Illustrations, from the original production of *The Dragon of Wantley*, for:
Above. "If that's all you ask." From Bickham, 2:8.
Below. "By the beer as brown as berry." From Bickham, 2:12.

Moore Coaxing Mauxalinda.

The Beggar's Opera may satirize the ills of society, and often bitterly, *The Dragon* may burlesque Italian opera, whose music and composers it respected. Carey and Lampe did not despise or hate Handel and the musical excellence of his heroic operas of the 1720s and 1730s. Rather, they attacked the pomposity and conventions of serious Italian opera itself and the foreigners who sang it. But the attack was not violent or angry; instead, it held up a mirror and irreverently laughed at the surprisingly clear image of reality. The humor of *The Dragon*, therefore, results not so much from the condemnation of opera seria conventions as from the use of them, and a very proficient use at that, since Lampe had learned the techniques through years of working and studying with Handel. As a result, *The Dragon* can be both more consistent and amusing than a work like *The Beggar's Opera*, which parodied not only Italian opera, but more openly, and many scholars would say primarily, satirized the Walpole government and contemporary social conditions.[21] *The Dragon* is more singleminded in purpose and employs direct rather than oblique burlesque. Also, its variety of burlesque would have been more in accord with the gregarious and funloving characters of Carey and Lampe, who believed, according to the inscription on the title page of *The Dragon*'s libretto, that "*Ridiculum acri, fortius & melius.*"[22]

Writers sometimes claim that *The Dragon* is a satire or burlesque of Handel's *Justino* (1737) because both works contain dragons,[23] but since *The Dragon* probably was written as early as 1734-35 such a relationship is unlikely. Heroic battles with monsters had been common from the beginning of London's Italian operas, and more likely the original and most famous of all of these encounters, the conflict between Hidaspes and the lion in Francesco Mancini's *Hidaspes* (1710), was being ridiculed.[24] The famous feud between Faustina and Cuzzoni that ended in a brawl during a performance of Buononcini's *Astianatte* (1727) seems undoubtedly to have been the basis for Margery and Mauxalinda and their less than amiable relationship. Their duet "Insulting gipsey" reenacts the fight, and its text "Your too much feeding has spoiled your breeding" likely is reminiscent of Cuzzoni's rotund figure. Even Mauxalinda's name is part of the parody, for the *Oxford English Dictionary* defines "Maux" as "a prostitute," and includes a 1706 definition as "a dirty nasty slut." The burlesque in this instance is the comparison with the high virtue of the usual opera seria heroines.

The conceited castrati received special consideration, and Mauxalinda's aria describing Moore, the *primo uomo*, with "He's a man ev'ry inch, I assure you" undoubtedly refers to them. From newspaper descriptions and the plates in Bickham's *The Musical Entertainer* (1738-40), Moore appears to have been dressed like Farinelli from the very beginning, to identify his ignoble character further with the strutting eunuchs.[25] Even the scenery seems

---

21 Walter H. Rubsamen, "Ballad Burlesques and Extravaganzas," *Musical Quarterly* 36 (October 1950): 551; Harold Gene Moss, "Popular Music and the Ballad Opera," *Journal of the American Musicological Society* 26 (Fall 1973): 377.

22 "Ridicule often settles an important affair better and more effectively than severity." The same inscription had appeared on James Ralph's *The Touchstone*, and is evidence of a possible connection between *The Touchstone*'s suggestion of the Dragon legend as an opera plot and Carey's use of the story.

23 E.g., Eric Walter White, *The Rise of English Opera* (New York: Philosophical Library, 1951), 70.

24 See an amusing description in *The Spectator*, no. 13; also see Zacharias Conrad von Uffenbach, *London in 1710*, trans. and ed. W. H. Quarrell and Margaret Mare (London: Faber, 1934), 18; and George Hogarth, *Memoirs of the Musical Drama*, 2 vols. (London: Richard Bentley, 1838), 1:263-69 and 2:77.

25 In his article "Reviving England's 18th-Century Operas," *Opera* 22 (March 1971), Roger Fiske laments the fact that although "it would be fascinating to attempt total authenticity in staging, it is almost impossible, since sketches of the scenery and costumes hardly ever survive for an opera that one might wish to produce." A unique opportunity

to have been part of the burlesque.[26] Burney mentions the parody of a particular Handel aria, "Impara ingiata" in *Atalanta*, by the Dragon's one aria,[27] but I can see little resemblance between the two.

The very language of the libretto burlesqued opera seria as well. Carey could write as fine an *ottonario* aria text as most Italians, and Lampe could set it to exquisite music, but the sum effect in such arias as "But to hear the children mutter when they lost their toast and butter" and "Zeno, Plato, Aristotle, all were lovers of the bottle" became lovably ludicrous. The latter aria, despite its calling upon classical authority (another common Italian practice of the time, even by Zeno himself), is a drinking song, the sentiments of which would be highly inappropriate for the lofty, idealistic, opera seria, as of course would have been the violence between Margery and Mauxalinda and between Moore and the Dragon.[28]

In spite of its caricatures of Italian opera, it is the non-Italian elements that actually make *The Dragon* come alive dramatically. The typical British plot has been mentioned earlier, but even more important are the musical aspects of the work. The chorus is a real chorus, not the simple, homophonic *coro* of soloists in an Italian finale, and Lampe's chorus appears at many important dramatic points throughout the opera with fine choral writing, often in fugal style. Ensembles are frequent and interesting, simile arias are nonexistent, and often the recitative-aria motion breaks down entirely for the sake of the drama. In fact, almost all deviations from general operatic conventions seem intended to enhance the dramatic impact of the opera and its characters. Especially impressive is Lampe's ability to combine the varied elements of Italian opera seria, English burlesque, and German counterpoint into a distinctive and individual style, and to use it to create a musically satisfying and theatrically enjoyable full-length piece of musical *comedy*! It seems that Pergolesi and *La serva padrona* were not unique in the 1730s, nor Britain's composers so backward, as sometimes has been thought.

Accomplishments of The Dragon

By the end of the 1737-38 season the fate of *The Dragon* and its composer were secure. The work had become standard in British music theater repertory and was performed during every theatrical season up through the time of Lampe's death. Even after the composer died, the opera remained so popular that it was republished in full score as well as in a new continuo-vocal arrangement, and the work continued to be performed for over thirty years after Lampe's death, the last performance being March 18, 1782 at Covent Garden.

The Dragon appeared at a good time in the history of English opera. Audiences were beginning to weary of the expense of supporting two Italian opera companies. Complaints

---

exists with *The Dragon*, however, for engravings of its scenes and costumes *do* survive. Bickham's *The Musical Entertainer*, for which Lampe was the musical editor, contains almost all of the important arias from *The Dragon*, and over the caption-title and music of each piece is a large and detailed engraving of the setting and characters of that particular aria. Since *The Musical Entertainer* was prepared during the heyday of *The Dragon*'s popularity and since Lampe edited the collection, the engravings likely represent the costumes and scenery of *The Dragon* fairly accurately.

26 Allardyce Nicoll, *A History of Early Eighteenth Century Drama* (Cambridge: Cambridge University Press, 1925), 33.

27 Burney, *History*, 2:802.

28 See Patrick J. Smith, *The Tenth Muse* (New York: Alfred A. Knopf, 1970), 63-100, for one of the better discussions of opera seria conventions.

against incongruous plots and a foreign tongue continued to be voiced, while politics threatened both opera companies. Through overwork and worry, Handel's physical and mental condition deteriorated, resulting in a stroke and mental disorientation. Although *The Dragon* cannot fully be credited, therefore, with causing the demise of the two Italian opera companies in London, it did nail down the lid on the coffin after their death, and Italian opera remained dormant in England until the advent of the newer gallant works of Galuppi and others.

The Dragon also accomplished what the English opera revival had never been able to do, at least on such a scale. The opera was a great and lasting theatrical success and established British plots and British singers. It was even more popular during its first years than *The Beggar's Opera* had been, making it the most successful piece of British vernacular music theater to its date. Exposing the weaknesses of opera seria much more effectively than had *The Beggar's Opera* and similar works, Lampe's opera helped to bring about the foreign form's temporary dissolution. Perhaps most important, *The Dragon* demonstrated that Lampe was a superior dramatist and composer, and that he was probably the best musical craftsman writing English comic works at the time. It is not surprising, therefore, that Carey and Lampe soon began work on a sequel, to be produced the next season. As 1737-38 had been "The Year of the Dragon," 1738-39 was to be "The Year of the Dragoness."

Illustration, from the original production of *The Dragon of Wantley*, for: "Oh, ho! Master Moore." From Bickham, 2:32.

Moore fighting with y^e Dragon.

CHAPTER 4 AFTER *THE DRAGON*: THE RISE AND FALL

1738-1739

The Dragon of Wantley opened the 1738-39 theatrical season at Covent Garden on September 15 for the first of seventeen performances, and the opera continued to be used at or near the beginning of theatrical seasons for several years, a record attesting to its lasting appeal. Early in December, however, *The Dragon* was withdrawn from the stage, except for a few scattered performances throughout the rest of the season, to make way for its sequel, Lampe's and Carey's newest creation entitled *Margery, or A Worse Plague than the Dragon* and later called *The Dragoness*.

The new opera was another triumph for the pair. At a time when Italian operas or oratorios were considered extremely successful if they achieved eight or ten performances, *Margery* was performed twenty-one times during its first season, and on eleven of the first twelve possible nights. The plot takes up where *The Dragon* ends, and Carey's own Argument from the 1738 libretto furnishes perhaps the best synopsis:

> *Mauxalinda*, enraged at the Falshood of *Moore*, retires disconsolate to a Desart, unable to bear the Triumphs of her rival *Margery* (now Lady *Moore*) who from the meekest of Creatures, is so elevated with her present Grandeur, that she becomes a very *Virago, a worse Plague than the Dragon*; and leads her Husband such a confounded Life, that he runs away from her on the very Wedding-Night, and flies, for Quiet-sake to the Desart; where meeting with *Mauxalinda*, they renew their former Loves, and grow fonder than ever. Lady *Moore* pursues them with the utmost Fury, surprizes them in the height of their Endeerments, and sends *Mauxalinda* to Prison. *Moore* makes a second Elopement, and send *Gubbins* to release *Mauxalinda*; which being done, *Gubbins*, who has long loved her in secret, courts her, and gains her consent. *Moore* wants to renew his former Acquaintance with *Mauxalinda*, but is repulsed by her, and furiously attack'd by his Lady: After a smart Scolding-Bout they make up: *Moore* is friends with his Lady; *Gubbins* is married to *Mauxalinda*; and the Opera concludes, according to the Custom of all Operas, with the General Reconciliation of all Parties, no matter how absurd, improbable, or rediculous.[1]

The amusing story provides opportunity for all sorts of silliness, to which Lampe adds music using new and different techniques in the overture and opening chorus, in aria forms, and in over-all formal organization. Nevertheless, *Margery* proved to be of a less enduring character than *The Dragon*. Perhaps the plot was too silly or was too closely tied to the parent work for *Margery* to exist alone. Londoners, after all, had a wide variety of equally funny pantomimes and farces available almost any night of the week, and *Margery* may soon have lost its identity. Lacking many of the distinctive and appealing elements of *The Dragon*, such

---

[1] Henry Carey, *Margery; or, A Worse Plague than the Dragon* (libretto) (London: J. Shuckburgh, 1738), Argument.

as the direct burlesque of opera seria, the use of familiar English folklore, and the Dragon himself, *Margery* had to rely on comedy and its relationship to the parent opera for success, and these simply may not have been enough. In addition, *Margery* is not as satisfying and interesting a work, either musically or dramatically, as is *The Dragon*. Carey must bear much of the blame, for the silly libretto provided little opportunity for continuity of dramatic expression, one of the strong points of Lampe's operatic style. Also, few occasions existed for writing the fine choruses that had helped to distinguish *The Dragon*, and in fact *Margery* contains few important choruses at all.

From the very beginning Lampe and Carey seem to have been aware of the shortcomings of their sequel and of the difference between the reception of it and of *The Dragon*, for *Margery* remained in an almost constant state of revision, with new arias, recitatives, or ensembles being added for each revival. A definitive, workable arrangement of the work, such as had existed from very early in the life of *The Dragon*, was never achieved with *Margery*, perhaps because of the inherent and inescapable problems resulting from its subject matter and its necessary tie to *The Dragon*.

Too dismal a picture should not be painted, however, for *Margery* was by all the standards of the time quite a success. It helped to increase the popularity of the composer, author, and performers, and established Lampe all the more firmly as a leading theatrical composer of his day. During 1739 it was printed, minus the recitatives, in full score, as had been *The Dragon*, and the new opera undoubtedly not only increased Lampe's artistic reputation but improved his financial security as well.

Possibly because of his prosperity and because of his continued close relationship with the same cast throughout the long runs of both *The Dragon* and *Margery*, Lampe married Isabella Young, his leading lady, probably sometime during the week of December 4, 1738.[2] Lampe had enjoyed a close relationship with the Young family for some time, and probably had met them through opera acquaintances. Cecilia Young, Isabella's older sister and a student of Geminiani, had sung the leading roles in Lampe's *Amelia*, *Britannia*, *Dione*, *Cupid and Psyche*, and *Aurora's Nuptials*. This elder Young sister was a popular concert and entr'acte artist and had sung for Handel as early as January 8, 1735, when her fine performance had aroused the jealousy of Anna Strada, Handel's Italian prima donna from 1729 to 1737.[3] In 1736 or 1737 Cecilia married Thomas Arne, although her father, the organist at All Hallows Church, Barking, disapproved of the marriage for religious reasons. Arne was a Roman Catholic and his new wife soon became a convert. The father might well have disapproved of the match on other grounds, too, for the marriage was destined never to be a happy one. Arne apparently married Cecilia mostly because she, or rather her voice, promised to be a professional asset, but when her voice failed and she became a liability, he left her. In all fairness, however, Mrs. Arne's character seems to have been far from exemplary.[4]

Isabella Young probably was a few years younger than Cecilia, who was born in 1711,[5]

---

[2] Lampe likely was married between Tuesday, December 5, and Saturday, December 9, 1738, since all advertisements from the Tuesday and before list Isabella as Miss Young and all advertisements from Saturday and afterwards list her as Mrs. Lampe.

[3] Paul Henry Lang, *George Frideric Handel* (New York: Norton, 1966), 251-53.

[4] Julian Herbage, "Arne: His Character and Environment," *Proceedings of the Royal Musical Association* 87 (1960-61): 19-22; Hugh Arthur Scott, "Sidelights on Thomas Arne," *Musical Quarterly* 21 (July 1935): 301-10.

[5] Mollie Sands, *Invitation to Ranelagh, 1724-1803* (London: John Westhouse, 1946), 75; the Youngs and their relatives are discussed on pp. 74-82.

since Isabella's singing debut lags Cecilia's by that length of time. I can find no justification for Mollie Sands's assertion that Isabella was "apparently the eldest."[6] The first probable reference to her on the stage is in a Drury Lane advertisement in *The Daily Advertiser* of November 26, 1733, which mentions "a Grand Dance of Spirits as perform'd before the Emperor of Constantinople at the Feast of Bairam . . . Amphritrite—Miss Young, who has never appeared on any stage before." Both Lampe and Cecilia were at Drury Lane during this season as part of a company formed to replace the Drury Lane revolters. The first advertisement to include her first name is for a concert at Mercer's Hall, December 13, 1734, where she and Cecilia sang and Handel's opera musicians played. Isabella sang in many such concerts during the next few years, and they constituted the majority of her stage experience prior to *The Dragon*. At another Mercer's Hall concert on February 11, 1736, Esther Young, a third sister and the future Mauxalinda, first appeared on stage.

Unlike the Arnes, the Lampes remained a close family, both within their marriage and with their Young relatives. Esther Young, who never married, at least not until after Lampe's death, lived with the Lampes, since advertisments always list the

ROGER *and* JOAN;

OR THE

Country Wedding.

A

COMIC MASK:

As it is ACTED at the

Theatre-Royal in *Covent-Garden.*

With several New SONGS;

Set to Mufick by Mr. LAMPE.

LONDON:

Printed for T. COOPER, at the Globe in *Pater-noster-Row*, and Sold by the Bookfellers of *London* and *Weftminfter*. MDCCXXXIX.

Title page of *Roger and Joan*.

sisters at the same address, and Cecilia sometimes lived with them as well. Lampe's only son, Charles John Frederick, carried on both the Young family tradition as a church organist, succeeding his grandfather at All Hallows, Barking, as well as the Young family name of Charles. This practice of giving different members in different generations of the family the same first name, plus the fact that most members of the family were musicians who often were referred to only by surname, had made the Young family geneology especially confusing for both modern and eighteenth-century writers. Fortunately, much of the difficulty has been unravelled by Mollie Sands in various articles and writings.[7]

In 1738-39 another short Lampe work appeared at Covent Garden, although *The London Stage* and some other major sources fail to mention it. A libretto exists, however, for *Roger and Joan*[8] (above and overleaf), which according to Nicoll and Genest was

---

6 Mollie Sands, "Some English Musical Clans," *Monthly Musical Record* 73 (October 1943): 181.

7 See the two works cited above plus Roger Fiske, *English Theatre Music in the Eighteenth Century* (London: Oxford University Press, 1973), 130-31.

8 At the University of Michigan.

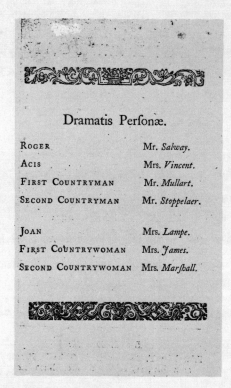

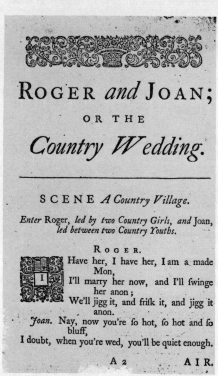

Dramatis Personae and first page of text from *Roger and Joan.*

performed on March 20, 1739.[9] Whether the work ever was performed again is uncertain, although since such short items in the evening's program often were not listed in advertisements (which explains their absence from *The London Stage* and elsewhere), subsequent performances were not only possible but likely. The libretto was advertised in *The London Magazine* in October 1739, so perhaps the work was revived or continued to be performed at that time. The anonymous author of the text seems to have taken his material mostly from the comic section of Pierre Antoine Motteaux's *Acis and Galatea* libretto, written for a 1701 Drury Lane masque by Eccles. None of Lampe's music is extant.

1739-1740

The 1739-40 season was another successful year for the Lampes at Covent Garden. *The Dragon* remained popular, being performed five times in September to help open the

---

9 Allardyce Nicoll, *A History of Early Eighteenth Century Drama* (Cambridge: Cambridge University Press, 1925), 382; John Genest, *Some Account of the English Stage*, 10 vols. (Bath: H. E. Carrington, 1832), 3:589.

season and fourteen times throughout the year. *Margery* was revived for two performances. Since Lampe's old pantomime *Cupid and Psyche/Columbine Courtezan* continued to be used at Drury Lane, there were times during this season when one could find three different Lampe works being presented during the same week at two different London theaters.

Mrs. Lampe also was in demand as a singer. John Rich, the owner/manager of Covent Garden, frequently cast her in the serious sections of his famous pantomimes, such as *The Necromancer*, *Cupid and Bacchus*, and *The Four Seasons*. She performed as a singing actress in comedies like *The Rehearsal*, as well as in serious works such as *Macbeth*, and both she and her sister Esther also did a good deal of entr'acte singing, sometimes of Lampe songs. When Lampe's version of *The Opera of Operas* was revived at Covent Garden on May 30, 1740 (possibly because Fielding's *The Tragedy of Tragedies* recently had been revived by both Covent Garden and Drury Lane), Mrs. Lampe sang the leading female role. She sang Nancy in Harry Carey's *Nancy, or the Parting Lovers,*[10] along with other singers from *The Dragon*, when the new work was first staged at Covent Garden.

Mrs. Lampe also sang the lead in her husband's newest work *Orpheus and Euridice*, and the pantomime soon became a favorite of both the audience and Rich, who starred in his usual role of Harlequin. Although *Orpheus* was not put into production until February 12, 1740, by the end of the season it had received forty-six performances, and had become Lampe's third great musical success in as many years.

The one extant song from the work, "The parent bird," is delightful, and appeared in journals, magazines, song collections, and broadsides. Still, the appeal of *Orpheus* may have resulted as much from its lavish scenic effects as from its music or humor. Rich, with

---

[10] This short intermezzo is musically one of Carey's more important works; see Fiske, *English Theatre Music*, 155-56.

Title page of a collection of instrumental music arrangements from the pantomime *Orpheus and Euridice,* 1740.

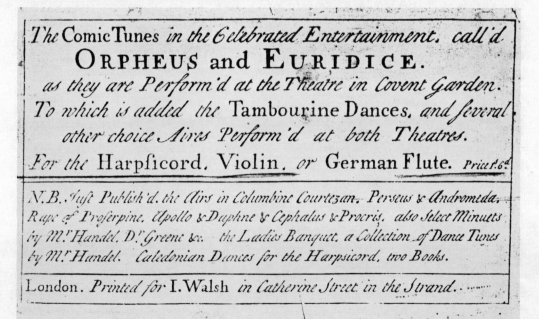

much confidence in his composer's and his own ability, spent over £2000 on all of the scenery,[11] the most famous element of which was a seventeen-foot long clockwork serpent designed to attack and kill Euridice (Mrs. Lampe). About a month after its first performance, *Orpheus* and its scenery were described by one of the audience in a letter to the Edinburgh *Scots Magazine*:

> Orpheus and Euridice, an opera, draws the whole town to Covent-garden Theatre; whether for the opera itself, (the words of which are such miserable stuff) or for the pantomimical interlude with which it is intermixed, I cannot determine. The musick is pretty good, and the tricks are not foolisher than usual, and some have said that they have more meaning than most that have preceeded them. — The performance is grand, as to the scenery. What pleases almost every body, is, a regular growth of trees, represented more like nature than what has yet been seen upon the stage; and the representation of a serpent so lively, as to frighten half the Ladies who see it. It is, indeed, curious in its kind, being wholly a piece of machinery, that enters, performs its exercise of head, body, and tail, in a most surprising manner, and rushes behind the curtain with a velocity scarce credible. It is about a foot and a half in circumference, at the thickest part, and far exceeds the former custom of stuffing a boy into such likeness. It is believed to have cost more than 200 l.; and when the multitude of wheels, springs, etc. whereof it consists, are considered, the charge will not appear extravagant. — The whole Royal Family have seen this performance; and, from what can be judged, every body else will see it before the end of the season: the house being every day full at three o'clock; though seldom empty till after eleven.[12]

The famous serpent, unfortunately, proved to be the downfall of its builder, for the man became so infatuated by his creation that he built dozens of smaller versions for his toy shop, but soon lost his trade and his fortune through having hoards of unsold serpents on his hands.[13] The pantomime also caused some trouble for Rich; the cantankerous Sir John Hill accused Rich of stealing the idea for the pantomime from a similar libretto Hill had submitted to Rich a few years earlier. After a pamphlet war, Rich and his libretto, which probably had been written by Lewis Theobold, emerged the victors, and *Orpheus* and its serpent continued to run as one of Rich's major pantomime attractions for several years.

During the successful runs of his stage compositions, Lampe had continued to work with songs, writing them to be sung by his students at home or by his company in the theaters, and collecting and editing them for publication. In 1739 the London engraver and publisher Benjamin Cole brought out *British Melody; or, The Musical Magazine*, a collection of sixty songs, each with a beautiful engraving above the caption-title. Lampe had been asked to edit the collection, at least one-fourth of which is his own music. Cole describes Lampe's role in the preface to the work, which also speaks of Lampe's high reputation at the time:

> In order therefore to answer the End proposed, and render the following laborious and expensive Undertaking as valuable as possible I could, I prevailed on the

---

11 R. J. Broadbent, *A History of Pantomime* (London: Simpkin, Marshall, Hamilton, Kent, 1901), 158.

12 *The Scots Magazine* 2 (March 1740): 113-14.

13 See Broadbent, *Pantomime*, 160; Genest, *English Stage*, 3:619; Albert Edward Wilson, *King Panto, the Story of Pantomime* (New York: E. P. Dutton, 1935), 59.

ingenious Mr. *Lampe* (whose Character is too well known to need any thing to recommend it) not only to direct me in the Choice of the most favourite Words, but to revise the whole Musick, and introduce into the Body of the Work some *Select Pieces* of his own Composition; and for that Reason alone, if no other, I flatter myself that this *Magazine* will be acknowledg'd by all Impartial Judges to be preferable to any Thing of the like Kind hitherto extant.

Two of the Lampe songs in the collection provide clues about some of his activities outside the theater during the 1730s and 1740s. One song, "Farewell to Vaux-Hall" (no. 33), is a setting of a 1733 text written by Sam Godwin, which laments the winter closing of the gardens after the extremely successful first *ridotto* festival of 1732.[14] The engraving style of the plate is much different from that of the rest of the collection, indicating that the song probably had been issued previously as a single broadside and implying Lampe's connection with the London pleasure gardens from early in his career.

Another Lampe song whose engraving does not match most of the rest of the book is "The Fellow Craft's Song" (no. 45), a Masonic song that, it seems, could only have been written by a fellow Freemason. The song must have been held in high regard by the Masons, for an inscription under the caption-title reads, "To be Sung & Sounded w.th Trumpets, French Horn, &c &c at y.e Grand Feast," an occasion for which a song by a non-Mason hardly would have been appropriate. Two other Masonic songs (nos. 8 and 54) are printed anonymously in the collection and may or may not be by Lampe, but they demonstrate his interest in the organization and appear to indicate a relationship with or membership in it.

The 1739-40 season seems to have been an especially important one for Lampe songs, for in addition to *British Melody* one finds in the July 19, 1740 issue of *The London Daily Post and General Advertiser* an announcement of another Lampe song collection, to be composed entirely of Lampe's own works:

> *This Day is publish'd* Number I. of LYRA BRITANNICA, being a Collection of Ballads and Arietta's, the Words and Musick entirely New. The Musick composed, with a figured Thorough-Bass, adapted to the German Flute and Common Flute, by JOHN FREDERICK LAMPE.
>
> As often as these Songs are publish'd, Four Songs are to make a Number, and these Numbers will always be engrav'd by the best Engravers of Musick, and in the most intelligible Manner, and every Number deliver'd, stitch'd up in Covers, to the Subscribers at the Price of 6d.
>
> To be sold at the Musick-shops and Musick-sellers in Town and Country.
>
> Such persons as are willing to subscribe to this Work, are desired to give Notice to C. Corbett, Bookseller and Publisher, at Addison's Head, against St. Dunstan's Church, Fleet Street.
>
> *To prevent Imposition of incorrect Copies by pyrating these Songs, each Number will be sign'd at the Bottom of the Title-page by Mr. Lampe.

Work on *Lyra Britannica* continued for the next few years, and a cumulative edition of the fascicles, containing twelve songs, was issued in 1745.

---

[14] Walter Sidney Scott, *Green Retreats—The Story of Vauxhall Gardens, 1661-1859* (London: Oldham's Press, 1955), 68. Visiting the public *ridottos* (sometimes called a *ridotto al fresco* if outdoors) at the London pleasure gardens, with their lavish music, dancing, food, and other entertainment, became one of the major and more popular social activities of the eighteenth century.

Less than a week after the above advertisement appeared, the announcement of a third new Lampe song collection was printed in the London papers. *The London Daily Post and General Advertiser* of July 25, 1740 contains the following:

> *The Copper-Plates being entirely finished of that beautiful Work, entitled* THE MUSICAL ENTERTAINER; consisting of the most Favourite Italian, English, and Scots Songs, Cantatas, &c. &c. extant. The Words by the best Poets; and set to Musick by PURCELL, HANDELL, CORELLI, GREEN, And other EMINENT MASTERS.
>
> Adapted to the Voice, Violin, German and Common Flute, Harpsichord, &c. all neatly engraved on Copper-plates; at the Head of each of which is a beautiful Picture adapted to each Song, designed by GRAVELOT and others and engrav'd By G. BICKHAM, jun. Now carefully Corrected, and a figured Thorough Bass added to each Song, and made entirely complete. By JOHN FREDERICK LAMPE —
>
> Just publish'd Price 2s. 6d. The Art of Music; By John Frederick Lampe.

Bickham's collection had been begun several years earlier and issued in fascicles, but although the book had included several Lampe works, notably most of the arias from *The Dragon*, Lampe's name had not been associated with it in its early forms. Lampe appears to have been asked to correct and write thoroughbass parts for the final, cumulative version of *The Musical Entertainer*,[15] probably because of his fame as teacher, writer on thoroughbass, and composer.

Also in July of 1740 Lampe's second theory treatise, *The Art of Musick*, appeared (his *A Plain and Compendious Method of Teaching Thorough Bass* had been printed in 1737). While no advertisement mentioning the date of publication can be found, the notice for *The Musical Entertainer* quoted above reports that *The Art of Musick* had been "Just publish'd." The book was highly esteemed by Lampe's contemporaries and is quite a learned work, demonstrating Lampe's familiarity with the theoretical writings of Euclid, Zarlino, Vicentino, Mattheson, Rameau, Pepusch, and others.

Lampe bases many of his theories on the overtone series, his use of which apparently was developed independently of Rameau; throughout the treatise there also is a heavy emphasis on "Nature" as it applies to practical musical situations. Unlike Rameau and his concept of Nature, however, Lampe believes that any attempt to reduce music to mathematics is a fallacy, derived from erroneous ideas of the ancients, and he states that to follow only mathematics and rules "would deprive us of the greatest Part of the Beauties of Musick."[16] Reasoning from the belief that the human passions music depicts and evokes cannot be described mathematically, Lampe writes that "to know only the right Use of Concords, the Preparations and Resolutions of Discords, or to make Subject upon Subject, without knowing how to touch the Passions, the Work most probably will be dull, flat, and insipid."[17] The treatise also gives clues on some matters of Lampe's performance practice — he suggests, for example, a crescendo and diminuendo on a long, held note[18] — as well as insights into his attitude toward the voice, choruses,[19] and other aspects of music.

---

[15] A modern facsimile edition of the cumulative 1740 London edition in two volumes, printed by Charles Corbett, is published (New York: Broude Bros., 1965).

[16] John Frederick Lampe, *The Art of Musick* (London: C. Corbett, 1740), 33.

[17] Ibid., 5.

[18] Ibid., 7.

[19] Ibid., 11.

1739-40 had been a very good year for Lampe. He had written a great theatrical success for the third season in a row, he had issued a second respected theory treatise, and he had advertised three new song collections. He was esteemed in most musical quarters of the city and was at the height of his prosperity and popularity. Unfortunately, fate was to take a turn for the worse, with the ensuing few years becoming hard times for the Lampes and most other London musicians.

1740-1744

"The years 1740 and 1741 mark a dividing point in the English theatre. . . . In February 1741, Macklin played Shylock for the first time, and eight months later Garrick conquered London with his blazing performance of Richard III."[20] The era inaugurated by Charles Macklin and David Garrick was one of revolution in acting style. In the early eighteenth century, tragic acting in spoken drama was as stylized as in opera seria. Actors strutted, bellowed, and declaimed in stentorian tones while either striking a position at the front of the stage or accompanying their pondorous rhetoric with equally heavy and conventional stage motions. Lifelike impersonation of a character did not exist. The new style of Garrick and Macklin was founded on the realistic portrayal of tragic characters, and the style soon took London theater by storm.

One result of the change in emphasis from the work to the way it was being performed was a drastic reduction in the number of new works that were scheduled. In the seasons 1741-47, Drury Lane produced a total of only eighteen new plays (seven main plays and eleven afterpieces) while Covent Garden brought out only three new works, even though during this period both companies were performing about seventy different plays in a given season. As the main tragedy grew more and more important, emphasis on other parts of the evening's entertainment—music, pantomimes, and afterpieces—decreased, so that not only authors but also dancers, composers, and other musicians found themselves out of work. The appeal of ballad opera had waned, and Italian opera was dead for the time being. Although Handel's new oratorios often were applauded, they certainly did not enjoy consistent success or reap substantial financial rewards, as the following passage from *The London Stage*'s introduction to the 1744-45 season makes clear:

> Handel made a desperate effort to get subscriptions for some oratorios and eke out a program in a pitiful attempt climaxed on 17 January by his famous letter in praise of the English language. Even so, he gave only sixteen performances throughout the season.[21]

With the theater in such a state, Lampe's position became increasingly precarious. His new one-act work for the 1740-41 season at Covent Garden, *The Sham Conjuror*, while a delightful piece and of high musical quality, failed after only three performances on April 18, 21, and 22, 1741. Under the circumstances it could have suffered no other fate, even though a success evidently had been anticipated and a printed full score prepared and published. *The Dragon* again had opened the season, but was presented only nine times. The pantomime

---

[20] William W. Appleton, *Charles Macklin* (Cambridge, Mass.: Harvard University Press, 1960), 43.

[21] *The London Stage, 1660-1800*, 5 parts (Carbondale: Southern Illinois University Press, 1960-68), 3:1115-16.

Title page of the printed full score of *The Sham Conjuror*, 1741.

THE

GRAND

CONCERTO,

Favourite Songs, Dueto's, Trio & Chorus

IN THE

NEW MASQUE

call'd the

SHAM CONJURER

As it is now perform'd at the

THEATRE ROYAL

in

COVENT GARDEN

Set to Musick by

John Frederick Lampe

London Printed for; & Sold by **John Simpson** at y Viol and
Flute in Sweeting's Alley opposite the East Door of the Royal Exchange.

Orpheus and Euridice retained some popularity and appeared on thirty-four evenings, but the use of the musically weak pantomime could hardly have given Lampe much pleasure or encouragement, although it probably did insure his employment.

During the summer of 1741, perhaps as an attempt to find greener pastures or merely to supplement his dwindling income, Lampe organized a tour of the provinces, where his company performed *The Dragon*, *Margery*, *Amelia*, and other works. *Amelia*, almost ten years old by then, possibly was rewritten somewhat for the occasion, and the only extant manuscript score of *The Dragon* probably dates from this time. Although it is unknown whether or not Carey was a member of the company, his music was performed, testifying to a continuing collaboration and friendly relationship between him and Lampe. The young Charles Burney heard the group frequently at Chester, where he was in school, and remarked later on the enjoyable experiences.[22]

In the 1741-42 season Lampe wrote no new work for Covent Garden, although he probably helped in a revision of *Orpheus* that took place and composed some songs for a revival of Shakespeare's *The Winter's Tale*, which began on November 11, 1741. The revision of *Orpheus* was seen on thirty-seven evenings, but *The Dragon* and *Margery* lay nearly dormant, the former being given six times while the latter appeared only once—its last performance until 1755. The state of music theater became so unbearable in London that Arne and his wife made a trip to Dublin to check out conditions abroad. After a few successes and a return to London to make arrangements for an extended stay, they were back in Dublin in time for the beginning of the 1742-43 season for an engagement of two years. Handel also had left London for Dublin and there presented the first performance of *Messiah*. Arne's sister, Mrs. Cibber, had sung in *Messiah* and was still in Dublin when the Arnes arrived.

The 1742-43 season in London saw the Lampes leave their five-year position at Covent Garden, where no further opportunities seemed to exist, and replace the Arnes at Drury Lane. The new situation proved to be little better, however, for *The Dragon* was given only seven performances, and no new Lampe works were staged. It seems that Garrick, who had come to Drury Lane, and Fleetwood, the manager, had little use or desire for new music. Probably unable to get a benefit at Drury Lane, Lampe rented the Little Theatre on March 24, 1743 for a single benefit performance for his wife and staged a production of *Amelia* there.[23] Lampe was to see the inside of that theater quite a bit during the coming year.

The situation at Drury Lane had become unpleasant for more people than the musicians. Charles Fleetwood, the manager, had accumulated great financial difficulties for his theater, and as one biographer of Garrick describes, he "seemed to his alarmed company to be getting rather depraved."[24] The manager's promises for improvements were continually broken, salaries were months in arrears, and the personnel were treated with insolence and contempt by one Pierson, the house treasurer. Eventually, during the summer of 1743, the principal players decided to secede under leadership of Macklin and Garrick; all determined to remain

---

[22] Charles Burney, *A General History of Music* (London, 1776-89), new ed. in 2 vols. with critical and historical notes by Frank Mercer (New York: Harcourt, 1935; reprint, New York: Dover, 1957), 2:1007.

[23] According to benefit advertisements, the Lampes had moved. Notices for benefits in 1740 and 1742 indicate that throughout those years Lampe had lived in the same house—May 30, 1740: "Tickets at Lampe's House, Brownlow Street"; and May 30, 1742: "Tickets at . . . Mrs. Lampe's and Miss Young's Lodgings, at the Golden Ball, in Brownlow Street." Brownlow Street was near Covent Garden and a frequent home of musicians and others from the theaters; see "An Eighteenth-Century Directory of London Musicians," *Galpin Society Journal* 2 (1949): 27-31. The address for the March 24, 1743 benefit was "Mr. Lampe's at the Golden Unicorn in Hanover St., Long-Acre," a few blocks away.

[24] Carola Oman Lenanton, *David Garrick* (Bunga, Suffolk: Hodder & Stoughton, 1956), 64.

First page of MS full score of *The Dragon of Wantley,* MS 927, Parry Room Library, Royal College of Music, London; likely copied about 1741 for Lampe's use and containing his personal corrections and annotations.

together until the manager agreed to accept them back on their own terms. The new company hoped that Garrick could obtain a royal patent for them from the Lord Chamberlain, and they set up shop in the Little Theatre. No patent was forthcoming, however, so that the company, which without the patent could not legally perform, soon asked Garrick to intercede with Fleetwood for them. The manager agreed to allow all to return except Macklin, whom Fleetwood considered to be the ringleader, but Macklin, who had not been informed of the arrangement, branded Garrick as a traitor to the cause. By early December 1743, Garrick and the others were back at Drury Lane, and Macklin was left out of the theatrical ranks entirely, although to his credit Garrick tried several times to help his friend.[25]

The Lampes' position in the revolt is not clear. During the 1743-44 season Esther Young and Isabella Young Lampe were back at Covent Garden, although Mrs. Lampe's name is not listed in advertisements until January 14, 1744. J. F. Lampe's whereabouts are extremely uncertain. *Orpheus* was revived at Covent Garden and *Cupid and Psyche* at Drury Lane, but it is unknown whether Lampe was connected with either production. He may have been with the Little Theatre company, or perhaps he had been so shocked and demoralized by the suicide of his close friend Harry Carey on October 4, 1743 that he was unable to work for awhile.[26] His despair of the entire London theater situation seems to have led him to lend Arne the score of *The Dragon* for production in Dublin, and 1743-44 is conspicuous as the only season during Lampe's life in London and after its debut that *The Dragon* did not walk the boards of London theaters.

Early in 1744 there was again activity in the Little Theatre. Both Lampe and Macklin were involved, possibly, Fiske believes, in some form of partnership.[27] Macklin had devised a method of evading the Licensing Act of 1735, and although a partnership cannot be documented, it is understandable that Lampe might have been willing to work with Macklin in return for the opportunity of performing his new works that had been rejected by the two patent theaters. Lampe's first contribution to the joint effort, an opera called *The Queen of Spain; or, Farinelli at Madrid*, was performed four times, beginning January 19, 1744. Although some newspapers give the author as James Ayres, a work of the same title had been produced in Dublin in 1741 by Carey's and Lampe's friend James Worsdale, who is listed as the author of the London production in other eighteenth-century sources.[28] Advertisements also list James Ayres as the librettist of Lampe's other new opera *The Kiss Accepted and Returned*, which was presented at the Little Theatre on April 16 and 19 along with *The Queen of Spain*. Neither music nor libretto survives for either piece, and, given the conditions under which they were performed, there was no possibility of the works enjoying

---

[25] The confusing events surrounding the stage revolt are explained in the following works: Arthur Murphy, *The Life of David Garrick*, 2 vols. (London: J. Wright, 1801), 1:57-69; Thomas Davies, *Memoirs of the Life of David Garrick*, 2 vols. (London: Thomas Davies, 1780), 1:60-80; Lenanton, *Garrick*, 64-68; James Thomas Kirkman, *Memoirs of the Life of Charles Macklin*, 2 vols. (London: Lackington, Allen, & Co., 1799), 1:273-91; William Cooke, *Memoirs of Charles Macklin, Comedian* (London: James Asperne, 1804), 133-36; Edward Abbott Parry, *Charles Macklin* (London: Kegan Paul, Trench, Trübner, 1891), 69-79; Appleton, *Macklin*, 60-65; Walter James MacQueen-Pope, *Theatre Royal, Drury Lane* (London: W. H. Allen, 1945), 160-63.

[26] Lampe may have participated in the Covent Garden benefit for Carey's widow, given on November 17, 1743.

[27] Fiske, *English Theatre Music*, 157.

[28] W. J. Lawrence, "Early Irish Ballad and Comic Opera," *Musical Quarterly* 8 (July 1922): 405; David Erskine Baker, *Biographia Dramatica*, 3rd ed., ed. Isaac Reed and Stephen Jones, 3 vols. (London: Longman, Hurst, Rees, Orme, Brown, 1812), 3:189; William Rufus Chetwood, *The British Theatre* (London: R. Baldwin, 1752), 185; and many later sources.

anything approaching a successful season. During the rest of the spring Lampe possibly provided music for Macklin, while Mrs. Lampe occasionally sang in Macklin's productions, but no more new Lampe operas appeared.[29] He could hardly have been encouraged about his prospects for the future.

Lampe's years immediately following *The Dragon* had seen both triumphant achievement and deep, discouraging disappointment. He had produced three extremely successful new works in three seasons, had become respected as a theorist and author, and was in demand as an editor and composer of song collections. But through the capricious changes of public taste and an emphasis on the interest in a novel acting style rather than music, the fortunes of Lampe as well as those of his fellow musicians and authors began to crumble. Some musicians, like Arne and Handel, left the country. Lampe's closest friend, Harry Carey, in a fit of despondency over theatrical dilemmas and the death of his son, committed suicide. Although unable to find a satisfying musical position in the theaters, Lampe remained in London and probably eked out a living, along with his wife, through teaching and performing. Finally in the middle and later 1740s the plight of the Lampes and other London musicians would begin to improve.

---

[29] For accounts of Macklin's activities at the Little Theatre, see Kirkman, *Macklin*, 292-95; Cooke, *Macklin*, 148-50; Parry, *Macklin*, 78-83; Appleton, *Macklin*, 68-70.

List of characters and first page of text from libretto of *Pyramus and Thisbe*, 1745.

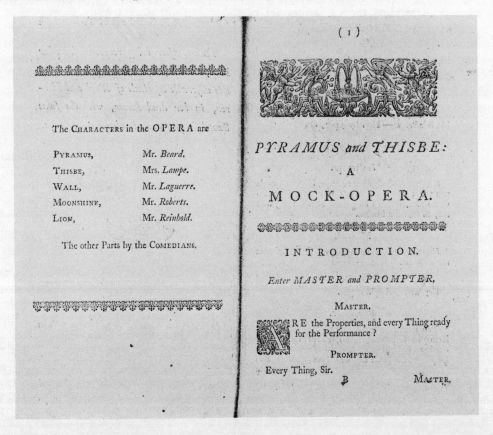

5 THE FINAL YEARS IN LONDON AND ABROAD

1744-1748

By the fall of 1744 Arne and his wife had returned from Ireland to their old positions at Drury Lane and Lampe was again the composer for Covent Garden.[1] Rich of Covent Garden finally accepted a new Lampe opera, and *Pyramus and Thisbe* ran for twenty nights during its first season, even though performances did not begin until January 26, 1745. In testimony to its success, the full score was available almost immediately, being advertised by Walsh in the *General Evening Post* of February 14-16. This virtual chamber opera was another burlesque, and is described as a "mock-opera" on its title page. The libretto probably was adapted by Lampe from an earlier piece of the same title written by Richard Leveridge, the famous bass.[2] Leveridge, who was over thirty years Lampe's senior and had sung for Purcell, had worked together with Lampe at Covent Garden and had sung the leading role in Lampe's *The Sham Conjuror.*

What little plot exists in *Pyramus* is taken from the rustics' short play in *Midsummer Night's Dream.* There are only two main characters, Pyramus and Thisbe, plus a wall, a lion, and a moon, all of which sing. The whole thing is extremely silly, in the style of the pompous tragedies of the time, and Lampe must have felt some satisfaction in successfully burlesquing styles and conventions of a genre that had helped to bring about the decline of music in the London theaters. *Pyramus and Thisbe* became quite popular and was performed by companies in Bristol, Kent, and probably elsewhere in the provinces, in addition to its runs in London.[3]

During the 1744-45 season at Covent Garden, Lampe also was asked to write new songs for a revival of John Gay's *The What d'Ye Call It*, which was performed on April 4 and 22. *Orpheus* retained some favor and was given nineteen performances. *The Queen of Spain* was revived for a February 14 benefit for Daniel Sullivan at the Little Theater. Also notable during this season and the next was the appearance of *The Dragon* at Drury Lane instead of Covent Garden, even though Lampe was at the latter theater. Perhaps Rich had tired of the piece and Arne was able to intercede for Lampe and get the popular work produced at Drury Lane. Lampe likely, however, still would have conducted his opera, even though it was presented in Arne's theater and with a new cast.[4]

---

[1] Young Burney came to London in 1744 as apprentice to Arne, and therefore not only had intimate and first hand knowledge of the general theatrical situation at the time but also of the Lampes, the in-laws of the Arnes. Burney's comments about 1744 come from his *A General History of Music* (London, 1776-89), new ed. in 2 vols. with critical and historical notes by Frank Mercer (New York: Harcourt, 1935; reprint, New York: Dover, 1957), 2:1007-08.

[2] For a good, short biographical sketch of Leveridge, see Roger Fiske, *English Theatre Music in the Eighteenth Century* (London: Oxford University Press, 1973), 633.

[3] Sybil Rosenfeld, *Strolling Players & Drama in the Provinces* (Cambridge: Cambridge University Press, 1939), 210, 236.

[4] Esther Young, who sang her old role of Mauxalinda, was an exception; in 1744-45 she seems to have worked with the Arnes at Drury Lane, while Mrs. Lampe remained at Covent Garden with her husband.

TABLE 1

Lampe Works Performed in London during the 1744-45 Season

1745/Date		Work	Theater
January			
1	Tuesday	Orpheus and Euridice	Covent Garden
2	Wednesday	Orpheus and Euridice	Covent Garden
4	Friday	Orpheus and Euridice	Covent Garden
5	Saturday	Orpheus and Euridice	Covent Garden
7	Monday	Orpheus and Euridice	Covent Garden
11	Friday	Orpheus and Euridice	Covent Garden
19	Saturday	Orpheus and Euridice	Covent Garden
23	Wednesday	Orpheus and Euridice	Covent Garden
25	Friday	Pyramus and Thisbe	Covent Garden
26	Saturday	Pyramus and Thisbe	Covent Garden
28	Monday	Pyramus and Thisbe	Covent Garden
29	Tuesday	Pyramus and Thisbe	Covent Garden
31	Thursday	Pyramus and Thisbe	Covent Garden
February			
1	Friday	Pyramus and Thisbe	Covent Garden
2	Saturday	Pyramus and Thisbe	Covent Garden
4	Monday	Pyramus and Thisbe	Covent Garden
5	Tuesday	Pyramus and Thisbe	Covent Garden
6	Wednesday	Pyramus and Thisbe	Covent Garden
7	Thursday	Pyramus and Thisbe	Covent Garden
8	Friday	Pyramus and Thisbe	Covent Garden
9	Saturday	Orpheus and Euridice	Covent Garden
11	Monday	Pyramus and Thisbe	Covent Garden
12	Tuesday	Orpheus and Euridice	Covent Garden
13	Wednesday	Orpheus and Euridice	Covent Garden
14	Thursday	Queen of Spain	Little Theater
15	Friday	Dragon of Wantley	Drury Lane
16	Saturday	Dragon of Wantley	Drury Lane
18	Monday	Dragon of Wantley	Drury Lane
28	Thursday	Orpheus and Euridice	Covent Garden
March			
2	Saturday	Pyramus and Thisbe	Covent Garden
5	Tuesday	Dragon of Wantley	Drury Lane
5	Tuesday	Pyramus and Thisbe	Covent Garden
9	Saturday	Orpheus and Euridice	Covent Garden
12	Tuesday	Pyramus and Thisbe	Covent Garden
16	Saturday	Orpheus and Euridice	Covent Garden
23	Saturday	Orpheus and Euridice	Covent Garden
25	Monday	Pyramus and Thisbe	Covent Garden
26	Tuesday	Orpheus and Euridice	Covent Garden
30	Saturday	Pyramus and Thisbe	Covent Garden
April			
1	Thursday	What d'Ye Call It	Covent Garden
6	Saturday	Orpheus and Euridice	Covent Garden
16	Tuesday	Pyramus and Thisbe	Covent Garden
20	Saturday	Orpheus and Euridice	Covent Garden
22	Monday	What d'Ye Call It	Covent Garden
25	Thursday	Pyramus and Thisbe	Covent Garden
May			
21	Tuesday	Orpheus and Euridice	Covent Garden

All performances of Lampe works that were given during the 1744-45 season in London, according to theater advertisements, are listed in Table 1. The table demonstrates that, with one exception, all of the works were presented on different nights, and that Lampe could have conducted all of their performances. The one exception is on March 5, 1745, when *The Dragon* was advertised at Drury Lane and *Pyramus* at Covent Garden, but this conflict is not unresolvable. *The London Stage* warns that newspaper advertisements occasionally can be misleading, for sometimes an announced work is known not to have been performed, another piece being given in its place.[5] I believe that such was the case with the Lampe overlap, especially considering his rather possessive attitude toward the score of *The Dragon*.

The Lampes were always at Covent Garden during the next season, 1745-46. Perhaps the performing of *The Dragon* at Drury Lane made Rich appreciate Lampe the more. *Pyramus* survived a revival well, with thirteen performances, and *The What d'Ye Call It* was presented three times. *Orpheus* again was one of Rich's important pantomimes of the season, being seen on thirty evenings, but *The Dragon* appeared only once, as a benefit for Mrs. Lampe. Lampe seems to have been asked for no new major work that season — Covent Garden did not produce a single new work during the entire year — although a number of new songs by him were sung at the theater. 1745-46 brought a renewal of interest by Lampe in song collections as well, for *Lyra Britannica* finally was completed, and Lampe made important contributions to Walsh's multivolume work *The Vocal Musical Mask*.

Many of Lampe's new individual songs were inspired by the Jacobite rebellion and performed in the theaters in support of the monarchy. He also composed a lengthy thanksgiving anthem, "The King Shall Rejoice," performed at the German Lutheran Chapel in the Savoy, October 9, 1746, in honor of the supression of the revolt. Perhaps he had been associated with the church at other times as well. A full score of the work soon was published, with two title pages, one in English and the other in German, with a Hannover/Göttingen imprint.

The years 1745-46 also saw other changes in Lampe's life that were to affect his music, for he and his wife met and came under the influence of the Wesleys. On October 26, 1744, John Rich had married for the third time, to Mrs. Priscilla Stevens, a minor actress at Covent Garden and a devout Methodist, and it appears that Lampe became acquainted with the Wesleys in Rich's home. An entry in John Wesley's diary for October 29, 1745, reads: "I spent an hour with Mr. Lampe, who had been a Deist for many years, till it pleased God, by the *Earnest Appeal*, to bring him to a better mind."[6] The *Earnest Appeal* mentioned is John Wesley's *Earnest Appeal to Men of Reason and Religion* (1743). The Wesleys defined a Deist as "one who believes there is a God distinct from matter; but does not believe the Bible," i.e., he acknowledges the existence of God upon the testimony of reason, but rejects any sort of revelation, through the Bible or by other means.[7] English Deistic philosophy had developed in the latter seventeenth and early eighteenth centuries among such thinkers as Lord Herbert of Cherbury, Thomas Hobbes, Charles Blont, John Locke, David Hume, and others, as a product of the Age of Reason, and it was quite influential in Continental thought and philosophy, especially among the French Encyclopedists and in certain areas of Saxony. The philosophy was appealing to an age that exalted reason and nature, but the Methodists declared

---

5 *The London Stage, 1660-1800*, 5 parts (Carbondale: Southern Illinois University Press, 1960-68), 3:ix.

6 John Wesley, *The Journal of the Rev. John Wesley*, standard ed., ed. Nehemiah Curnock, 8 vols. (London: Epworth Press, 1912), 3:226.

7 Quoted in *The Oxford English Dictionary*, ed. Sir James A. H. Murray, 12 vols. (Oxford: Clarendon Press, 1888-1933), s.v. "Deism."

SONGS and DUETTO's
IN THE
Burlesque OPERA, call'd,
THE
Dragon of *WANTLEY*,
IN SCORE.

COMPOS'D BY

JOHN FREDERICK LAMPE.

London. *Printed for* I. Walsh *in Catharine Street in the Strand.*

Of whom may be had Compos'd by Mr Lampe.

1. The Overture and Choruses to the Dragon of Wantley. in Score.
2. The Dragon of Wantley Set for a German Flute or Guitar.
3. Margery. or the Sequel to the Dragon of Wantly. in Score.
4. The Overture and Choruses to Margery. or the Sequel to the Dragon of Wantley. in Score.
5. Pyramus and Thisbe. a Mock English Opera, in Score.
6. A Collection of Songs and Cantata. and a medley Overture in 4 Parts.
7. The Comic Tunes in Columbine Courtezan for the Harpsicord.
8. The Cuckow Concerto for Violins and German Flutes in Parts. also Set for the Harpsicord.
9. Six Solos for a German Flute and a Bass.

Title page of the full score publication of the songs and duets in *The Dragon of Wantley.*

The score was first published in 1738 and reissued in the mid-1740s using the same plates.

This title page is from the later printing and lists many of Lampe's publications available at the time.

war upon and succeeded in containing Deism among the middle and lower classes. Lampe's Deistic philosophy is apparent in *The Art of Musick*, with its great emphasis on nature.

Of the two brothers, Lampe seems to have enjoyed a closer personal relationship with Charles Wesley. Mrs. Rich, in a 1746 letter to Charles, wrote, "I gave a copy of the hymn to Mr. Lampe, who at the reading, shed some tears, and said he would write to you; for he loved you as well as if you were his own brother."[8] Because of their friendship and in gratitude for the Wesleys' spiritual help, Lampe wrote tunes for some of Charles's hymns and edited a tune collection for the brothers. His *Hymns on the Greater Festivals and Other Occasions* (London, 1746) contained the first group of original tunes written specifically for Methodist hymns, and Lampe possibly paid for its publication himself.[9] The book became

---

[8] Quoted in Frederick C. Gill, *Charles Wesley, The First Methodist* (New York: Abington Press, 1964), 120-21.

[9] Frank Baker, *Representative Verse of Charles Wesley* (London: Epworth Press, 1962), 82.

widely used, and Lampe's work was highly respected by the Wesleys. A letter of Charles Wesley dated December 11, 1746 includes the following passage: "Tell Mrs. Dewal not to mind that envious gentleman who slandered Lampe. His tunes are universally admired here among the musical men, and have brought me into high favour among them."[10] As late as 1755 John Wesley was writing to his brother asking whether more Lampe hymn tunes might be printed, and Charles was writing to his wife asking how many of Lampe's tunes she could play, offering to buy her a fine harpsichord if he was encouraged at her progress.[11]

Charles Wesley is said to have celebrated Lampe's conversion with a hymn, "For a Musician," and to have commemorated Lampe's death by another hymn, "'Tis done! the sov'reign will's obey'd." The first stanza of each is quoted below.

For a Musician

With Tubal's wretched Sons no more
I prostitute my sacred Powers,
   To please the Fiends beneath;
Or modulate the wanton Lay,
Or smooth with Musick's Hand the way
   To everlasting death.[12]

Tis Done! the Sov'reign Will's Obey'd

'Tis done! the sov'reign will's obey'd,
The soul by angel guards convey'd
   Has took its seat on high.
The Brother of my choice is gone
To music sweeter than his own,
   To concerts in the sky.[13]

For the 1746-47 season Rich assembled at Covent Garden perhaps the greatest cast of actors and actresses of the century, including the rising star David Garrick, James Quin, the foremost proponent of the older school of tragic acting, and Mrs. Hannah Pritchard and Mrs. Cibber, the two greatest tragic actresses of their day. Audiences flocked to see the excellent acting. But pantomimes, other afterpieces, and most musical works virtually disappeared, so that regardless of how desirable the high state of acting and tragedy might have been for spoken drama it brought about a musical decay in the theaters. No new Lampe theater music appeared that year, and the usually popular *Orpheus* was performed only fourteen times. Lampe's other works lay silent at Covent Garden. He took *The Dragon* to Drury Lane again, where throughout March and April it received fourteen performances.

By the next season the tables had turned upon Rich, for Garrick, who had become part owner of Drury Lane, returned to that theater, taking the best actors and actresses with him. The lot of musicians was little better, though, for Rich's attitude toward music had not changed, and Garrick's regard for the art never was high (he eventually drove Arne from Drury Lane). Both managers apparently viewed music as a purely utilitarian, albeit sometimes delightful, accessory to legitimate drama. Garrick seems to have had a high opinion of *The*

---

[10] Quoted in James Love, *Scottish Church Music: Its Composers and Sources* (Edinburgh: William Blackwood & Sons, 1891), 190.

[11] John Wesley, *The Letters of the Rev. John Wesley*, standard ed., ed. John Telfold, 8 vols. (London: Epworth Press, 1931), 3:130; Gill, *Charles Wesley*, 165.

[12] Quoted in Edward Leonard Oldfield, "The Achievement of Henry Carey (1687-1743)" (Ph.D. dissertation in English Literature, University of Washington, 1969), 234.

[13] Quoted in Love, *Scottish Church Music*, 190.

Dragon, however, for it was performed a dozen times at Drury Lane during the year. For the most part, nevertheless, Lampe and his wife remained at Covent Garden, and in April Lampe's last work for the London stage was presented there. The piece was a new masque scene for a revival of *The Muses' Looking Glass*, originally by Thomas Randolph and rewritten by Lacy Ryan for his benefit performance on March 14. The work was not performed again, and neither music nor words survive. The day before, *Pyramus* had seen its single performance of the year as part of a benefit for Mrs. Lampe.[14]

Real musical opportunities continued to elude Lampe, Arne, and other London composers. Handel's oratorios had become mildly successful, but he so dominated that genre, which he had created virtually alone, that other London composers could hardly become involved in it. All of Lampe's successful, mature works had been comedies or burlesques, and he appears to have had too much respect for Handel and too strong a religious conviction to have attempted to burlesque the oratorios. Even the ambitious and egotistical Arne declined to compete in the field of oratorios until after Handel's death. Although it is interesting to speculate as to whether or not Lampe also would have tried his hand at an oratorio had he lived longer, the chance presented itself for him to go to Dublin, and he soon was on his way to Ireland, not knowing that he would never see London again.

1748-1750: Dublin

Dublin had suffered something of a musical drought during the mid-1740s, after Arne's departure, but the scarcity of good theater music had begun to be alleviated somewhat by performances of Handel's *Samson* and *Judas Maccabaeus* early in 1748. Encouraged by public reaction to the oratorios, Thomas Sheridan, the young manager of Dublin's Smock-Alley Theatre, journeyed to London during the spring of 1748 in search of more and better theater musicians — and he met Lampe. When approached with the prospect of going to Ireland, Lampe must almost have jumped at the chance, remembering Arne's and Handel's successes there a few years earlier. Besides the Lampes, Sheridan also engaged a number of other actors, singers, and instrumentalists, and the September 24-27, 1748 issue of the *Dublin Journal* described for the public the new company and some of the preparations being made to accommodate it:

> The Orchestra [pit] is much enlarged, in order to render it capable of containing the extraordinary Number of Hands who are engaged this Season. The Band is to consist of 10 Violins, a Harpsichord, two double Bases, a Tenor [viola], a Violenchello [*sic*], two Hautboys, two Bassoons, two French Horns, and a Trumpet. The Musical Performances will be conducted by Signior Pasquali, who will also lead the Band. Mr. Lampe, the celebrated Composer, from the Theatre-Royal in Covent-Garden, will accompany all his own Performances on the Harpsichord.

Benjamin Victor, Sheridan's more experienced partner, did not, however, approve of

---

14 The advertisements for this benefit, printed on April 13, 1748, show that the Lampes had moved again: "Tickets to be had at the Lampe's at the sign of the Holy Lamb, Drury Lane, near Long Acre." This is the first address given in any advertisement since March 24, 1743, and is the Lampes' last known address in London.

the expensive "Musical Tribe,"[15] and in his *The History of the Theatres of London and Dublin* Victor gave his own opinion of Sheridan's arrangements.

At the End of *March* the Manager took another trip to *London*, to provide for the following Season, 1748. . . .

The Manager, at this Expedition, instead of bringing over a profitable Freight as before, this Trip overloaded his Vessel, even to the Danger of sinking. He engaged Mr. and Mrs. *Macklin*, Mrs. *Vincent*, Mrs. *Bland*, (now *Hamilton*) Miss *Minors*, Mr. *Mozeen*, and Mr. *Storer*; and in the musical Way, Mr. *Lampe* and Wife, Signior *Pasquali*, Mr. *Sullivan*, Mr. *Howard*, Mrs. *Storer*, and Mrs. *Mozeen*. All this musical Party were articled for two Years.

Mr. *Lampe* was a good Composer, and Signior *Pasquali* a fine Performer on the Violin; and some of the Singers in Reputation. But admitting all this to be true, what was the Consequence? I attended carefully to the Product of this musical Bargain; and the Profits did not amount to the Sum paid for the Article of writing the Score for their Performances, which was over one hundred and Fifty Pounds! So that the Tot of their Salaries, which was near fourteen hundred Pounds a Year, was a dead Loss to the Manager.[16]

Regardless of the possible economic sense of Victor's business-like observations, Lampe's company provided Dublin audiences with some of the best music heard in years. It should also be noted that in addition to the other performers listed above, Mrs. Arne accompanied the Lampes to Dublin, and she occasionally sang with her sister Mrs. Lampe when her health permitted.

Lampe's music was already known in Dublin before he arrived. Some version of *The Dragon* had been given there as early as January 26, 1738, shortly after the full score (*sans* recitatives) had been published in London, and *Margery* had appeared on January 25, 1739, less than seven weeks after its first production at Covent Garden.[17] Arne also had presented *The Dragon* in Ireland during his visit, and on December 19, 1746 *Pyramus and Thisbe* had been performed there, presumably from the printed full score.[18] Dublin theater audiences, therefore, probably eagerly anticipated the famous composer being on hand to conduct these and other of his works in person, as well as writing new music for their own theater.

The Dublin season opened on October 3, 1748,[19] and less than a month later the first new Lampe work appeared. The *Dublin Journal* advertisement for the November 2 performance had included: "After the Play will be performed, the Birthday Ode, set to Musick by Mr. Lampe, as it was done last Night at the Grand Festino Room in Aungier-street." Early in the 1748-49 season, Sheridan began opening the unused Aungier-Street Theatre, which he also controlled, for Grand Festinos, modelled on the London ridottos and consisting of music, dancing, and refreshments. The festinos became the rage in Dublin that year as major social

15 Benjamin Victor, *The History of the Theatres of London and Dublin*, 2 vols. (Dublin: T. Davies, 1761), 1:143.

16 Ibid., 135-37.

17 T. J. Walsh, *Opera in Dublin, 1705-1797: The Social Scene* (Dublin: Allen Figgis, 1973), 57-58.

18 Esther K. Sheldon, *Thomas Sheridan of Smock-Alley* (Princeton: Princeton University Press, 1967), 453.

19 Lampe may still have been in London as late as September 9, 1748, when the first advertisement of his *A Cantata and Four English Songs Sung at Ranelagh Gardens* appeared in the *General Advertiser*, thus partially explaining the late start of the 1748-49 season in Dublin.

events. Sheridan's festinos usually were monthly affairs, and the first festino, in celebration of His Majesty's birthday, was highlighted by Lampe's birthday ode, mentioned above. Since the festino activities seem to have been similar to those of the London pleasure gardens, such as Vauxhall and Ranelagh, where festinos and similar events had been popular since the early 1740s,[20] the Lampes' experiences in the London gardens undoubtedly were a great boon to the success of Sheridan's and Victor's enterprise.

The festinos also helped to keep Sheridan's "woeful Bargains" (Victor's term[21]) busy, and Lampe and his musicians also occasionally performed, as had Handel earlier, for the Charitable Musick Society to aid in the release of persons from debtors' prison. During the next season Lampe and the orchestra had an agreement to perform for the society on a weekly basis, and by the middle of 1750 had raised enough money to release about 1,200 prisoners.[22]

On February 16, 1749, the Dublin public heard Lampe's first new music written specifically for the Smock-Alley Theatre, a set of songs for a scene in Act II of *Oroonoko*, a Restoration tragedy by Thomas Southern (1696). In the following months new Lampe songs, duets, and cantatas frequently were advertised for the theater, and near the end of the season he set the songs for another tragedy, Nathaniel Lee's *Theodosius*, first performed April 29, 1749. Of course, throughout the year Lampe also presented his old works that originally had won him recognition in Dublin; *The Dragon* and *Margery* both were popular, and the Lampe *Tom Thumb* was revived in May for three performances.

The summer of 1749, when the theaters were closed, probably provided Lampe his first opportunity to collect and edit some of his new music for publication. The result was *The Ladies Amusement*, which included the settings from *Theodosius* (the *Oroonoko* songs had been published earlier as broadsides), plus some other songs and a cantata, likely among those mentioned in the 1748-49 theater advertisements.[23] The texts for these songs came from Lampe's theater colleagues, as well as from other people who appear to have been patrons, and those songs in the collection not composed for Smock-Alley probably were written, as had been many of Lampe's earlier ballads, for patrons and students. During 1749 Lampe also edited a new Methodist hymnal entitled *A Collection of Hymns and Sacred Poems*, which was published by Charles Wesley in Dublin; the work appears to have been the first Methodist hymnal ever printed in Ireland.[24]

During the 1749-50 season in Dublin, Lampe's activities were much the same as the previous year. To performances of *The Dragon*, *Margery*, *Tom Thumb*, *Theodosius*, and *Oroonoko* Lampe added other of his works from London, such as *The What d'Ye Call It* and *Pyramus and Thisbe*. Also in this season and the previous one a number of Carey works

[20] From contemporary descriptions the Dublin festinos seem to have resembled the programs in the famous rotunda at Ranelagh somewhat more than the usual activities at Vauxhall, although ridottos and other such entertainments were common at both establishments. See Edwin Beresford Chancellor, *The Pleasure Haunts of London* (Boston: Houghton Mifflin, 1925), 215-17, 238-41, and T. Lea Southgate, "Music at the Pleasure Gardens of the Eighteenth Century," *Proceedings of the Royal Musical Association* 38 (1911-12): 149-51.

[21] Victor, *History*, 1:143.

[22] William H. Grattan Flood, *A History of Irish Music*, 4th ed. (Dublin: Brown & Nolan, 1927), 293; see also Sheldon, *Sheridan*, 132.

[23] *The British Union-Catalogue of Early Music Printed before the Year 1801*, ed. Edith B. Schnapper, 2 vols. (London: Butterworths Scientific Publications, 1957), dates *The Ladies Amusement* as ca. 1748, but the work must be from the middle or latter part of 1749 since it includes music written for the 1748-49 season from as late as April 29, 1749, but omits any new music Lampe wrote for 1749-50.

[24] Flood, *Irish Music*, 295.

Title page from Lampe's song collection *The Ladies Amusement,* 1749, written for his Dublin audiences and containing music from his Dublin performances.

THE
LADIES AMUSEMENT:

BEING

A *new* COLLECTION of SONGS, BALLADS, &c. with SYMPHONIES and THOROUGH BASS.

The MUSIC by

JOHN FREDERICK LAMPE.

DUBLIN:

Printed by JAMES HOEY,

For the AUTHOR, and sold at Mr. MANWARING's Musick Shop in *College-Green,* and at Mr. JOHNSON's, Musick-seller in *Cheap-side,* LONDON. Price Half a Crown *English.*

Song from Lampe's song collection *The Ladies Amusement,* 1749, written for his Dublin audiences and containing music from his Dublin performances; the song is one of several settings for the play *Theodosius.*

A Song in Theodosius.
Sung by Mrs Lampe & Mrs Mozeen at the Theatre Royal.

Andante

In humble weeds but clean Array your hours shall sweetly pass a way In humble weeds but clean Array your hours shall sweet...ly pass a : way, and when the Rites di..vine are past to pleasant Gardens you shall haste and when the Rites di..vine are past to pleasant Gardens you shall haste.

2
Where many flowry beds we have
 That Emblem still to each a Grave
And when withing the Stream we look
 With Tears we use to swell the Brook.

3
But oh! when in the liquid Glass
 Our Heav'n appears we sigh to pass
For Heav'n alone we are design'd
 And all things bring our Heav'n to mind.

were presented, including *Chrononhotonthologos*, *Nancy*, and *The Honest Yorkshireman*, as well as *The Beggar's Opera*, Arne's *Comus*, Handel's *Acis and Galatea*, and other pieces with which Lampe had been associated in London. Lampe seems to have written less new music for this second season in Dublin, though, the first being a setting of a serenata, *Damon and Anathe*, for the March 10, 1750 benefit of his old London associate Theophilus Cibber, who penned the libretto. Neither music nor text survives. Also, an announcement of a performance of Shakespeare's *King John* later in the season includes, "At the end of each Act will be performed a new Chorus in the manner of the Antients, set to Musick by Mr. Lampe."[25] Production of new songs by Lampe seems to have slowed if not ceased.

It appears that during his second season Lampe grew disenchanted with Dublin and the theater there. Niccolo Pasquali, the first violinist and hence the leader of the orchestra, had become more prominent than Lampe as a performer, and Pasquali's masques and pantomimes (genres of which Lampe was not at all fond) or perhaps his willingness to serve as Sheridan's intermediary, sometimes in unpleasant business, had made the violinist a personal favorite of the manager. Since Lampe's *Oroonoko*, however, had been one of the two most successful productions of the 1748-49 season (the other was the Shakespeare/Dryden/Davenant *Tempest* with Purcell's music), and his *Theodosius* also had been quite popular, Sheridan's lack of encouragement of Lampe hardly seems justified. It is understandable, therefore, that at the end of his two-year contract Lampe decided to try his luck elsewhere, much to the detriment of Smock-Alley's musical establishment. During the following season in Dublin the fine music of the previous two years would be replaced by a troupe of dancers, a balancing artist, and fireworks, plus an occasional violin solo from Pasquali, who remained with Sheridan. Throughout the remainder of Sheridan's tenure at Smock-Alley the quality of the music never seems to have equalled that of the Lampe years.

1750-1751: Edinburgh

Having resolved to leave Dublin, the Lampes and a number of their colleagues were engaged by the new proprietor of the theater in Edinburgh for the 1750-51 season. In the September 24, 1750 Edinburgh *Caledonian Mercury* a notice appeared announcing subscriptions for the new season, scheduled to begin on October 29 with a performance of *The Beggar's Opera* and a concert. Lampe was to play the harpsichord, his wife was to sing Lucy, and Mrs. Storer, one of his leading singers in Dublin and Edinburgh, would be cast as Polly. The season did not begin, however, on the evening planned. In the following day's paper was printed an explanation, a letter dated October 15, 1750, from Mr. Storer in Dublin, who appears to have been acting as the company's agent, to Henry Thompson, one of the proprietors of the Edinburgh theater:

> Sir, — I had the favour of both your obliging letters, but the pleasure I received from the contents of them, was very soon soured by the unlucky and most mortifying accident that possibly could have happened. Mrs. Lampe has kept her bed these sixteen days in a high fever, one day given over, the next the greatest hopes of recovery, and so alternately for above a fortnight past.
>
> As to setting out before her, the very thoughts of being left alone would

---

25 Quoted in Sheldon, *Sheridan*, 344.

absolutely kill her; nor could the entertainments be the least forwarded without Mr. Lampe. We are doing all we can in this situation, we have engaged a man singer, he is an agreeable figure, and (except low) has a better voice than any man on the stage. Mr Lampe has a high opinion of his capacity; he is already perfect in the *Moor of Moor-Hall*; and sings with great spirit. I have secured all the musick of *Romeo and Juliet*; *Merchant of Venice*; *Tempest*, &c., and have only this to say, that as we are out of all manner of business, our inclination and interest both join us to make us set out with the utmost expedition. — I am, Sir, your most obedient, &c.

Charles Storer

Mrs. Lampe possibly had been ill longer than was implied in the letter, for two performances of *The Beggar's Opera* with her, Mrs. Storer, and others of the company had been announced in Edinburgh for late July and early August, but undoubtedly never had taken place. The Lampes, Storers, and others arrived (Mrs. Lampe may have come slightly later, since newspaper accounts do not mention her by name) in Edinburgh on November 5, 1750, and soon were actively performing concerts, music for plays, and operas. Information concerning the actual works presented is quite sketchy, but both *The Dragon* (on February 21, 1751) and *Tom Thumb* (on March 12, 1751) are known to have been performed.[26] Probably much of Lampe's repertory from Dublin also was used, especially *Pyramus and Thisbe* and *Margery*. On March 18, 1751, Lampe conducted an especially noteworthy production of Handel's *Acis and Galatea*, with Mrs. Lampe and Mrs. Storer singing; this is the only documented performance of a major Handel work in Edinburgh during Handel's lifetime.[27] Lampe also can be credited with attempting to introduce open-air concerts in Edinburgh pleasure gardens similar to those of London's Vauxhall and Ranelagh, an endeavor that seems to have continued throughout most of June 1751.[28]

Besides his performing activities, Lampe had been preparing a new edition of his music for *The Dragon*, arranged for voice and continuo. He never lived to see the project completed, however, for in July he became ill with what was described as a fever, and died on July 25, 1751.[29] He was buried in Cannongate Churchyard three days later, and the following words were inscribed on his tombstone:

Here lye the mortal remains of John Frederick Lampe, whose harmonious compositions shall outlive monumental registers, and with melodious notes, through future ages, perpetuate his fame, til time shall sink into eternity. His taste for moral harmony appeared through all his conduct. He was a most loving husband, affectionate father, trusty companion. On the 25th of July, 1751, in the forty-eighth year of his age, he was summoned to join that heavenly concert with the blessed

---

[26] David Fraser Harris, *Saint Cecilia's Hall in the Niddry Wynd* (Edinburgh: Oliphant, Anderson, & Ferrier, 1899), 266-67; see also Dibdin, *Annals*, 67-69.

[27] Otto Erich Deutsch, *Handel: A Documentary Biography* (New York: Norton, 1955), 704.

[28] Fraser Harris, *St. Cecilia's Hall*, 266; Dibdin, *Annals*, 66.

[29] Not July 23 as is stated in James Duff Brown, *Biographical Dictionary of Musicians* (Paisley & London: A. Gardner, 1886), 373. Hawkins errs, stating that Lampe died in London, and Burney gives the wrong age. See Sir John Hawkins, *A General History of the Science and Practice of Music* (London, 1776), reprint of the 1853 Novello ed. in 2 vols. with a new introduction by Charles Cudworth (New York: Dover, 1963), 2:895; Burney, *History*, 2:1014.

First page of music from the continuo/vocal score of *The Dragon of Wantley,* prepared by Lampe before his death, but published posthumously in 1752 with the help of Thomas Arne.

choir above, where his virtuous soul now enjoys that harmony which was his chief delight upon earth. *In vita felicitate dignos mors reddit felices.*[30]

On Lampe's death his friend Charles Wesley wrote the hymn "'Tis done! the sov'reign will's obey'd," cited earlier in this chapter.

After Lampe's Death: His Widow and Son

Mrs. Lampe returned to London and her friends at Covent Garden after her husband's death. Her brother-in-law Arne seems to have helped care for her and to have assisted in preparing Lampe's last work, the continuo-vocal score of *The Dragon,* for publication. The Edinburgh *Caledonian Mercury* of March 6, 1752 carried the following advertisement of the work:

New Musick. Now in the press and will be ready for the beginning of April next, and delivered to subscribers. All the Songs, Duettos, and Trios in the Masque of

---

30 Happy in life, death brings deserved happiness.

Comus composed by Thomas Augustine Arne, as adapted to the Harpsichord and Voice, and all the Songs, Duettos, and Trios in the Burlesque Opera, called the Dragon of Wantley composed by the great John Frederick Lampe, likewise adapted to the Harpsichord and Voice. The above works may occasionally be accompanied with Violin or German Flute and Violoncello. This manner of reducting them to avoid the Perplexity of the different parts on a score which confound young practitioners was finished by Mr. Lampe in his lifetime, and the proofs of the Plates have been revised and corrected by Mr. Arne.

Mrs. Lampe's address is given on the title page of the score as "Broad Court near Bow Street Covent Garden." She seems to have remained living in the vicinity of Covent Garden and sometimes sang at that theater, especially in her husband's or Arne's works. She also occasionally sang in the minor theaters, appearing in the new, enlarged Sadler's Wells at least as late as 1766,[31] and performed in the pleasure gardens. Determining the events of her later career, though, is rather complicated, since her daughter-in-law also sang under the name of Mrs. Lampe.

Because of such confusion, Mrs. Isabella Lampe's death date is uncertain. The *European Magazine and London Review* for January 1795 includes the following item under "Monthly Obituaries": "5. Mrs. Isabella Lampe, relict [i.e., widow] of Charles Frederick Lampe, the celebrated composer. She formerly was a singer at Covent-garden theatre." This obituary is intriguing, for although the first name of Charles's wife is unknown, it seems improbable that it would have been the same as his mother's. (Isabella Young Lampe, however, had a niece, Isabella Young, who sang in Arne's *Comus* and elsewhere.) Perhaps the writer of the obituary had confused the son with his more famous father, since both had been dead for awhile in 1795, or the Isabella mentioned was his mother, not his widow. At least some confusion in the late eighteenth century between Charles and his father can be documented, for Charles was listed in *The Piano-Forte Magazine*, vol. 4, no. 6 (1798) as the composer of his father's Cuckoo Concerto. Hogarth states that the three Young sisters, Cecilia, Isabella, and Esther, were alive in 1789 when the last volume of Burney's *History* was published, although Cecilia died later that year, on October 5.[32] It seems possible, at any rate, that Mrs. J. F. Lampe may have lived until 1795 and may be the Isabella Lampe mentioned in the obituary above.

The Lampe's only child, Charles John Frederick Lampe, carried on the tradition of both his families as a musician. Fiske states in *New Grove* that he was born in "?1739," but I believe that late 1742 or 1743 is more likely. Mrs. Lampe was absent from London theater roles from May 30, 1742 until February 2, 1743, and again for about the same period of time a year later, and these were the only periods she seems to have stopped singing long enough to have had a child. Little is known of the boy's youth. In 1758 he succeeded his grandfather, Charles Young, as the organist of All Hallows, Barking, one of the major churches in London, and in 1763 he also became organist at Covent Garden.[33] He married a singer, Miss Smith, on May 7, 1763, and a year later published a collection of songs written for her and Thomas

---

[31] Dennis Arundell, *The Story of Sadler's Wells* (New York: Theatre Arts Books, 1956), 24-25.

[32] George Hogarth, *Memoirs of the Musical Drama*, 2 vols. (London: Richard Bentley, 1838), 2:72-73.

[33] Roger Fiske, "Lampe, Charles John Frederick," *The New Grove Dictionary of Music and Musicians*, ed. Stanley Sadie, 20 vols. (London: Macmillan, 1980). 10:419; see also Oscar Thompson, ed., *The International Cyclopedia of Music and Musicians*, 10th ed., ed. Bruce Bohle (New York: Dodd, Mead, 1975), s.v. "Lampe, Charles John Frederick."

Lowe to sing at the London pleasure gardens. Several single songs and catches of his also appeared in print in the 1760s. In 1769 his post at All Hallows, Barking, became vacant, possibly due to his death, since nothing is known about him after this time.

With her singing and the proceeds from his publications and performances of his music, J. F. Lampe's widow probably continued to live reasonably well, for Lampe's works remained popular and often were performed at Covent Garden after his death. *Pyramus and Thisbe* appeared in 1751, 1752, and 1754. After an absence during Lampe's years in Dublin and Edinburgh, *Orpheus and Euridice* was revived in 1755, receiving almost ninety performances during the next three years. *The Dragon* and *Margery* were presented during almost every benefit season in the years immediately following Lampe's death, with Mrs. Lampe in her old role as Margery, and her last performance in one of her husband's works seems to have been in *Margery*, April 13, 1758. *The Dragon* remained an attraction, however, being presented in 1762, 1763, 1765, 1767, 1768, 1769, and 1782, for a total of at least thirty performances after Lampe's death. *The Dragon* also appeared again in Edinburgh in 1762, and Lampe's medley overture from *Cupid and Psyche* continued to be so much in demand that it was republished in 1763 as part of a set of six medley overtures. The last performance, however, of *The Dragon* or of any other major Lampe opera seems to have been at Covent Garden, April 20, 1782, and with this performance, except for a few scattered references to Lampe by Burney, Hawkins, Hogarth, and a few others, the era of Lampe and his Dragon can be said to have ended, and since then they became almost completely forgotten.

PART II LAMPE'S MUSICAL STYLE

CHAPTER **6** BASIC STYLISTIC ELEMENTS

Stylistic Background

John Frederick Lampe was a composer for the theater, and his is a dramatic and eclectic musical style. His musical education and experiences were wide and varied, so that one can find in his music elements of Italian opera seria and cantata, the British broadside ballad, German and English vernacular opera and church music, comic pantomime music and ballet, and genteel parlor songs, all combined to produce carefully calculated dramatic and musical effects. Also, one must remember that Lampe was a scholar as well as a composer and performer, and his theoretical considerations also influenced his music.

For simplicity in terminology and discussion, Lampe's theater music has been divided into operas, plays with music, and pantomimes. The difference between the first two lies in the relative quantities of music and spoken text, and an opera is a work that is all or mostly sung and which may employ either spoken dialogue or sung recitatives, while a play with music is mostly spoken drama with interspersed songs and other music. This is not to imply that the music of plays is in any way inferior to that of opera — on the contrary, the style and quality often are indistinguishable — but that the play with music is basically a spoken drama, whose major purpose is not necessarily musical. Since the difference between the two is a matter of overall form and emphasis, not of musical style, Lampe's music for plays will and should be considered here alongside that of his operatic works.

Little music exists from Lampe's pantomimes, and none from the more operatic, serious sections of the works. His undistinguished comic tunes, which he seems to have thought worth little time and trouble, will be discussed along with his other instrumental theater music, and the few delightful, extant comic songs deserve their place beside those of his comic operas.

Lampe's known theater compositions are listed by genre (Table 2), indicating the librettist, date and theater of first performance, and whether music or libretto survives. While the list of operas may be assumed to be complete, Lampe probably wrote music for more pantomimes and plays than are given here, even though no others can be identified. In spite of scattered lacunae, however, all of the mature operas, *The Dragon*, *Margery*, *Pyramus and Thisbe*, and (probably) *The Sham Conjuror*, survive virtually complete, along with significant sections of *Britannia* and *Dione*, and arias from *Amelia*. All exist in full score, except perhaps the *Amelia* arias, printed for violins, voice, and bass/continuo. A majority of the vocal music for plays is extant as well, printed in continuo-vocal score, and librettos exist for many of those works from which no music survives. Thus it is possible to examine an excellent cross section of Lampe's music and to obtain a good idea of the style and structure of his works.

Melody

In *The Art of Musick* Lampe writes: "Melody, I think, is a Series of Sounds, whose regular and agreeable Succession are expressed by a *single* performing Part and arise from,

TABLE 2
Lampe's Major Theater Works

Work	Librettist	First Performance	Theater
OPERAS			
Amelia*†	Carey	13 Mar 1732	L.T.
Britannia*†	Lediard	15 Nov 1732	L.T.
Dione†	Gay/?	23 Feb 1733	L.T.
Opera of Operas	Fielding/Haywood	7 Nov 1733	D.L.
Aurora's Nuptials*	?	15 Mar 1734?	D.L.
Dragon of Wantley	Carey	16 May 1737	L.T.
Margery*†	Carey	9 Dec 1738	C.G.
Roger and Joan*	Gay/?	20 Mar 1739	C.G.
Sham Conjuror†	?	18 Apr 1741	C.G.
Queen of Spain	J. Worsdale	19 Jan 1744	L.T.
Kiss Accepted and Returned	J. Ayres	16 Apr 1744	L.T.
Pyramus and Thisbe*†	Lampe/Leveridge	25 Jan 1745	C.G.
Damon and Anathe	Th. Cibber	12 Mar 1749	S.A.
PANTOMIMES			
Diana and Acteon	Roger	23 Apr 1730	D.L.
Cupid and Psyche*†	?	4 Feb 1734	D.L.
Orpheus and Euridice*†	L. Theobald	12 Feb 1740	C.G.
PLAYS			
(In Which Songs Were Set)			
Fatal Falshood*†	John Hewitt	11 Feb 1734	D.L.
Cornish Squire*	Vanbrugh/J. Ralph	23 Jan 1734	C.G.
Winter's Tale†	Shakespeare	1745	C.G.
The What d'Ye Call It*	A farce by Gay, with additional songs; Lampe re-set all of the musical sections	4 Apr 1745	C.G.
Muses Looking Glass	Randolph/Ryan; Lampe set new masque scene for end	14 Mar 1748	C.G.
Oroonoko*†	Th. Southern	16 Feb 1749	S.A.
Theodosius*†	Nat. Lee	29 Apr 1749	S.A.
King John	Shakespeare	4 Apr 1750	S.A.

*	Some music survives	D.L.	Drury Lane Theatre
†	Libretto survives	L.T.	Little Haymarket Theatre
C.G.	Covent Garden Theatre	S.A.	Smock Alley Theatre (Dublin)

EXAMPLE 1. Chorus, Act II finale, *The Dragon of Wantley*.

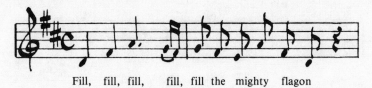

Fill, fill, fill, fill, fill the mighty flagon

EXAMPLE 2. "The lion in battle," *Margery*.

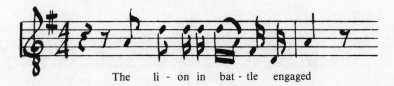

The li - on in bat - tle engaged

EXAMPLE 3. "Bright Cynthia's Pow'r," *Oroonoko*.

Bright Cynthia's Pow'r di - vine - ly great

EXAMPLE 4. "Let's go to his dwelling," *The Dragon of Wantley*.

Let's go to his dwell - ing

are comfortable to, or grounded upon Species of Harmonies, which are mutually related."[1] Given this definition, it is not surprising that the most noticeable characteristic of Lampe's melodies is the triad. Triadic melodies can be found in arias and choruses, songs from plays, pantomimes, and overtures, and they contribute to the highly dramatic character of Lampe's music.

The triad frequently is outlined at the beginning of Lampe's melodies, often with an upward flourish and return to the starting note (Example 1) or an ascent, descent, and return (Example 2). Occasionally the melody may descend first and then return (Examples 3 and 4).

Members of the triad may be omitted or passing and neighboring tones may be added, especially after the initial triadic statement, to produce a more conjunct line

---

[1] John Frederick Lampe, *The Art of Musick* (London: C. Corbett, 1740), 46.

EXAMPLE 5. "Amelia wishes when she dies," *Amelia*.

EXAMPLE 6. "Or else this cursed dragon," *The Dragon of Wantley*.

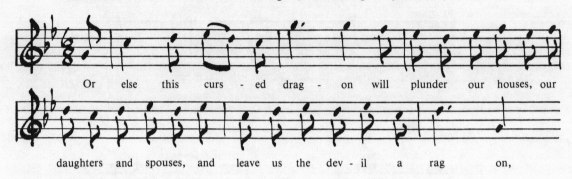

EXAMPLE 7. "The swain I adore," *Margery*.

(Example 5). Such diversity is consistent with Lampe's theories, for he states that variety in the size of intervals that make up a part is important, and that one should use just enough variety to make the performance brilliant, but not glaring.[2] Often melodies are spun out to create flowing cantabile lines, but Lampe employs the same *fortspinnung* techniques with equal ease to produce vigorous fugue subjects, especially in his choruses (Example 6). Whether smooth or disjunct, fast or slow, however, Lampe's melodies frequently encompass at least an octave within the first few measures, and sometimes cover an even greater interval (Example 7), which adds to the melody's strength and energy. Such strong melodic beginnings, with a wide sweep and gesture, share many characteristics with the melodies of Handel, which also swiftly and strongly traverse a wide range.[3]

---

[2] Ibid., 31.

[3] See the discussion in Paul Henry Lang, *George Frideric Handel* (New York: Norton, 1966), 592.

Not all of Lampe's melodies are so elaborate and sophisticated as the above examples. He wrote a number of simple, folk-like songs for his collections, for the pleasure gardens, and for the theater, and like Schürmann, Keiser, and Handel (i.e., "You ask if yon damask rose be sweet," in Handel's *Susanna*, Act II, Scene 2), he included a few of them in his operatic works (Example 8). Though such simple songs certainly are not the rule in his operas and seldom appear except when they serve a dramatic purpose, their triadic melodies often are quite pronounced.

In addition to their initial triadic statement, Lampe's melodies internally are consistent with the harmonic implications in his definition of melody given above, often strongly outlining the primary triads of the key or confirming the tonality in other ways. Usually both the tonic and the dominant are solidly established, frequently with a cadence on the dominant (Example 9). In the minor mode the customary motion is to the relative major, and can occur quite quickly (Example 10). Such a quick change of tonality is unusual in the melodies of Lampe's English contemporaries, especially Arne, although with Lampe it is fairly ordinary and even occurs during the opening ritornello of an aria. I believe that these melodic differences result from differences in harmonic practices, for Lampe's harmonic rhythm generally was much quicker and his range of modulation much wider than was Arne's. One may note that in the beginning of the same example, "So Hercules of old," Lampe moves from the tonic to the relative major, goes sequentially to the dominant, but is firmly within the minor dominant, as if the major form had never occurred, by the sixth measure. One can compare Arne's well-known "By dimpled brook" from *Comus*, where by the sixth measure Arne never has left the tonic, and finally arrives at the dominant several measures later.

Lampe's love of variety—in melodic contour, intervals, range, harmony, and elsewhere—also manifests itself in the relationship of melodies within his arias. For unlike some of his German contemporaries and Handel,[4] the theme of the second main section of his full-scale da capo arias often is of a quite different character from that of the first, especially when such contrast is implied by the text. If the first theme is robust, the second theme generally is more lyric (Example 11), and when the first theme is conjunct and florid, the melody of the second section often is simpler and more triadic (Example 12). Sometimes the themes can be of a similar character if the mood of the aria is constant throughout, such as in "Furies of Orcus," a rage aria from *Britannia*. Occasionally the two sections of the aria may even be thematically related (Example 13). Exact transpositions from one section to another, such as can be found in the works of Hasse and Graun, virtually never occur in Lampe's arias, however. Nor are the extreme and jarring changes of meter, tempo, and character so frequent in Arne (e.g., in Pallas's "The glorious voice of war" from *The Judgment of Paris*).

Melodic Embellishments and Coloratura

Coloratura passages occur in many of Lampe's arias, especially those in da capo form, and often are quite Italianate and florid, as in "Gentle knight" and "Dragon, dragon" from *The Dragon*. Like Handel, but unlike his younger Neapolitan contemporaries, Lampe's coloratura exists neither for mere vocal display nor as part of an over-all florid melodic

---

4 Gustav Friedrich Schmidt, *Die frühdeutsche Oper und die musikdramatische Kunst Georg Caspar Schürmanns*, 2 vols. (Regensburg: Gustav Bosse, 1933), 2:352ff; Anthony Lewis, "Handel and the Aria," *Proceedings of the Royal Musical Association* 85 (1958-59): 105; Michael Robinson, "The Aria in Opera Seria, 1725-1780," *Proceedings of the Royal Musical Association* 88 (1961-62): 33ff.

EXAMPLE 8. "Then come to my arms," *Margery.*

Then come to my arms old Dad, old Dad, and

fondle thine own dear honey

EXAMPLE 9. "Who to win a woman's favour," *Cupid and Psyche.*

Who to win a Woman's Favour, Would solicit long in vain?

EXAMPLE 10. "So Hercules of old," *Margery.*

So Her-cu-les of old, the va-liant and the bold, who made the fierce giants and

monsters to rue, who made the fierce giants and monsters to rue, was forced to rock and reel, and turn the spin-ning wheel,

92

EXAMPLE 11. "Dragon, dragon," *The Dragon of Wantley*.

Drag-on, drag-on, thus I dare ———— thee

But re - gard - ing where my dear is

EXAMPLE 12. "Fortune ever changing," *Britannia*.

MAIN THEME

Fortune ever changing now shall keep from ra-

SECOND THEME

Inspired to lasting glory

EXAMPLE 13. "Tho now she scorns," *Dione*.

FIRST SECTION

Tho now she scorns, her blooming face

SECOND SECTION

Then shepherd she your loss will mourn

EXAMPLE 14. "Quel amor," Keiser's *Jodelet*.

Piu so - ven - te an - cor sa-

ga - ce nell' a - mo - re

EXAMPLE 15. "Artige Kinder," Keiser's *Jodelet*.

ge - fähr — — — — — lich, ge-

fähr - lich sein

style, such as Bach's. Rather, Lampe's coloratura usually is prompted by the text or dramatic situation, and thus is not a standard ingredient to be found in a predictable spot in every aria.

Lampe's coloratura passages are well written for the voice, employing good vowels and idiomatic melodic figures. In this respect he differs significantly from Keiser and other Germans, such as J. S. Bach, whose coloratura writing often is more instrumental and rhythmic. This difference in character can be seen in four excerpts (Examples 14-17), which include coloratura sections from both Italian and German arias by Keiser, and from Lampe's *Britannia*. Music from *Britannia* is chosen to demonstrate that even early in his career Lampe had a fine feeling for the voice, and the *Britannia* examples are undoubtedly easier to sing than are those of Keiser.

EXAMPLE 16. "Britannia, heav'nly blest," *Britannia*.

There may I e — — — — ver rest

EXAMPLE 17. "Royal daughter, only treasure," *Britannia*.

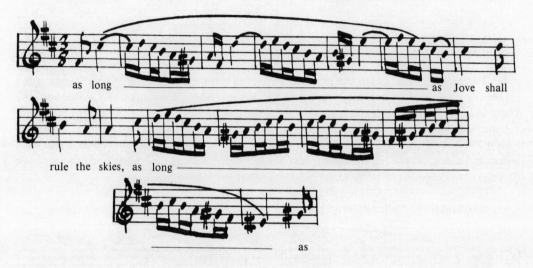

as long ————————————————————— as Jove shall

rule the skies, as long ——————————————

———————————————— as

EXAMPLE 18. Simplified version of the melody of "Britannia heav'nly blest" excerpt in EXAMPLE 16.

Lampe's coloratura technique seems to be related to the melodic embellishment practices demonstrated in his thoroughbass book, where a simple melody is "varyed" by the addition of passing and neighboring tones, passage work, and arpeggiation of triads. The coloratura example from "Britannia, heav'nly blest" (Example 16) is one such passage, and there is also a possible simplified version of that melody (Example 18). Such examples and his thoroughbass book illustrate that the basis of Lampe's coloratura technique is to be found in his own melodic and theoretical practices, and is a natural outgrowth of his overall musical style.

In addition to the serious functions of coloratura, in Lampe's hands the device sometimes becomes intentionally funny. This is especially true of florid passages in bass arias

EXAMPLE 19. "Ladies, don't fright ye," *Pyramus and Thisbe.*

gen - tle   roar ——————————————————————————

such as when the dragon growls at Moor (in "Oh ho! Master Moore"), when Moore threatens the dragon (on "work" in "Pigs shall not be so fond as we"), or when the lion in *Pyramus and Thisbe* roars (Example 19). But even in these amusing examples, the coloratura still serves dramatic purposes, and admirably so.

Text Setting

Lampe generally treats the text quite carefully and thoughtfully. Great concern for text setting was characteristic of Schürmann and Keiser, whose ideas probably influenced the young Lampe. This is in sharp contrast to the practices of many opera seria composers, who often, it seems, considered their texts mere vehicles for the music, a suspicion affirmed by the not infrequent contrafacta and substitute-text arias in their works. One never finds such devices in Lampe, whose respect for the text also reflects his sense of drama, nurtured through his years with Handel.

EXAMPLE 20. "What horror fills my soul," *Dione.*

and light ————————————————————————————————————

———————————————————————— ning crush me   dead.

Lampe's command of English, even in his early works, seems to have been better than that of Handel, whose frequently misaccented English and troublesome text setting have led some scholars to believe that the master occasionally even misunderstood the texts he was setting.[5] Lampe, however, is quite careful with accentuation, placing melismas on important words and providing good vowels for the singer where such vowels would be especially necessary, such as in the bass aria "What horror fills my soul," from *Dione* (Example 20). Arne's declamation, on the other hand, can be rather awkward, as in the bravura arias of *Judith*, where there are long divisions on such words as "assuage" and "preside."

---

[5] Winton Dean, *Handel's Dramatic Oratorios and Masques* (London: Oxford University Press, 1959), 64; for a further comparison of their respective use of English one might compare Lampe's two theory treatises with the extant Handel letters and other writings.

Rhythm and Phrasing

Rhythm is always an important element of Lampe's melodies, and as a result of his concern for accentuation Lampe sometimes utilizes strong and distinctive rhythms. The technique is especially apparent in the fugue subjects of the *Dragon* choruses, and results in fine and dramatic declamation in both duple ("Houses and churches") and triple ("Let's go to his dwelling") meters (Example 21). Such strong melodies as in these choruses and in "Or else this cursed dragon" — the fugue within "O save us all" — can seldom be found in the works of Arne and other English composers, who usually preferred a sweeter and more lyric style, although a rare exception exists in Arne's "Rule, Britannia."

EXAMPLE 21. "Houses and churches," *The Dragon of Wantley.*

While many Lampe melodies are built of four-measure phrases, his phrasing, like that of Handel and Telemann, frequently is asymmetrical. Some pieces, such as "I go without delay" in *Pyramus and Thisbe*, are based on three-measure phrases, and the first section of "Ah, traitress" in *Amelia* is built of seven-measure phrases. In "Cease complaining" from *Dione*, irregular phrasing is the rule, with one and a half-, two-, and three-measure phrases common. Not one four-measure phrase is to be found in the entire aria. Often a four-measure phrase will be extended by repeating the last measure or two, especially if the phrase occurs before an important cadence point. Phrases also are extended at cadences by increasing the value of the last few notes, a technique frequent in *The Dragon* and elsewhere (Example 22). This example also includes a sequence, another common element of Lampe's melodies.

EXAMPLE 22. "Who to win a woman's favour," *Cupid and Psyche.*

Along with asymmetrical phrase patterns in Lampe's music, hemiolas sometimes occur, although not nearly so frequently as in the works of Handel. A particularly interesting example is in the second section of the "Wall's song" in *Pyramus and Thisbe*, where a long passage in 3/4 exists within a 2/4 aria (Example 23; the bar lines implied by the rhythm and text are indicated by dotted bar lines). At the point marked with an asterisk, the section returns to 2/4, but with the feeling of the bar line displaced by half a measure. Another short 3/4 passage exists at the final cadence.

EXAMPLE 23. "Wall's song," *Pyramus and Thisbe.*

An additional rhythmic figure of Lampe's melodies that deserves discussion is the Scotch snap rhythm (♪.). Although infrequent in most of Lampe's music, it occurs with agonizing regularity in *Pyramus and Thisbe* and contributes much to the disagreeable first impression that the *Pyramus* songs may make upon a listener. The Scotch snap became a common and indiscriminate mannerism in the popular songs and ballads of the mid-eighteenth century, such as Arne's. It is also found in other Lampe music of around 1745, the year of *Pyramus*, particularly in the songs of the last fascicle of the *Lyra Britannica* collection. The over-use of the figure in *Pyramus and Thisbe* may be deliberate, however, resulting from the burlesque character of the opera, since the Scotch snap rarely recurs in Lampe's subsequent theater music, such as *Theodosius* and *Oroonoko.*

Harmonic Vocabulary

Lampe's music is written totally in the major/minor tonal system of the late Baroque. The chief chromatic chords found are the diminished seventh, the Neapolitan sixth, and the augmented sixth (usually an Italian sixth), all of which function in their usual manner. More interesting, however, is the general chromaticism of Lampe's style and his harmonic adventurousness, both of which contrast greatly with the practices of his English contemporaries.

EXAMPLE 24. "Fortune ever changing," *Britannia*.

Remote modulations occur frequently in Lampe's arias, especially in the middle sections of the early works. "Fortune ever changing" in *Britannia* contains one such middle section, which begins with a G-minor chord and concludes with its dominant (D), but certainly weaves an indirect route between the two. (Example 24, reproduces the melody and bass line of the entire middle section of the aria; the bracketed figures indicate the harmonies of the omitted upper instrumental voices.) The example also demonstrates another common technique in Lampe arias: the use of a long dominant pedal. Many such instances exist in *The Dragon* and elsewhere, especially in its "Zeno, Plato, Aristotle." Also noteworthy (in Example 24) is the near canon at the fifth within the sequence, beginning at "long."

In addition to the functional and sequential chromatic modulations, Lampe's chromatic melody or bass lines often produce modulations to remote keys, and strange progressions, whose constituent chords are determined not by normal functional relationships but by the dictates of the chromatic melody. Such chromatic lines usually are ascending and occur at instances of sorrow or fear, such as in the middle sections of "Sure my stays" in *The Dragon* (Example 25), and "Wretched is a wife's condition" in *Margery*. Lampe's use of ascending chromatic lines possibly was influenced by the practice in such Schürmann operas as *Alceste*, where such themes are prominent.

EXAMPLE 25. "Sure my stays," *The Dragon of Wantley.*

Lampe's harmonic practice and style can be said to be of the late Baroque period rather than of early Classicism, which Arne and the younger Neapolitans represent. Grout's differentiation between the two is pointed, appropriate, and enlightening:

> In the older style the harmony was comparatively rich and changeable, the bass lines fairly active, the melody spun out in long phrases of variable length (except in pieces based on dance rhythms), and the forms still somewhat free despite the tendency toward exclusive use of the da capo pattern. In the newer style, harmony was simplified to a few fundamental chords with the bass changing relatively seldom and the whole texture functioning solely as a support for the melody; the latter came to be organized in symmetrical short phrases, though with considerable variety of rhythmic patterns within the phrase; variety of form gave way to the almost exclusive dominance of the full five-part da capo scheme.[6]

---

6 Donald J. Grout, *A Short History of Opera*, 2nd ed. (New York: Columbia University Press, 1965), 182.

In terms of this description, Lampe's melodic and harmonic practices clearly belong to the late Baroque. His rich and substantial music never relies on mere tunefulness or melodic sweetness to carry it forward, as often is the case with Arne. Lampe's melodies are strong and exciting, his harmonies are varied and interesting, and he combines some of the better elements of both the older and newer styles to produce attractive and dramatic works of significant artistic value, which at the same time provide delightful theater for the present, as well as they did for his own age.

Lampe's Use of the Aria

Judging from the sections that survive, Lampe's early operas seem to have been more Italianate than his mature works. This resemblance to opera seria probably was intentional, for, as described earlier, the aim of Lampe, Carey, and the other experimenters of 1732-33 seems to have been the creation of an English vernacular school of opera that would equal the Italian in excellence of music and performance. Italian forms and conventions possibly were retained in order to lend these novel operatic efforts some validity and respectability, and newspaper advertisements emphasized their Italianateness, with *Amelia*, *Britannia*, and *Dione* all described as being "Set to Musick after the Italian Manner." Thus one could expect and one finds in these three early operas a preponderance of da capo exit arias, few choruses or ensembles, and little dramatic development or depiction of characters. In spite of such constraints, however, Lampe was already beginning in these early works to break down Italian conventions, especially the reliance on the da capo form and the exit aria, creating a more dramatic style. His efforts are most evident in the latest of the three, *Dione*.

Although no libretto of the Lampe setting exists, Gay's original *Dione* is much more dramatic than either *Amelia* or *Britannia*, and is not very adaptable to the use of exit arias. None of the extant *Dione* arias, in fact, would seem to make good exit arias, although admittedly it is difficult to define just what constitutes a good exit aria. More important than their function, however, is the great variety of da capo forms within *Dione* when compared with *Britannia* and *Amelia*, where all of the extant arias seem to be cast from the same mold. The *Dione* arias differ from their predecessors in the variety of lengths of sections, treatments of orchestral ritornellos, and harmonic and tonal relationships. Most striking is the presence of the first extant non-da capo structure written by Lampe. The cavatina "Cease complaining," set to a single strophe of text, appears at the most dramatic and emotional point of the opera, Dione's death. Dione's beautiful and expressive siciliano lament is constantly interrupted by the orchestra, as if she is sighing or gasping for breath (she has been stabbed), a realistic "suspirato" technique[1] quite dissimilar to most contemporary Italian practice, and unexpected even in much of Handel's drama (Example 26).

From *Dione* on and throughout the rest of Lampe's operatic career, the aria forms become more varied, probably because of his desire for dramatic contrast and propriety. The diversity of forms is greatest in *The Dragon* and *Margery*, but even in them an interesting trend begins to appear, which becomes more evident throughout Lampe's later music. In his mature works Lampe seems to devote each new opera to a study of a different aria form, which then will be found more often in that opera than in any other work. Additional aria forms may occur, depending on the dramatic situation, but the chosen form will be most frequent and predominant. Of the eleven arias in *The Dragon*, which encompass five different forms, seven arias are in some type of da capo design — an appropriate arrangement if one

---

[1] See Athanasius Kircher's discussion of the device in his *Musurgia universalis*, 2 vols. (Rome, 1650).

is burlesquing Italian opera. In *Margery*, however, there are no da capo arias at all, nor is it possible to find a single example of a true da capo aria written after *The Dragon*. The chosen form in *Margery* is the cavatina, and nine out of sixteen arias are so cast. *The Sham Conjuror* uses modified da capo forms for five out of its seven arias, and in *Pyramus and Thisbe* seven out of the ten arias are binary. The songs for plays and pantomimes are all in a strophic binary form. In addition, the ensembles of an opera often rely heavily on that work's particular form, so that three of the five ensembles in *The Dragon* are da capo and three of the five *Margery* duets resemble cavatinas.

EXAMPLE 26. "Cease complaining," *Dione.*

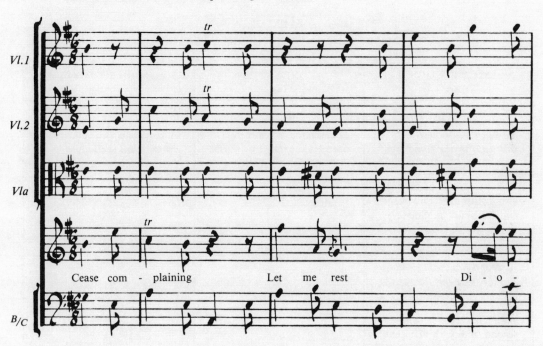

Therefore, as is true with the works of Schürmann, Keiser, Telemann, and others, it is more appropriate to discuss Lampe's arias in terms of their forms, rather than according to the standard opera seria classifications of *aria cantabile, aria di portamento*, etc., as given by Brown[2] and quoted in Hogarth,[3] Grout,[4] and elsewhere. The Italian classifications actually were concerned more with performance affections than with the music, and are of little help even in the study of Handel's Italian arias. Beginning with the da capo aria, the different forms will be discussed according to their relationship with one another. This results in an order very similar to the chronology of Lampe's study and emphasis on the various forms.

---

[2] John Brown, *Letters on the Italian Opera*, 2nd ed. (London: T. Cadell, 1791), 36-39.

[3] George Hogarth, *Memoirs of the Musical Drama*, 2 vols. (London: Richard Bentley, 1838), 2:105-13.

[4] Donald J. Grout, *A Short History of Opera*, 2nd ed. (New York: Columbia University Press, 1965), 187-88.

Da Capo Arias

The da capo is the earliest aria form known to have been used by Lampe, and by his day it had become a standard element of German, English, and Italian vocal music. Developing in seventeenth-century Italy, the da capo aria had been found in England at least as early as the late works of Purcell, such as *The Fairy Queen*. The form was popular in both sacred and secular German music, and important strides had been made in its development by Schürmann, who was one of the earliest to expand its first main section into two parts. In the first half of the eighteenth century, under the influence of Zeno and Metastasio, the da capo aria became the most important and virtually the only aria form in Italian serious opera, and its dominance continued for decades.

TABLE 3
Standard Da Capo Aria Form, 1720-1760

MAIN SECTION (A)	SECOND SECTION (B)	MAIN SECTION (A)
Ritornello 1 *An opening orchestral ritornello in the tonic.* Part a The first stanza of the text is sung through completely, and the music modulates, usually to the dominant. *Ritornello 2* *A second ritornello, usually shorter than the first.* Part b The first stanza is sung a second time with different and often more elaborate music, coloratura, and text repetition, and the music returns to the tonic. *Ritornello 3* *A closing ritornello, often similar to the first, and ending in the tonic.*	Part c This section is shorter, is not divided into two parts, and ends in a key different from the tonic.	A complete da capo of the entire main section, with free ornamentation added by the singer.
or simplified:		
A	B	A
a b	c	a b

The da capo aria in its simplest form consists of two sections, the first of which is repeated after the second has been finished. Such simple da capo arias are first found with frequency in the cantatas of Luigi Rossi and had become common in Italy by the middle of the seventeenth century. The form gradually was lengthened and expanded, so that the first section of the aria was composed of two parts, separated and delineated by orchestral ritornellos. With this main section repeated, the result was a five-part rather than a three-part structure, which remained the standard da capo form from about 1720 to 1760 (see Table 3).

The da capo aria was especially popular with singers, because during the repeat of the first section they were given the opportunity, and actually were expected, to demonstrate their skills and felicity at vocal embellishment. But the repetition of the earlier music and its text also led to the condemnation of the form as antidramatic. The da capo need not necessarily be considered static and retrogressive, however, for the repeat could be utilized to emphasize and intensify the emotions and character of an individual or situation, and in the hands of a master like Handel became a dramatic advantage. A fine example of Handel's dramatic da capo technique is to be seen in "Ah! mio cor," from Act II of *Alcina* (1735), in which the form is modified slightly, with the opening ritornello omitted during the repeat. Lampe writes modified da capo arias of a similar sort, especially in *The Sham Conjuror*.

Since Lampe consciously was imitating Italian models in *Amelia*, *Britannia*, and *Dione*, and parodying them in *The Dragon*, it is only logical that those works should emphasize da capo arias. J. C. Smith, Jr., Lampe's associate in the opera revival, also relied almost solely on da capo arias for his operas of 1732-33. In *Amelia* and *Britannia* Lampe's arias follow the form outlined above quite closely. The first main section of all the arias, except "Furies of Orcus" in *Britannia*, is in two parts, with the parts both separated and framed by ritornellos. The middle ritornello may be quite short, only a measure or two, and the opening and closing ritornellos often are almost identical. The two parts of the first section usually are of approximately equal length, although in the two *Amelia* arias the second part is longer, being made up of two smaller parts separated by another ritornello. The middle sections of the *Amelia* and *Britannia* arias, as well as Lampe's other da capo arias, are all relatively short in comparison with the main sections (see Table 4), a trait his music shares with that of Smith, Pepusch, Handel, and others. The middle sections also differ from the main sections in a number of other ways, especially in text setting and tonal organization.

A large number of the early Lampe da capo arias are in triple or compound meters, rather than duple ones (as shown below). This high proportion of 3/8 arias is difficult to explain, but possibly may be related to similar practices by Handel.[5] Arias in 3/8 meter are common in Handel's operas of the late 1720s and early 1730s, when Lampe was in his orchestra, and numerous examples might be cited. "Gioja sì, speri sì" from *Scipione* (1726), "La sorta mia vacilla" from *Admeto* (1727), and "Come il candore" from *Poro* (1731) are all minuet-like 3/8 arias that resemble the Lampe 3/8 arias closely in mood and rhythmic treatment. By the latter 1730s Handel's preference had switched to duple meter, as a comparison of such works as *Alessandro* (1726) and *Giustino* (1737) demonstrates. It is interesting to note that *The Dragon*, which premiered in the same year as *Giustino*, also shows a preference of duple over triple meter in its arias. Lampe's early partiality for 3/8 meter may therefore have been a trait of the general style of the time, and no evidence exists to indicate that his practice was extraordinary.

---

[5] For a detailed discussion of Handel's aria techniques see Michael F. Robinson, "The Aria in Opera Seria, 1725-1780," *Proceedings of the Royal Musical Association* 88 (1961-62): 31-43; and Bruno Flögel, "Studien zur Arientechnik in den Opern Händels," *Händel Jahrbuch* 2 (1929): 50-156.

TABLE 4
Length of Sections and Metric Distribution in Lampe's Da Capo Arias

Aria	3/8	6/8	4/4
Amelia		50 m.-10 m. 61 m.-13 m.	
Britannia	116 m.-22 m. 80 m.-20 m. 92 m.-17 m. 79 m.-27 m. 85 m.-21 m.	39 m.-13 m.	43 m.- 9 m. 19 m.- 9 m. 54 m.-12 m. 52 m.-11 m.
Dione	100 m.-22 m. 56 m.-19 m. 66 m.-16 m. 75 m.-21 m.		38 m.- 8 m. 64 m.-10 m. 39 m.- 7 m.
The Dragon		36 m.-12 m. 56 m.-13 m.	52 m.-13 m. 23 m.- 9 m. 21 m.- 7 m.

During the 1720s and 1730s Handel customarily employed 12/8 meter for siciliano arias and reserved 6/8 for faster gigue-like arias. Lampe, on the other hand, wrote both siciliano and gigue arias in 6/8. Perhaps Lampe's preference of 6/8 over 12/8 can be explained as his having adopted the more recent Italian practice of the 1720s and 1730s, when the number of time signatures began to be restricted and when the 12/8 signature common with Scarlatti's generation virtually disappeared. Handel preserved the older tradition, as he also did in plots, forms, etc.

In Lampe's da capo arias the meter never changes for the second section, although such a change is common with Arne, as in "Hark, hark, the glorious voice of war" from *The Judgment of Paris*, or "Now Phoebus sinketh in the west" from *Comus*. Nor is the contrast of mood between the sections so great in the Lampe arias as in Arne's, and often one finds the mood and accompaniment of Lampe's two sections quite similar (Example 27). Lampe's contrasts of mood in his arias resemble Handel's techniques, and are achieved through a different tempo or a change in orchestration for the middle section of the aria. One example is "But to hear the children mutter" from *The Dragon*, which opposes a Larghetto with oboes, four-part strings, and continuo in the main section to an Allegro for voice and continuo alone in the second section.

As mentioned in Chapter 6 above, Lampe's early arias usually do not employ the same theme or melody for the two main sections, although similar themes were basic to the aria style of Handel, Schürmann, Graun, and the younger Neapolitans. Lampe's main themes of each section are more often of contrasting characters, so that, for example, when one is triadic, the other is more lyric. Occasionally, if the mood is similar, the melodies of the two sections may also be of similar characters, and similar melodies in the two sections are the rule in the da capo arias of *The Dragon*, designed to burlesque the Italian practice. New melodic

EXAMPLE 27. "Favourite Neptune," *Britannia.*

OPENING, MAIN SECTION

Favour - ite Nep-tune darl-ing God, great com - man-der of the seas,

OPENING, SECOND SECTION

Guardian to my victo - rious fleet, ev - er honour'd ev - er great

material also occurs in the second sections of some of those arias, however, as had become the practice in Handel's da capo arias of the 1730s.

In addition to differences in melody, the main section and the middle section of Lampe's da capo arias differ in their treatment of the text. In the second section the text setting basically is syllabic and little text repetition occurs, but the main section includes much text repetition and often long coloratura passages. Similar contrast in text treatment is characteristic in the works of Keiser, Schürmann, and other German composers, as well as in the music of Handel and some Italians, so that Lampe probably had become familiar with the technique even before he arrived in London.

Tonally, the two major sections of the Lampe da capo arias differ because of their distinct structures and purposes. The main section, actually a binary form within itself, generally modulates to a closely related key, but begins and ends in the tonic, for the sake of tonal unity—a typical Baroque binary form but without the customary repeats. Lampe's binary main sections in major tonalities generally modulate to the dominant by the middle of the section. This is also standard in the arias of other composers, although in some cases, such as in "Gentle knight" in *The Dragon*, the motion can be to the mediant. In minor keys the middle cadence of the main section usually is to the relative major, but cadences to the dominant, subdominant, and even the minor dominant occur as well.

TABLE 5
Tonal Relationships in Lampe's Da Capo Arias

ARIAS IN MAJOR KEYS		
Main Section	*Middle Section*	*Number of Arias*
I - V - I	iii	10
I - iii - I	iii	1
I	iii	1
ARIAS IN MINOR KEYS		
Main Section	*Middle Section*	*Number of Arias*
i - ♭III - i	V	6
i - V - i	V	2
i - v - i	V	1
i - iv - i	V	1
i	V	2

The tonality and structure of the middle sections of the arias are both more variable and more predictable than the main sections. The middle sections modulate constantly in almost every conceivable progression, and sometimes without a strong cadence in any key until the final chord of the section. But no matter what key begins the middle section or how the music progresses, in all cases the final cadence of the middle section of major arias is to the mediant and that of minor arias to the dominant.

The various tonal relationships found in the twenty-four extant da capo arias of *Amelia*, *Britannia*, *Dione*, and *The Dragon* (there happen to be an equal number of major and minor arias) are shown in Table 5. Lampe's variety of tonal form in the first section, especially in the minor arias, is somewhat greater than his contemporaries, although two-thirds of his arias are in the two most standard tonal arrangements. His tonal consistency in the middle sections is striking, however, especially when compared to a composer such as Carl Heinrich Graun, whose arias often went to the subdominant in their middle sections, but could end almost anywhere except the leading tone triad.[6] Also it should be noted that Lampe's middle section is never in the same key as the main section, or even in the parallel major, such as one sometimes finds in the works of Hasse, Graun, Jomelli, and Gluck.

Modified Da Capo Arias

For dramatic as well as musical reasons, Lampe, like Handel, often modified the da capo form. Lampe's first modified da capo arias[7] occur in *The Dragon*, the last work to include strict da capo numbers. The middle section of "Sure my stays," an otherwise strict da capo aria, is a Baroque binary form in the relative major of the main section, complete with repeats of each part and a modulation to its own dominant in the center of the section. Such a second section, longer than the first (35 measures in the first section, 18 plus 24 in the second) and a closed form within itself, differs markedly from Lampe's usual formal practice described above, as well as from the custom of Handel and others. In "Dragon, dragon," the other modified da capo aria in the opera, the da capo is omitted altogether, undoubtedly so that the dramatic flow into the battle scene between Moore and the Dragon will not be interrupted. This aria ends in the mediant, which certainly seems unusual until one considers it a da capo aria without its repeat and compares it to the customary tonal plan of Lampe's other da capo arias mentioned above. The contrasts in tempo, meter, orchestration, and mood between these two sections is greater than in most Lampe da capo arias, although not some of Handel's (e.g., see Alcina's aria early in Act III of *Alcina*, 1735), and the extremes probably occur to intensify this most dramatic point of the opera. Lampe's complete omission of the da capo, however, resembles the work of the continental Germans of the 1720s and 1730s much more than Handel.[8] This demonstrates that Lampe did not merely follow Handel's examples slavishly, but kept up with and used the more recent stylistic innovations of other countries and opera centers. Perhaps, in fact, he had become acquainted with the practice of omitting the da capo while he was in Brunswick or Hamburg.

The one modified da capo aria in *Margery*, "Thus the damsel," combines elements of binary and da capo forms, but in a different way from "Sure my stays" or "Dragon, dragon" described above. The *Margery* aria is a fairly simple and standard da capo, with the main section as a single part. But that main section ends in the dominant, so that the reprise must be written out and altered to enable the aria to conclude in the tonic. Even more unusual is Lampe's imposing a pair of repeats on the aria, almost transforming it into a binary form, with the usual cadence to the dominant ending the first section. In addition, a short coda is attached to this binary form (as shown in Table 6).

---

[6] Albert Mayer-Reinach, "Carl Heinrich Graun als Opernkomponist," *Sammelbände der internationalen Musikgesellschaft* 1 (1899-1900): 489-90.

[7] Lampe did not use this or any other formal label to describe his arias, being content with the general term "air." Nevertheless, he apparently was quite conscious of the differences in his aria forms, which helps to justify somewhat the terminological distinctions I have found to be useful in my discussion.

[8] See examples in Keiser's *Jodelet* (1726) and Schürmann's *Ludivicus Pius* (1734). See also Gustav Friedrich Schmidt, *Die frühdeutsche Oper und die musikdramatische Kunst Georg Caspar Schürmanns*, 2 vols. (Regensburg: Gustav Bosse, 1933), 2:319, 397.

TABLE 6
Form of "Thus the damsel," *Margery*

8 m.		10 m.		9 m.	10 m.		2 m.	2 m.
opening ritornello	‖:	A	:‖:	B	A'	:‖	*voice alone* (coda)	*closing ritornello*
		I - V		-	I			

The modified da capo is the most frequent type of aria in *The Sham Conjuror*. After Lampe's concentration on the cavatina in *Margery,* his return to the da capo aria is intriguing, since it implies a renewed interest in the da capo form when it could be altered somewhat for musical and dramatic purposes. The modified da capo arias of *The Sham Conjuror* resemble the form Lampe had developed in *Margery*, but without repeats, although the opening section of one aria, "God of love" (but not the second and the reprise), is repeated. The main sections of these *Sham Conjuror* arias end in the dominant or relative major and the da capo is written out, so that the arias end in the tonic. The middle sections are more varied tonally than the first, and can be in the dominant, mediant, relative minor, and even the major mediant (in "When you smile"). The aria "What pastime" presents an interesting exception to the above description, however. While it resembles the other modified da capo arias of the opera in harmony, texture, and length of sections, the music of the final section is different from that of the first, resulting in a combination of through-composed and da capo forms.

In Lampe's last opera, *Pyramus and Thisbe*, there are no true da capo arias, although the Moon's song, "The man in the moon," is related to some of his earlier modified da capo practices. The aria has a da capo of its text, but musically is a binary form resembling "Thus the damsel" in *Margery* and demonstrating Lampe's continuing love of variety and experimentation with musical structure.

Lampe's enduring interest in some aspects of the da capo aria form indicates a conscious and enduring link between his works and opera seria. It emphasizes his willingness to use Italian forms and conventions, even in his mature operas, when they could be modified to intensify or complement the dramatic situation. But Lampe's arias were not restricted to varieties of the da capo type. Because of his experience with German and English musical theater, both of which included many different aria and song forms not commonly found in Italian opera, his works could employ great diversity, with the type and form of solo song tailored to the dramatic situation.

Cavatinas

Of all of the Lampe aria types, the one most closely related to the da capo aria is the cavatina. The previous discussion of da capo arias mentions that in Lampe's time the first section of the da capo aria generally was in two parts, creating a small binary form with no repeats. Beginning in the 1720s, this section sometimes appeared alone in operas, in situations where there was only one stanza of text to be set. The term generally applied to this single-stanza aria was "cavatina." For my purposes I have classified as cavatinas Lampe's short binary arias that formally and tonally resemble the opening sections of his da capo arias. These cavatinas are all in two sections, although the sections are not always separated by ritornellos. In all cases but one, "Agree, agree" from *Margery*, they also follow the standard tonal arrangements of the main sections of Lampe's da capo arias.

Lampe's cavatinas are shorter than his da capo arias and their text setting is simpler, with less coloratura — practices common in the cavatinas of his contemporaries. Text repetition varies, from an extreme amount in Lady Moore's nagging aria "You coxcomb" in *Margery*, to his standard practice of stating the stanza of text once in each of the two parts, as in "Oh, ho! Master Moore," in *The Dragon*, and even to using a different stanza of text for each section, such as in "And thou, oh Wall" from *Pyramus and Thisbe*. This latter organization may at first not seem consistent with earlier statements about the derivation of the cavatina from the single first stanza of the da capo aria, but it should be noted that Lampe's da capo arias sometimes employ more than four lines or one stanza of text in a single musical section. Arias in *The Dragon* frequently use at least six lines in the aria's first section (e.g., in "Zeno, Plato, Aristotle" and "But to hear the children mutter") or in its second (e.g., "Gentle knight"). Six or even more lines of text for his cavatinas should not seem extraordinary, especially since the cavatina's text setting is much more syllabic than that of the aria.

Lampe's first extant cavatina is from *Dione*, the heroine's death aria "Cease complaining," although a number of single-stanza aria texts exist in the libretto of *Amelia*. A single cavatina occurs in *The Dragon*, "Oh, ho! Master Moore," which along with the following accompanied recitative and the intervening battle piece forms a scene that resembles the cavatina/cabaletta scenes of Handel. A better cavatina/cabaletta-like pairing, more similar to Handel's own practice, occurs in *Pyramus and Thisbe*, with "And thou, oh Wall" and "Oh wicked Wall." The first is a slow, sostenuto piece for Pyramus, extolling the virtues of the wall and asking to be shown the chink in it through which he might look for Thisbe. When he can not see her, he curses the wall in a fiery 6/8 allegro number, "Oh wicked Wall," set in the relative minor of the first cavatina.

In *Margery* the cavatina is the basic aria form, chosen for nine of the sixteen arias. The form is handled with considerable freedom, and most of the variants mentioned above can be found. An interesting aria is "O piercing anguish," which has three complete repetitions of the text that modulate in turn to the dominant, the mediant, and back to the tonic, resulting in a structure exactly like the opening sections of the two *Amelia* arias. The cavatinas "O wicked Wall" and "Approach ye furies" in *Pyramus* are similar.

It is notable that Lampe's interest in the cavatina began with his first opera, *Amelia*, if the single-stanza arias in its libretto actually were set as cavatinas, and continued through his last opera, *Pyramus and Thisbe*. His emphasis on the cavatina in *Margery* is quite progressive, for Grout singles out Carl Heinrich Graun's *Montezuma* (1755), written almost twenty years later, as being of considerable historical significance because of its remarkable two-to-one ratio of cavatinas to da capo arias.[9] *Margery*, however, contains nine cavatinas, only one modified da capo aria, four binary arias, one fugal aria, and a cavatina-like aria with chorus, and another *Margery* cavatina exists in the extant manuscript score of *The Dragon*. Thus, *Margery's* ratio of cavatinas to da capo arias is ten (or eleven) to one, and the opera contains twice as many cavatinas as all other aria forms combined. Because of such a high proportion of cavatinas, both *Margery* and its composer deserve considerably more attention

---

[9] Grout, *Short History of Opera*, 211. It might also be noted that the preference of the cavatina over the da capo aria in *Montezuma* was not Graun's own innovation, but was a change dictated by his employer Frederick the Great, who also had written the opera's libretto. See Eugene Helm, "Graun, Carl Heinrich," *The New Grove Dictionary of Music and Musicians*, ed. Stanley Sadie, 20 vols. (London: Macmillan, 1980), 7:645.

than they have previously been accorded, since the opera pushes back the early appearance of the cavatina by about twenty years, and serves as yet another example of the progressiveness and innovation of Lampe.

Binary Arias and Songs

The frequency of cavatinas in Lampe's later operas declined in favor of other forms such as the binary, which was closely related to the cavatina, but older than either it or the da capo aria. By the middle of the seventeenth century, bipartite arias had been common in Italian cantatas and operas, such as those of Cesti, and the binary aria often had been used by later composers like Scarlatti before the era of the da capo aria's dominance. In England, Purcell had written many binary songs and arias for his stage works, and short binary arias, sometimes with repeats, could even be found in Handel's operas (e.g., the set of three binary arias sung by Bajazet, Andronico, and Irene in Act II, Scene 2 of *Tamerlano*, 1724).

Lampe would have known the binary aria through his association with Handel, but he undoubtedly first encountered it in Germany, where the form had been the foundation of early German opera song and occurred quite frequently in the works of Keiser, Schürmann, and Telemann. In such arias the two parts usually were of about the same length, were both repeated, and were each set to from two to four lines of text. The middle cadence was to the dominant, and the works were often strophic. These early German arias also exhibit a close relationship to both folk song and the dance, and often were written in dance rhythms.[10] Lampe would have discovered that binary songs and arias were popular in England as well, both within and without the British theater. Almost all English popular songs and ballads published in the British Isles during Lampe's time were binary, and the form was standard in the operas and playhouse music of Arne and his British contemporaries.

Lampe's bipartite songs and arias can be divided into two groups, strophic and nonstrophic, and Lampe's distinction between the two is quite careful. Strophic songs never are found in his operas, but all surviving play and pantomime songs are cast in strophic form. Other composers, both German and English, did not make such a clear differentiation within the form, and in fact the strophic aria was especially favored in Hamburg opera.

Two reasons probably account for the absence of strophic songs from Lampe's operas. First, he likely found the strophic song to be of too popular a character to suit his concept of opera as a serious art form. The influence of the high musical ideals of Italian opera, of Handel, and of Schürmann likely remained too strong to allow the degeneration of Lampe's operas into a mere series of pretty and catchy tunes, as sometimes was the case with the operas of Arne and Keiser. Thus it also is noteworthy that Lampe never wrote in the highly popular genre of the ballad opera—he had higher tastes and aspirations. Even such works as *Pyramus and Thisbe*, which at first glance may seem silly, trite, and of little musical consequence, under closer scrutiny reveal careful and imaginative musical and theatrical craftsmanship.

In addition to objecting to the strophic song in opera for aesthetic reasons, Lampe probably disapproved of the form dramatically. For a composer as conscious and careful of text setting and drama as Lampe seems to have been, the task of writing music that would fit several stanzas of text equally well and continue to move the dramatic action forward would

---

[10] A good example is "Auf die Gesundheit" from Keiser's *Circe* (1734), which may be found in Ernst Otto Lindner's *Die erst stehende deutsche Oper*, 2 vols. (Berlin: Schlesinger'sche Buch & Musikhandlung, 1855), 2:17.

have become impossible. Other German composers and theorists had realized for a long time the dramatic and musical problems inherent in strophic songs, and Mattheson had expressed in rather definite terms his opinion on the subject when writing in his *Critica musica*:

> Odes [i.e., strophic songs] are in my opinion not at all musical; and hymns, in so far as they are sung by the congregation, are even less so. My reasons are, that if in composition one wishes to set these pieces like songs, suitable music and good melodies can never be achieved except in a melismatic style, because of the different strophes, since all strophes must be treated exactly alike.[11]

Even earlier, Christian Friedrich Hunold, one of Keiser's librettists, had stated:

> A composer can set no more than the first stanza of an ode [to a given melody], after which the other stanzas must accommodate themselves to it. How terrible it is when different affections have the same melody or when musical variation occurs on contradictory or incommodious words can be judged easily by anyone.[12]

In pantomimes and plays, however, the musical and dramatic purpose of a song differed from that in opera, for the song served as an adjunct to the actual drama, providing decoration or a point of reflection or contrast. Thus the strophic form was adequate, and was the customary form of pantomime and play songs long before Lampe. Besides his songs for pantomimes and plays, Lampe wrote many other strophic songs of a popular nature to be sung in the playhouses, performed in the pleasure gardens, and enjoyed in the homes, and these songs constitute the majority of works in his song collections. His German contemporaries also realized the values of the strophic song in certain situations. Although Mattheson criticized the strophic song severely on dramatic grounds, he could write in *Der vollkommene Kapellmeister* that:

> One should not invariably classify drinking songs, lullabies, gallant pieces, and such as trifling; they often give more pleasure and perform greater service than do powerful concertos and imposing overtures, because they prove to be more genuinely natural. Neither style requires any less mastery of its own sort than does the other.[13]

Lampe wrote an even stronger, though similar, defense of the strophic song, i.e., ballad, in the preface to his first song collection *Wit Musically Embellish'd*:

---

[11] "Oden sind bei mir gar nicht musicalisch; Kirchen-Lieder, in so weit sie von der Gemeine gesungen werden, noch viel weniger. Meine Ursachen sind, dass sich jene, wenn man sie in der Composition Liedermässig behandeln will, wegen der verscheidenen Strophen, nimmermehr zur Music und guten Melodie schicken, ausser im melismatischen Styl, da alles über einen Kamm geschoren wird." Johannes Mattheson, *Critica Musica*, 2 vols. (Hamburg: Mattheson, 1722-25), 2:309.

[12] "Und ein Componist kan in einer Ode ebenfalls nicht mehr als den ersten Satz componieren wonach sich die übrigen accomodieren müssen. Allein wie übel es lässt wenn unterscheidene Affectus einerley Melodie haben oder die Musicalische Variation auf widrige und incommode Wörter fällt kann jeder leicht judicieren." Quoted in Richard Petzold, *Georg Philipp Telemann, Leben und Werk* (Leipzig: VEB Deutscher Verlag für Musik, 1967), 108.

[13] "Trink- und Wiegen-Lieder, Galanterie-Stücklein u. darff man eben nicht immer ohne Unterscheid läppisch nennen: sie gefallen offt besser, und thun mehr Dienste, wenn sie recht natürlich gerathen sind, als grossmächtige Concerte und stoltze Ouvertüren. Jene erfordern nicht weniger ihren Meister nach ihrer Art, als diese." Johann Mattheson, *Der vollkommene Kapellmeister* (Hamburg: Christian Herold, 1739), 73.

> I am not insensible that some Persons are so strongly prejudic'd against ye Word Ballad, that notwithstanding the best Modulation & Harmony is compendiously couch'd under that Denomination, yet they will despise them merely upon Account of the Name they are distinguish'd by; but I may venture to assert, that many of the sublimest Taste are Friends to this particular Branch of the Musical System, as well for its easy Conciseness as advantageous Contrivance, there being a great Variety of Words adapted to one short specimen of Musick, which other kinds of Vocal Composition will not admitt of; . . .

Other statements of the same nature were written by Lampe's close friend Carey in the prefaces to his *Six Songs for Conversation* (1728) and *Six Ballads on the Humours of the Town* (1728).

Lampe's binary arias and songs share many characteristics with their German and English counterparts. For arias in the major mode, the first section ends in the dominant and the second returns to the tonic; in the minor mode the motion is to the relative minor and back. Similar tonal motion is the rule in Schürmann, Telemann, and Keiser, as well as Arne. Lampe differs from Arne, however, in his preference of the minor mode. Arne's early binary numbers are almost all in major keys with triple meters and are closely related to the dance. In contrast, well over half of Lampe's binary songs of the same time are in minor keys and their meters are much more varied. While Arne's songs are often light, gallant, and dance-like in character, Lampe's binary numbers more closely resemble the short and sometimes serious two-part German songs and keyboard pieces of the period, such as in Telemann's *Singe-, Speil- und Generalbass-Übungen* and the *Anna Magdalena Bach Notebook* (Example 28).

TABLE 7
Form of "Wretched is a wife's condition," *Margery*

Rit. 1	A B	Rit. 2	‖: A :‖: B :‖	Rit. 2 *repeated*
	strophe 1		strophe 2	

In terms of their structure, the two main sections of the strophic songs in Lampe's plays and pantomimes are more nearly the same length than are those in his binary opera arias, where the second section usually is longer. The songs and arias often have short ritornellos at the beginning and end of the first section and the end of the second and, in cases where an opening ritornello or introduction does not appear in the print, one likely was added or improvised in performance. Songs and arias often seem to have been printed without their opening ritornellos, as is the case with all the arias from *The Dragon* that appear in Bickham's *The Musical Entertainer* (London, 1740), which Lampe edited.

As was mentioned above, both main sections always are repeated in Lampe's binary opera arias, although his practice in the strophic binary songs of the plays and pantomimes is less strict. The sections sometimes are both repeated, as in "Bright Cynthia's pow'r" from *Oroonoko*, or only one is repeated, as in "Hail to the mirtle shade" from *Theodosius*, or neither is repeated, as in "The parent bird" from *Orpheus and Euridice*. In *Margery*, treatment of the form also varies. Sometimes a repeat is written out to allow for a change in the closing ritornello, as in "Then come to my arms." Another binary aria, Margery's "Wretched is a wife's condition," is exceptional in several ways, for it combines strophic elements with repeated and unrepeated sections of the binary forms (see Table 7). The ritornellos are based,

EXAMPLE 28. "He's a man every inch," *The Dragon of Wantley.*

as is usual, on the vocal material, Rit. 1 equalling section A, and Rit. 2 equalling the last half of section B. Another variant of the binary song, found first in *Margery* in "Mauxalinda thus admiring" and "Then come to my arms," and later in *Pyramus and Thisbe* in "Where is my love," involves the addition of a short vocal and instrumental coda after the repeat of the second section. Although present in Lampe's operas, this technique never appears in his pantomime and play songs. It is found, however, in Arne's theater music, occurring several times in *Comus* ("Come, come bid adieu" and "Fame's an echo") and other works.

As in his da capo arias and cavatinas (and also like Arne), Lampe rarely bases the two main sections of his binary arias and songs on the same motive. Occasionally the two sections may employ similar rhythmic patterns and phrase lengths, especially in the incipits of the sections, although these similar rhythms usually are coupled with different melodic contours (Examples 29 and 30). In some cases the melodies of the two sections contrast considerably (Example 31). But at the other extreme, it is possible to find one, and only one, example in Lampe's binary songs and arias of the original motive being transposed exactly to form the basis of the second section (Example 32).

Whether occurring in operas, plays, or pantomimes, however, Lampe's binary songs and arias generally remain operatic in style. Their tessitura is similar to that of his da capo arias and cavatinas, although in the binary songs of other composers such as Telemann tessituras often are lower than in their arias. In addition, Lampe's phrasing in all of his arias and songs is not nearly so symmetrical and predictable as is that of the binary arias of Hamburg and Brunswick, or of England, and the folk and popular elements so common in the melodies of his German and English contemporaries can only be found occasionally in Lampe's arias. The textual treatment in Lampe's binary arias is similar to that of his other operatic forms, the chief difference being the absence of many long melismas in the binary pieces. Lampe's binary arias, therefore, fit well into the total musical and dramatic texture of his operas, and never create the dramatic and musical jolts commonly caused by the binary strophic aria in Keiser, or that are so detrimental to the overall effect of Arne's *Artaxerxes*. In Lampe's operas as well as in his pantomimes and plays, the binary aria can justifiably take its place alongside the more serious forms in opera.

Other Aria Forms

Although almost all of Lampe's arias belong to one of the three major classifications discussed above, isolated instances of a few other forms exist, and two will be mentioned here. "Poor children three" in *The Dragon* is a short, through-composed aria that is unique in several ways, possibly because it was not an original part of the opera. It seems that soon after the premiere of *The Dragon* there were complaints that John Laguerre, a minor playhouse singer who played Gubbins, had no aria. A comic song, a genre in which he and his singing excelled, was added. The new work was so well liked that it soon became a standard part of the opera. The little aria is constantly in or close to the tonic, and appears to be one of the few examples of a Lampe work written merely as a display vehicle for the singer. Laguerre's highly ornamented performance became quite popular, and at least two different printed versions of his ornamentation for this song exist.[14]

---

[14] In George Bickham, *The Musical Entertainer*, 2 vols., ed. John Frederick Lampe (London: Bickham, 1734-40), 2:24; and John Frederick Lampe, *The Songs and Duetto's in the Burlesque Opera called the Dragon of Wantley, Adapted to the German Flute, Hautboy, or Violin, With a Thorough Bass* (London: Wilcox, 1738).

EXAMPLE 29. "The parent bird," *Orpheus and Euridice.*

The parent bird whose little nest But soon as na-ture plumes their wings

EXAMPLE 30. "In humble weeds," *Theodosius.*

In hum - ble weeds but clean array and when the rites di - vine are past

EXAMPLE 31. "Where is my love," *Pyramus and Thisbe.*

Where is my love, my Pyre, my dear The wheel of for - tune guide thee

EXAMPLE 32. "With sweet lillies," *The Sham Conjuror.*

With sweet lillies, pinks and roses What kind nature still composes

EXAMPLE 33. "Thus distracted," *Margery*.

Another unique Lampe aria is "Thus distracted" from *Margery*, the sole example of a fugal aria found in Lampe's operas. Fugal arias were almost unheard of in the Italian opera seria, but in the operas of German composers occasional fugal arias existed, such as "Numi stelle, per pietà" in Keiser's *Jodelet* (1726), a da capo, four-voice fugue. Lampe's fugue is based on a three-measure subject that appears in a complete, three-part fugal exposition in the opening ritornello, which is repeated to close the aria. During the vocal portion of the work, which maintains the character of a series of fugal developments and episodes, the subject appears in the tonic, dominant, subdominant, and relative major, and the interaction between the voice and the instruments is both frequent and interesting. The fugue is made even more intriguing by the presence of a quasi-canonic countersubject that always enters one beat after the main subject begins (Example 33).

*　　　*　　　*

As one surveys the corpus of Lampe arias, their variety in form is striking. In a day when opera seria was dominated by the da capo tradition and the British musical theater relied almost completely on simple songs, Lampe's operas and theater music include strict and modified da capo arias, cavatinas, binary, and fugal arias, and through-composed pieces in a consistent, dramatic, and operatic style. Many of his mature operas seem to constitute a study of a particular aria form, although the form may be modified considerably for dramatic reasons. Yet such tight organization and concern for drama were not limited to Lampe's arias, but permeated Lampe's entire musical style, and affected ensembles and other elements of his operas as well.

8 CHAPTER SOLO ENSEMBLES, CHORUSES, AND OTHER VOCAL FORMS

One important difference between Lampe's operas and Italian opera of his day lies in his treatment of choruses and ensembles. Ensembles are of considerable dramatic and musical importance in Lampe's compositions, as well as quite numerous, totalling over forty percent of the numbers in his mature works (see Table 8). In Italy, however, opera consisted of an almost endless series of recitatives and arias, with only occasional duets, few if any other ensembles, and no real chorus at all, only a *coro* of soloists. In London's opera seria the preponderance of arias was even greater, as described by Giuseppe Riva writing in 1725 to the Duke of Modena, "in England people like very few recitatives, thirty arias and one duet at least, distributed over the three acts."[1]

TABLE 8
Arias and Ensembles in Lampe's Mature Operas

Opera	Arias	Duets	Other Ensembles
The Dragon	11	4	1 trio, 7 choruses
Margery	15	5	4 choruses, 1 aria with chorus
The Sham Conjuror	7	2	1 trio, 1 chorus
Pyramus and Thisbe	10	3	1 chorus

Nor can English vernacular practice adequately explain the high percentage of ensembles in Lampe's works. Ensembles and choruses had been important in Purcell's stage music, but the forms were little used in English theater after him. In early eighteenth-century attempts at serious opera, such as Pepusch's *Venus and Adonis* (1715) and *Apollo and Daphne* (1716), one finds only an occasional duet, as in Italian opera, and no chorus of any sort. Comic works such as *The Beggar's Opera* and other ballad operas also consisted of a mere series of songs, with neither ensembles nor choruses. In addition, extant pantomime librettos from Lampe's time indicate that although choruses occasionally sang, most often in Lullian or verse anthem-like refrains within an aria, other ensembles were almost completely absent.

One must look to German rather than English or Italian practices to be able to account for Lampe's preference for ensembles. An examination of the use of ensembles at Brunswick and Hamburg is especially informative, for while opera in Vienna, Dresden, Berlin, and most

---

[1] Quoted in Richard A. Streatfeild, "Handel, Rolli, and Italian Opera in London in the Eighteenth Century," *Musical Quarterly* 3 (July 1917): 433.

other German centers was rather Italianate, with an Italian preference for solo arias, the Brunswick and Hamburg operas enjoyed much more musical and textual variety. Schürmann's operas generally had no fewer than four duets, one or two trios or quartets, and three or four choruses — and many of his works contained even more. His *Heinrich der Vogler* (1721), Part II, for example, includes seven duets, one trio, one quartet, and fourteen choruses, all in a work that Lampe almost certainly heard performed. In Hamburg, where Lampe also likely visited, the large number and wide assortment of ensembles was similar, probably resulting from the Hamburg love of operatic variety. Thus, Lampe's acquaintance with the operas of Brunswick and Hamburg in his youth, which can be reconstructed plausibly from extant biographical data, becomes virtually certain in light of elements of his musical style, such as his love of ensembles.

Duets

Lampe apparently held the duet in high esteem, for of his sixteen extant solo ensembles fourteen are duets and two are trios. His fondness for the duet may have been influenced by the continental Germans, who wrote about four times as many duets as other ensembles in their operas. In addition, the duet was the preferred, and almost the only, solo ensemble in Handelian and other Italian opera, possibly because of the popularity of the Italian chamber duet.

Like his German contemporaries, Lampe wrote his duets and trios in the same closed forms, with the same harmonic and thematic relationships, as the arias of his operas. In fact, Lampe's chosen aria form in a particular opera is also usually his preferred duet form, so that in *The Dragon* three out of the four duets are da capo (the other is binary), four out of the five *Margery* duets are cavatina-like (the other is a modified da capo), and *The Sham Conjuror* has one modified da capo and one binary duet. In *Pyramus and Thisbe*, however, only one duet resembles a binary form, and two are cavatina-like contrasts. The binary duet "I go without delay" is one of the more dramatic numbers of the opera, and in it the basic binary form is slightly modified, with the two sections being very short and the repeats written out. The written-out repeat of the first section transposes the original music exactly and entirely into the relative major, so that the first section eventually concludes in that key, as is usual with Lampe's binary movements in minor modes. The second section is repeated literally, although for some reason the repeat is written out and it is followed by a two-measure vocal coda and a three-measure ritornello. This coda can be compared to similar vocal codas in some of Lampe's arias (e.g., "Thus the damsel," in *Margery*).

More intriguing than the form of the duets is the variety of relationships and the drama that Lampe creates between the two voices. Many of Lampe's techniques are strikingly similar to those in Schürmann's duets and imply a direct influence by Schürmann upon the younger composer. In the duets of both men, one finds much contrapuntal imitation between the voices (a practice of Schürmann influenced by the duets of Steffani), including motives treated in echo fashion, quasi-canonic sections, freer imitation, and long phrases at the beginning of the duet that are sung first by one character, then by the other (often with different text), and finally by both together. Similar imitative duets also are common in the works of Telemann. The Lampe duets, however, are generally more carefully constructed than those of Schürmann, Keiser, and other continental Germans, whose ensembles often betray signs of haste and carelessness.

EXAMPLE 34. "Around the wide world," *Margery*.

In Lampe, the relationship between the two vocal parts is determined by the text and its dramatic implications. Frequently the two characters are either a pair of lovers or friends and share similar feelings and ideas. Hence, Lampe will set their thoughts with similar music. Sometimes the two voices echo the same sentiment (Example 34). Often duets will begin with whole phrases being repeated back and forth by the two characters, as in "Pigs shall not be" from *The Dragon*, where several short phrases are repeated in turn, or "Thus folding, beholding" from *Pyramus and Thisbe*, in which a thirteen-measure series of singing and ritornellos is repeated as a unit. The repetition can be quite literal, and among the numerous imitative passages one may find some strict canonic sections, as in "By these arms" (Example 35), which contains a canon at the fourth (actually the eleventh) at the distance of one measure. The interaction of the two voices is also of interest for its demonstration

EXAMPLE 35. "By these arms," *Margery*.

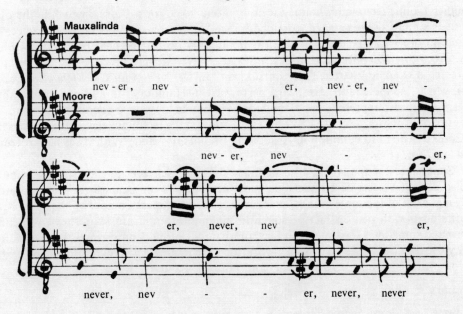

EXAMPLE 36. "Thus folding, beholding," *Pyramus and Thisbe.*

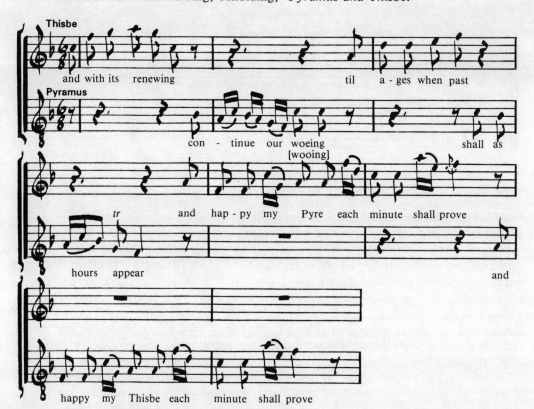

of another Lampe technique, holding a note in one voice for a short time while the other voice sings a more active passage. Analogous sections of alternation between the voices can be found in other Lampe duets as well, as in "Let my dearest be near me" and "Insulting gipsey" from *The Dragon.* Such strict canons also have German precedents, for Telemann had written a canonic quartet, "Mit Entzükken," in *Der neu-modische Liebhaber Damon* (1724), which Lampe could have heard performed in Hamburg. In addition to the above devices, Lampe also represents an affinity or harmony between two characters by a smooth series of parallel thirds and sixths, but his application of the technique never degenerates into the bird-like twitters so common in Arne, as in "To liberty" and "With roses be our temple bound" in *Eliza* (1754).

Sometimes Lampe writes true dialogue duets, which are much different from the so-called dialogue duets of Handel.[2] In most of Handel's dialogue duets the two singers merely make use of the same musical material at different times. Lampe, on the other hand, can write duets with two distinct personalities singing different music and text, sometimes together and sometimes separately. In fact, the dialogue often demonstrates the highest level of unity between the singers when they work together to create a single melodic and textual line, completing one another's thoughts and phrases (Example 36).

---

[2] Paul Henry Lang, *George Frideric Handel* (New York: Norton, 1966), 621-22.

The conversation can be amiable, as in the above example or in the beginning of "Let my dearest be near me" from *The Dragon*, which begins as a dialogue but ends in parallel thirds and sixths that symbolize the growing closeness between the two characters as the duet progresses. In other instances, the two parties may be less friendly or even hostile. Such duets, in which the two characters are in conflict, are uncommon in Handel's operas, but occur in Lampe fairly frequently, especially between Margery and Mauxalinda in *The Dragon* and *Margery*. Margery, who as Lady Moore seems unable to get along with anyone, even attacks her husband, especially after he is discovered with his former mistress Mauxalinda. The resulting duet, "O ungrateful," is a particularly glorious dialogue duet, with a long introductory epithet by each character, followed by short, sharp exchanges between them, as well as both singing at once. Near the end of *Margery*, in "Hear, oh! hear," Margery and Mauxalinda argue and quarrel constantly, without allowing a single measure of ritornello in the entire duet. The two women have sharply contrasting vocal lines and text, and sing sometimes in reply to one another and in other cases simultaneously. The following (Example 37) is taken from the very heart of the fight, and includes a fine variety of Lampe's conflict duet style.

EXAMPLE 37. "Hear, oh, hear my sad contrition," *Margery.*

Trios

Two Lampe trios are extant and, like the duets, exhibit the variety of form and dramatic content found in Lampe's arias. Most German opera duets, trios, and larger solo ensembles of Lampe's time were in da capo form, and therefore were called *arie à 2, à 3, à 4*, etc. in the scores and librettos. Neither of Lampe's trios, however, is in a strict da capo form.

In "O how easy is a woman," the trio from *The Dragon*, each character sings one stanza of text alone, after which all three join together for the final stanza. Although the singing of similar material, first separately and then together, is a common feature of Lampe's duets, especially near their beginnings, in this trio the repetition technique is expanded to encompass an entire section. Moreover, the repetitions here are not literal, as is customary in the duets. Moore, who has the second strophe, sings in the parallel minor, and in the final, three-voice strophe the original music is altered considerably. Hence, the term strophic variation probably is the most applicable and accurate description of the trio's form, and the presence of such a form in Lampe's music almost certainly is a result of similar practices in Brunswick and Hamburg.

Strophic variation had died out in Italian opera by the middle of the seventeenth century, but the form continued to be used in German opera, especially in Hamburg. As late as 1724 Telemann had included a strophic variation aria in *Der neumodische Liebhaber Damon*, and the form also appears in Keiser's works. An especially notable example is in his *Fredegunda* (1715), where in Act II, Scene 3, an aria by Hermenigild is followed by a variation over the same bass and harmonic background sung by Bazima. Both the original and the variation are then combined in a duet that immediately follows, forming a three-stanza strophic variation. The similarity between this Keiser duet and the Lampe trio is considerable and certainly suggests that Lampe learned of the strophic variation in Hamburg, especially since the form was so uncommon elsewhere.

The trio "Love me" in Lampe's *The Sham Conjuror* is not only interesting formally but delightful musically and effective dramatically. Like many *Sham Conjuror* numbers, the trio is in a modified da capo form. The reprise is written out, so that the main section, which originally ended in the relative major, can be altered to allow the trio to conclude in the tonic. The middle section and reprise are then repeated again, resulting in an almost rondo-like form (A B A' B A'), which is similar to the so-called double da capo arias sometimes found in Keiser (A B A B A, as in *Fredegunda*, 1715). The most exceptional quality of the trio, though, is its spirited dialogue, the setting of which amply demonstrates Lampe's excellent dramatic and musical craftsmanship and its enjoyable results. The following (Example 38) reproduces most of the last two sections of the trio in which Tom and Jamie are vying for Bell's affections.

Lampe's duets and trios generally are more influenced by their dramatic situations than are the solo ensembles of his contemporaries, whether Italian, German, or English. Such development and depiction of individual characters in ensembles (Examples 36-38) is more often associated with the latter eighteenth century and Mozart on the continent or Steven Storace in England rather than Lampe in London in the 1730s, fifty years earlier. Lampe's advanced ensemble practice appears to have been recognized by his English contemporaries and to have had a positive influence on their works written after *The Dragon*. Arne's music, for example, in parts of *Comus* (1738) and *The Judgment of Paris* (1742), when compared to his earlier compositions, seems especially indebted to Lampe.

EXAMPLE 38. "Love me," *The Sham Conjuror.*

Choruses

In *The Art of Musick* Lampe states that "grand Choruses" are "the most noble Pieces human Nature is capable of, to show Musick in its full Strength,"[3] and his opera choruses are intended to support his theories. His handling of the chorus differs considerably from practices in Italian and Handelian opera where there were no real choruses at all. The simple, homophonic *coro* that ended most Italian operas was sung by the soloists, not a chorus, and the soloists also sang whatever other short choruses might occur — often to the detriment of the drama. In Lampe's operas, however, an actual chorus sings the chorus parts, although the principals occasionally join in if the dramatic situation warrants, as in the final chorus of *The Dragon.*

Lampe's opera choruses are much more frequent than those of opera seria. While the final *coro* might be the only chorus-like section of an Italian opera, Lampe's operas include many choral numbers. For example, seven out of the twenty-four vocal numbers in *The Dragon* (not counting recitatives) are choruses. Lampe's preference for choruses possibly results from Schürmann's influence, for the latter's Brunswick operas include numerous choruses. Keiser's operas also contain many spectacular choruses but, like Schürmann, he does not seem to have thought the choruses worth much time and trouble. Rather, the chief purpose of the German opera chorus, even according to dramatic authorities,[4] was to get many people on the stage for a large spectacle such as the celebration of victory or peace, sacrifices, battles, sorceries, funeral processions, or rejoicings.

In England, Purcell's operatic choruses generally had been part of a spectacle as well, except in the case of *Dido,* where the chorus participates somewhat in and comments upon the action. In Handel, too, the attempted dramatic use of the chorus is exceptional, and is not always successful or convincing, such as in the *coro militare* that is sung twice in *Sosarme* (1732) and the chorus proclaiming Berengario king in *Lotario* (1729). Lampe's choruses, however, always serve an important function in the drama, carrying it forward, with the singers actually participating in the action.

Lampe's opera choruses, with one exception (the two-voice finale of *The Sham Conjuror*) are all written for only three voice parts — two high treble voices plus one in the baritone/bass range. Lampe often treats the two upper parts as virtually equal voices which, when added to the bass, form a trio sonata-like texture. The printed full score of *Margery,* in fact, labels the top two lines as "Canto 1" and "Canto 2," and the bottom one as "Bass." Such a trio sonata texture was common in early eighteenth-century Italian vocal and instrumental theater and chamber music, and also can be found in the Italianate opera choruses of John Christopher Smith Jr.'s *Teraminta* (1732) and *Ulysses* (1733). Keiser also wrote three-voice da capo opera choruses for *Tomyris* (1717), *Croesus* (1730), and other works, although his customary voicing was soprano, tenor, and bass. Handel's standard practice of the 1720s and early 1730s was to write for two to three high voices (castrati and women) plus one lower male part in the *coro* and other operatic choruses, and three sounding parts, two high and one low, were quite common, e.g., in *Ottone* (1723), *Alessandro* (1726), *Siroe* (1728), *Partenope* (1730), and other works, even though more written parts, doubling one another, might appear. In addition to the potential affect of general Italian practice, Lampe may have written three-voice choruses for the purely practical reasons that his chorus,

---

[3] John Frederick Lampe, *The Art of Musick* (London: C. Corbett, 1740), 11.

[4] Barthold Feind II, *Deutsche Gedichte* (Stade: H. Brummer, 1708), 102.

made up mostly of actors and dancers, was too small or of too inadequate musicianship to allow singing in more than three parts. He certainly could write for four or more distinct voices, and did so frequently in his instrumental works and in his nonoperatic choral works such as his *Thanksgiving Anthem* celebrating the suppression of the Jacobite revolution.

Lampe's preference for da capo choruses in *The Dragon* also can likely be explained by his association with Keiser, Handel, and opera seria. The da capo *coro* was prevalent in Handel's operas of the 1720s and early 1730s such as *Radamisto* (1720), *Ottone* (1723), *Admeto* (1727), *Siroe* (1728), *Ariodante* (1735), and others. Since Lampe was burlesquing Italian opera, his use of the customary chorus form is understandable. In *Margery,* where the element of burlesque is not so prominent, the form is freer, with two binary choruses and two through-composed choruses. Handel also wrote some binary opera choruses, as in *Partenope* (1730).

If Lampe's choral forms in *The Dragon* resemble those of Handel's operas, his choral style certainly does not. Instead of the simple, homophonic *coro* in Italian opera, Lampe, as a typical German, often prefers fugues, with *The Dragon* containing a number of fine ones, quite spirited and driving. The choral fugues of *The Dragon* are all preceded and followed by orchestral ritornellos, and the works sometimes have other internal ritornellos as well. In da capo choruses, the fugue forms the main section, with the second section often sung by a soloist alone. "Or else this cursed dragon" (Example 39) is of interest, since the chorus also takes over the performance of the opening and closing ritornellos, both of which, contrary to Lampe's usual custom, are unrelated to the following fugue and even are written in a contrasting tempo.

The Dragon and *Margery* both begin and end with a chorus, in accord with German dramatic theory[5] and Handel's own sporadic practice (as in *Giulio Cesare,* 1724). In *The Dragon,* the opening chorus helps to set the mood of the drama as well as to provide some background for the plot. In *Margery,* the first chorus is part of a grand tableau (the wedding of Moore and Margery), such as those frequently found in Handel of this period, as at the beginnings of *Siroe* (1728), *Partenope* (1730), *Sosarme* (1732), *Giustino* (1737), *Berenice* (1737), and *Faramondo* (1738), all of which preceded *Margery* and would have been known to Lampe. In the *Margery* chorus Lampe appropriates another of Handel's favorite tricks. The overture ends on the dominant and proceeds directly into the opening ritornello of the chorus, which is in the same key, so that the audience believes that it is still listening to part of the overture, when the chorus suddenly interrupts, with considerable dramatic impact (cf. Handel's *Giulio Cesare,* 1724).

The two internal choruses of *Margery,* "Oh sad, oh strange" and "Come wet your whistle," contrast both with one another and with the grand opening chorus. "Come wet your whistle" is a drinking song, a genre of which Carey was quite fond, and an enjoyable, madrigal-like, binary piece with freely imitative as well as homophonic sections. "Oh sad, oh strange," which ends Act I, is a lament over the breakup of Moore's and Margery's marriage, and the music actually is almost too good for the silly text. In the character of the best British laments, the slow, triple meter chorus begins with (but does not continue in) a descending Phrygian tetrachord in the bass, and employs a constantly falling melodic line, with appoggiaturas written in. (Part of this lament is reproduced in Example 40.)

Lampe's final choruses are more homophonic than his other choruses, probably because of the example of the Italian *coro* as well as the common German practice of Schürmann

---

[5] Feind, 102.

EXAMPLE 39. "Or else this cursed dragon," *The Dragon of Wantley*.

Adagio

Allegro

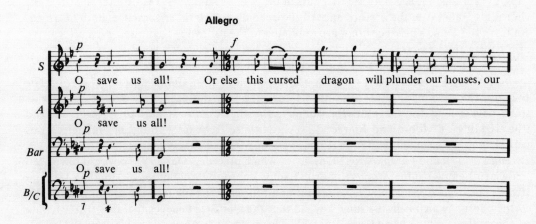

Example 39 — *continued*

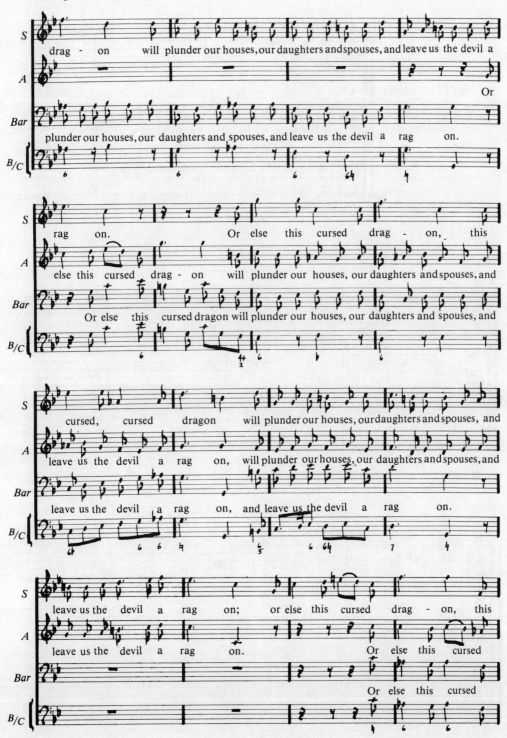

EXAMPLE 40. "Oh sad, oh strange," *Margery*.

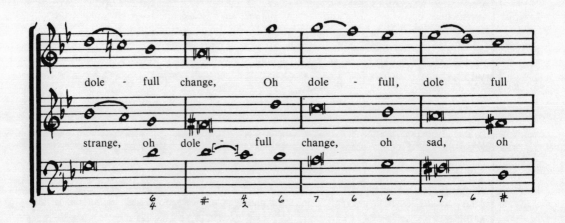

130

and others. The relationship between the last chorus of *Margery* and the *coro* is especially close, for the first section of the binary chorus is sung only by the soloists. Soloists also are present in the final chorus of *The Dragon*, where Lampe's technique of alternating the pair of soloists with the chorus has some precedent in Handel's operatic finales, e.g., in the final chorus of *Radamisto* (1720).

The closing chorus of *The Sham Conjuror* is written entirely for two voices instead of three, and resembles the so-called vaudeville finale, in which the various characters step forward and sing short solos between choral refrains. The term "vaudeville finale" was taken from the popular French comic operatic genre, which customarily ended with such a chorus. A vaudeville-like finale had been included in Telemann's *Socrates* (1721), which Lampe could have known, and the vaudeville finale later became common and quite popular in British theater, even in serious works such as Arne's *Artaxerxes* (1762). Fiske states that the first appearance of the vaudeville finale in England was in William Boyce's *The Shepherd's Lottery* (1751),[6] but since *The Sham Conjuror* antedates the Boyce piece by more than ten years it may provide yet another example of Lampe's innovative techniques being well ahead of his time.

On the whole, Lampe's choruses seem closer in technique to the Handel of the oratorios than to the Italians or some of his British contemporaries such as Arne. While Arne's simple theater choruses, such as those in *Comus*, are developed formally, Lampe's choruses, like Handel's, develop organically, continually growing, expanding, and pushing dramatically forward. In contrast to Arne's insipid choral melodies, the themes of the Lampe choruses, especially in the fugues of *The Dragon*, are strong and driving, and add to the excitement and drama of the entire work. Also like Handel, Lampe often interrupts quicker contrapuntal motion with heavy hammerstrokes, such as in "Fill, fill, fill" in *The Dragon* (Example 41). Lampe's choruses, therefore, make a major dramatic contribution to his operas, and in addition to containing some of his finest music, they are to a large extent responsible for the appeal and success of works such as *The Dragon*.

Recitatives

The only recitatives extant from Lampe operas are those of *The Dragon*, and they are almost all of a secco nature, probably because *The Dragon* sought to burlesque Italian opera where secco recitatives were the norm. The Lampe recitatives do follow the text cadences and dramatic sense well, however, and are by no means mere stereotypes that only link the arias together.

Most of Lampe's recitatives are short, covering scarcely a page of the score, but "O villain! monster! devil!" in *The Dragon* is both longer and more complex. Beginning with an agitated accompanied recitative for Mauxalinda, it moves smoothly into a secco dialogue between her and Moore, after which she sings a short melody from Moore's preceding duet with Margery to drive home her accusations of infidelity. Moore responds in another secco section that leads into his next aria, where he renews his declaration of love and faithfulness. It is tempting to hope that Lampe wrote other such extended and dramatic recitatives, but disappointing that they seem to have disappeared.

Even in Lampe's shorter recitatives, however, the dramatic and musical interest remains high. Unlike composers such as Arne, whose recitatives can boringly stagnate in one key

---

[6] Roger Fiske, *English Theatre Music in the Eighteenth Century* (London: Oxford University Press, 1973), 221.

EXAMPLE 41. "Fill, fill, fill," *The Dragon of Wantley.*

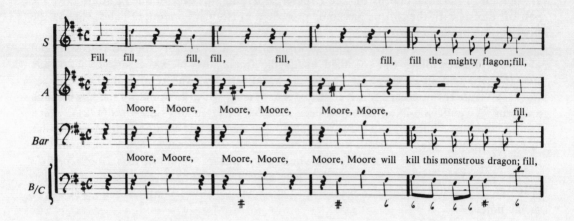

EXAMPLE 42. "Lauk, what a monstrous tail," *The Dragon of Wantley.*

(e.g., the opening recitative of *Britannia,* 1734), Lampe, like Handel, utilizes rich, varied, and expressive harmonies. His writing can be quite chromatic, even when the overall motion from beginning to end is only a fourth or fifth, as in the *Dragon* recitatives "O Father, father" and "Lauk! what a monstrous tail" (Example 42). Tonal relationships between the end of a recitative and the following aria also vary, unlike in the works of C. H. Graun and many of the younger Neapolitans where the relationship almost always is that of dominant to tonic. In Lampe the tonal relationship between recitative and aria can be either a fourth or fifth, and often a second, but only occasionally a third.

Even from the limited number extant in *The Dragon,* one can see that Lampe's recitatives are by no means mere copies stamped out of the same mold, but exhibit originality and inventiveness. He demonstrates his concern for the text and the continuity of drama and an understanding of the need to maintain musical interest, as well as the use of musical elements for maximum dramatic effect. One regret concerning Lampe recitatives remains — that more have not survived. One can be grateful for his other extant music, however, especially the choruses and solo ensembles, which contain some of the most delightful and dramatic music in his operas.

9 USE OF INSTRUMENTS

Overtures

Lampe's overtures from *The Dragon, Margery, The Sham Conjuror, Pyramus and Thisbe,* and *Cupid and Psyche/Columbine Courtezan* are all extant in full score. These overtures, like the rest of Lampe's operatic music, encompass a variety of forms, no two the same, and the overture for *Cupid and Psyche* is even one of the earlier examples of a new form—the medley overture. Lampe's boldness in experimenting with overture form contrasts with the usual practice of Handel, most of whose overtures are in a French style and form, or that of other Italian composers, who generally write the more modern sinfonia. Lampe's love of variety and experimentation may have been influenced by Hamburg customs, for unlike the rather standardized overtures of other major opera centers, Hamburg's operas by Keiser, Mattheson, and Telemann included overtures in some very uncommon, as well as in all the usual, forms and styles.

Lampe's overture to *The Dragon* is a French overture, a form that had been used by all the important German composers with whom Lampe had been in contact. Contrary to some definitions,[1] the late Baroque French overture that was written for English, German, and some Italian operas generally was not a two-part form (i.e., a slow section in dotted rhythms followed by a fugal Allegro), but a three-part one. And neither should these three-part French overtures be confused with the "French overture suite," as sometimes is the case.[2]

The three-part French overture actually developed quite early, from Lully's own practice, and the technique was further expanded and elaborated by others. Lully's two-part overtures often had been rounded off with a minuet episode. In Germany, the French overture had included a final minuet as early as Steffani's *Marco Aurelio* (1681), and the French overture plus minuet became the common overture form of Schürmann. The added movement was not as popular in Hamburg (it is found in Telemann's *Sieg der Schönheit,* 1732), but Mattheson admits that the practice existed quite early, even though he does not seem to have approved of it:

> Most French *overtures* close after the *Allegro,* or second part of the *overture;* in other cases, some close with a short *Lentement,* or serious movement; but it appears that this *fashion* is going to find few adherents.[3]

---

[1] Willi Apel, "Overture," *The Harvard Dictionary of Music,* 2nd ed. (Cambridge, Mass.: Harvard University Press, 1969), 635-36.

[2] Willi Apel, "Suite," *The Harvard Dictionary of Music,* 816.

[3] "Die meisten Frantzösischen *Ouvertüren* schliessen nach dem *Allegro,* oder anderen Theile der *Ouvertüre,* wiederum mit einem kurtzen *Lentement,* oder ernsthafften Satze; allein es scheinet, dass diese *Façon* nicht viel Adhaerenten finden will." Johann Mattheson, *Das neu-eröffneten Orchestre* (Hamburg: Mattheson, 1713), 171.

Future practice proved Mattheson's opinion incorrect, however, for in Handel's French overtures the added minuet, or sometimes another sort of section, became commonplace, appearing in *Ottone* (1723), *Partenope* (1730), *Arminio* (1737), *Berenice* (1737), *Imeneo* (1740), and elsewhere. The three-part form was even further expanded by some composers such as Carl Heinrich Graun, who occasionally replaced the customary minuet with a short, two-part Presto or Allegro section.

The appearance of two short sections (eight measures and twelve measures) at the end of the overture to *The Dragon,* therefore, is not as irregular as it might at first seem. It makes no difference that the additional sections are not dances, for Handel is by no means so strict as to employ only minuets and gigues in his own overtures. Marches end the overtures of *Scipione* (1726), *Ezio* (1732), and *Deidamia* (1741), all of which Lampe would have known. Also, there is the example mentioned above of C. H. Graun, who like Lampe was influenced by Schürmann, and whose overtures ending in a short bipartite Presto or Allegro bear a striking resemblance to Lampe's practice in *The Dragon.* Thus the pair of short sections at the end of the overture to *The Dragon* are neither an irregular quirk nor a set of act tunes that possibly belong somewhere else in the opera; they are an ordinary part of the overture and should be performed along with it.

Unlike the extended overture of *The Dragon,* with its woodwinds and brass, the single, short movement that constitutes the *Margery* overture is scored only for strings, and resembles the first movement of a sinfonia, a form and style with a much greater distinction from the French overture than the tempo and order-of-movements definition often used to contrast the two. Grout describes the two overtures thus:

> The essential difference was a matter of musical texture. The French overture was a creation of the late baroque, having a rich texture of sound, some quasi-contrapuntal independence of the inner voices, and a musical momentum bound to the nonperiodic progression of the bass and harmonies. The Italian overture was a characteristic preclassical form, light in texture, with busy activity in the upper voices accompanied by simple, standardized harmonic formulas.[4]

The *Dragon* and *Margery* overtures could almost serve as textbook examples illustrating the two extremes described by Grout. The overture to *The Dragon* begins with the slow, dotted movement typical in the French overture and written for a thick texture of trumpets, horns, oboes, and strings. The trumpets and horns often alternate on adjacent phrases, echoing the same melody, but in the middle part of the movement (in the relative minor) they are entirely silent. The fugal Allegro, like Lampe's choral fugues, is mainly in three actual voices, with much doubling. Three-voice fugues are frequent in Handel's French overtures as well, as in his *Berenice* (1737) overture or the familiar overture to *Messiah* (1742). Also, like Handel, Lampe concludes his overture with the short tunes mentioned above.

In the *Margery* overture, written for strings alone, the florid first violin part in continuous sixteenth notes is accompanied by the lower three voices in constant eighth notes. The relatively uninteresting second violin and viola parts merely fill in the harmony.

Even the first violin contains little that could be called a melody, relying instead on figuration, chord arpeggios, and scalewise passages. And while the harmonies are not necessarily stereotyped, especially in the rather chromatic second section, the harmonic rhythm is slower than in many of Lampe's other works.

---

[4] Donald J. Grout, *A Short History of Opera,* 2nd ed. (New York: Columbia University Press, 1965), 183-84.

The middle section of the *Margery* overture resembles the analogous part in the first movement of Graun's sinfonias, where the middle section may have the character of a development. In Lampe this "development" is built over a bass line that gradually ascends chromatically an entire octave, from tonic to tonic. This "development" (part of which is reproduced in Example 43) adds interest and musical tension to the overture, which with its persistent rhythms and florid passage work amply fulfills its purpose of building excitement and anticipation for the succeeding opera.

At the end of the overture a form of the opening motive is stated in the tonic with a strong tonic cadence, followed by a one-measure coda that concludes with a half cadence to the dominant. The opening ritornello of the first chorus immediately begins in the same key as the overture (D), and probably would have been thought by the listeners to be another movement or section of the overture. The dramatic effect when the chorus enters sixteen measures later would have been considerable, and had been exploited by Handel on several occasions. In *Giulio Cesare* (1724), for example, the final minuet of the overture is transformed abruptly into a chorus as Caesar and his army cross the Nile. These and similar passages in other Handel works probably served as Lampe's models for the *Margery* overture and opening chorus, although it must be admitted that the inclusion of the sinfonia instead of the French overture was a novel and personal innovation.

The overtures of both *The Sham Conjuror* and *Pyramus and Thisbe* are concertos, the first being a concerto grosso and the second an orchestral concerto. Concertos generally were not written as overtures to eighteenth-century Italian operas, although Italian composers, and especially Handel, sometimes experimented with concerto-like principles in their overtures. Concerto principles also had been combined with the French overture form in early English vernacular works, such as the overture to Pepusch's *Venus and Adonis* (1715), but concertos are found neither in his operas nor in the works of Arne, Smith, and other Englishmen. The Hamburg composers, however, wrote actual concertos for their opera overtures at least as far back as Keiser's *Nebuchadnezzar* (1704), which employs an oboe concerto, and Telemann's concerto overtures of *Emmaund Eginhard* (1708) and *Damon* (1724), which Lampe could have known. Also, Lampe would have been familiar with the common practice in the British playhouses of performing concerto grossos and similar music every evening before the "mainpiece."[5] Perhaps Lampe even hoped his concerto overtures would serve a dual purpose in the playhouses, by appearing before both operas and plays.

The concerto of *The Sham Conjuror* (for in the printed full score it is called a concerto rather than an overture) begins with a spirited Allegro movement in cut time. A pair of horns and a pair of oboes plus a bass (probably a bassoon) function as two distinct groups of concertino instruments, and the work contains some fine passages for horns or oboes (and bassoon) alone. The concerto grosso does not function merely as a ritornello, however, since it also participates in developing and expanding material through the dominant and mediant regions. At the end of the movement all instruments join together for the only tutti statement of the opening material.

A four-measure Grave section for strings alone follows the Allegro, and it resembles a similar short section, two measures long, that exists as the second "movement" of the concerto overture to *Pyramus and Thisbe*. Both sections cadence on the dominant. The presence of these short, slow sections may seem troublesome to explain until one remembers that in

---

5 Music was performed every evening for almost a half hour before the mainpiece began, and *The London Stage*, especially for the 1830s, often lists the titles of the compositions played, many of which were concertos. For a discussion of this "interval music" and of the popularity of the concerto, see Roger Fiske, *English Theatre Music in the Eighteenth Century* (London: Oxford University Press, 1973), 259-61.

EXAMPLE 43. Overture, *Margery*.

Corelli's *concerti da chiesa,* the first eight of his opus 6, each concerto contains a short Adagio section which serves as a transition between movements. The Corelli concertos were quite popular in the British theaters, and Lampe would have known them well; they provide the most logical source of the short, slow movements in the *Sham Conjuror* and *Pyramus and Thisbe* concertos. Similar short, slow, transitional movements also are found occasionally in other overtures of the time, such as Handel's overture to *Giustino* (1737), which probably also reflects Corelli's influence.[6]

TABLE 9

Form of Final Two Movements of the *Sham Conjuror* Overture

‖: A :‖ :B A¹ :‖	or	A A B A¹ B A¹

The overture of *The Sham Conjuror* includes two further movements, a 3/4 Larghetto and a 3/8 Minuet Allegro. Both are written out as modified da capo forms, the first section, which had ended in the dominant, being altered in the reprise so that it ends in the tonic. Superimposed upon each da capo form, however, is a pair of binary repeats, with the main section repeated as one unit and the middle section plus the reprise as the other (see Table 9). The result is similar to the Hamburg double da capos and the trio "Love me" that occurs later in the opera, both of which are discussed above. The orchestration of the two movements is similar, for the main section and its reprise are both played tutti, while in the shorter parts of the middle section the first is played by oboes and strings and the second by strings alone.

TABLE 10

Form of *Pyramus and Thisbe* Overture, Movement 2

8 m.	8 m.		16 m.	8 m.	
A	A¹		‖: B	A¹: ‖	
I	V	I	vi ii (I)	V	I

The overture of *Pyramus and Thisbe* (it is called an overture in the print) begins with a lively, gigue-like Allegretto alla breve for oboes and strings, the oboes doubling the first and second violins. In this short binary movement both sections are repeated, with a middle cadence on the dominant, and are followed by the two-measure Adagio mentioned above. The second actual movement is a 3/8 Allegro for two horns, violins and oboes in unison, viola, and bass. It also is binary, with the repeat of the first section being written out to cadence on the tonic rather than the dominant and the opening section reappearing at the end (see Table 10). One might compare this movement to Lampe's other modified da capo forms, such as the movements ending the *Sham Conjuror* overture (described in Table 9) or the aria "Thus the damsel" in *Margery* (outlined in Table 6 above).

The last two movements of the *Pyramus and Thisbe* overture form a unit, such as is uncommon in both concert and overture literature of the time. The penultimate movement,

---

6 Arthur Hutchings, *The Baroque Concerto* (London: Faber & Faber, 1973), 252-56, describes the strong Corelli concerto tradition and appeal in London.

a twelve-measure 6/8 Presto in binary form, is followed by a much longer 3/4 Affettuoso in the parallel minor. This latter is the only movement in Lampe's concerto overtures that is not in the tonic, and its form is similar to that of the second movement of this overture described above. After the repeat of the second two sections, however, the scores indicate a da capo return to the 6/8 movement (the third), with which the overture is intended to conclude. The origin of this complex, compound final movement structure is unclear. But Lampe had written a similar da capo in the overture to *The Dragon,* so that the elaborate da capo ending of the *Pyramus and Thisbe* overture possibly is related to the da capo of the minuet, which often concluded the French overture. The relationship to the minuet becomes even more startling upon examining the graphic representation of the end of the *Pyramus and Thisbe* overture (given in Table 11). This table reveals a form strikingly similar to the standard Classical minuet form — but written fifteen years before Haydn composed his first primitive symphony and ten years before Mozart was even born — so that the *Pyramus and Thisbe* overture may provide yet another example of Lampe's surprising innovation and creativity.

TABLE 11
Comparison of Last Sections of the *Pyramus and Thisbe* Overture
with the Standard Minuet Form in the Classic Period

Poco Presto 6/8 in F		*Affettuoso 3/4 in f*				*Poco Presto 6/8 in F*	
A		B				A	
a	b	c	c¹	d	c¹	a	b
Minuet			*Trio*			*Minuet*	
A			B			A	
a	b	(a)	c	d	(c)	a	b	(a)

Lampe's one extant pantomime overture comes from *Cupid and Psyche* and is a medley overture, a form in which Lampe was a pioneer. Lampe's is, in fact, the first medley overture whose performance can be documented (on February 4, 1734), although a medley overture by Richard Clarke probably was written a short time earlier. Fiske describes the English medley overtures of the time as follows:

> Their music is surprisingly sophisticated, and quite different from the Musical Switch overtures that came in later. The Medley Overture of the 1730s was no inane succession of tunes, but a piece of ingenuity that called for quick wits on the part of the audience. Though all the tunes were well known at the time, they occur only in fragments, often in the bass or middle parts, and sometimes two are being played at once.[7]

Lampe's medley overture is more sophisticated than most of the others of his time. At least his contains more sophisticated tunes, including melodies from Handel's *Ottone* (1732), *Giulio Cesare* (1724), *Rodelinda* (1725), *Admeto* (1717), *Siroe* (1728), and other works in

---

[7] Fiske, 161, which also contains a good discussion of the genre.

addition to traditional and ballad tunes. Also unlike other composers, he often sets at least two tunes simultaneously in different voices, and then reverses their positions in double counterpoint. For example, Lampe ingeniously combines Handel's "Lusinghe piu caro" with the street cry "Butter'd Pease," and a little later "Butter'd Pease" with "Over the hills and far away," a ballad tune that had been used in *The Beggar's Opera.*

Lampe's creative medley overture remained popular and almost certainly was performed before other stage works in addition to *Cupid and Psyche,* itself a perennial favorite. In addition to appearing in parts and in a keyboard version along with the comic tunes, demand for and popularity of Lampe's medley overture was of such duration that the work was included in a set of six medley overtures published in parts in 1763, almost thirty years later. In spite of its success, however, the overture is unique among Lampe's theater music, and one wonders why he never wrote another work in this form, or if he did and the music has been lost.

Other Operatic Instrumental Music

The only other instrumental music that exists from Lampe's operas and plays is a group of four short instrumental pieces in *The Dragon.* None of these are act tunes, in the sense of Purcell's act tunes, which serve as interludes between or introductions to acts. Nor are the Lampe movements similar to the Handelian act tunes, with which he frequently begins the second and third acts in his late operas. Lampe's instrumental music, like that of Handel's early and middle operas, always accompanies action on the stage.

Like Handel's similar movements, Lampe's instrumental symphonies are not especially distinguished musically but serve as a background for the action at the time. The two numbers that accompany the dragon's stalking about the stage are mostly in unison, one for strings alone and the other for strings and oboes, as is the dragon's single aria. Both instrumental movements are built on a persistent dotted rhythm, which perhaps had something to do with the way the dragon walked or moved. There are no repeats in either movement, and the second runs directly into a recitative by the dragon, the sole instance of such an arrangement in the opera.

The Dragon also includes a battle piece of the sort found in many Handel operas. It is in two short sections, both of which are repeated, with a cadence to the dominant between them. The writing is somewhat less strictly in unison than in the dragon's other instrumental numbers, but it offers ample opportunity for martial flourishes by the trumpets and other instruments during the conflict between Moore and the dragon.

The symphony that begins Scene 2 is probably the most interesting instrumental piece in *The Dragon* (except for the overture), both musically and dramatically. The number is almost twice as long as any of the other instrumental pieces (with repeats it is more than three times as long as some), it includes a da capo, and although it contains some unison writing it is mostly in three parts. In addition to its musical interest, however, the lively piece performs a very necessary dramatic function. As the only one of Lampe's instrumental numbers that opens a scene, this number provides music during the only scene change in the opera that occurs on an open stage during the action rather than between acts. And this particular scene change was a considerable undertaking, for it included not only sliding flats back and forth, but also bringing on furniture, glasses and bottles, and other decorations, allowing the entire chorus to leave and Moore and his companions to enter and preparing the mood for the following scene. The short symphony fills the necessary time, but delightfully creates the appropriate atmosphere as well. One can almost see the servants bustling about lighting candles and preparing for Moore's party as his guests enter noisily, similar to the beginning of "Fate presto o cari amici" in *Così fan tutte* (Example 44).

EXAMPLE 44. "Symphony," *The Dragon of Wantley*.

Pantomime Music

The comic tunes of Lampe's pantomimes are of relatively little importance, and their quality seems to indicate that Lampe shared such an opinion. Since the purpose of the tunes was merely to provide a background for the pantomime action and to fill up space, and since the emphasis in the pantomimes was far more on the spectacle than on the music, there was little incentive for Lampe to waste much time on the tunes. Lampe's practice or attitude probably differed little from those of his contemporaries, and his tunes were no worse than average. They were popular enough to have been published by Walsh in their own volume, as were the tunes of all the other famous Covent Garden pantomimes of the time.

Everything considered, however, the tunes from *Orpheus and Euridice* really are not very good, and Fiske finds them so poor that he suggests that they may not be by Lampe at all.[8] Lampe's name, in fact, is not mentioned on the title page of the publication. It is possible, though unlikely, that the printed tunes of *Orpheus and Euridice* date from after the extensive revisions of the pantomime for the 1741-42 season, in which Lampe may or may not have participated.

The tunes printed for *Orpheus and Euridice* are almost all in binary form, usually with each section repeated (one has a da capo and no other repeats), a form typical of pantomime dance tunes. They are quite short, usually having just two or three phrases in each section and occupying only one page each in the print. The tonal motion is characteristic of the Baroque binary form, from the tonic in the first section to the dominant at the beginning of the second section and returning to the tonic; in minor tunes the motion usually is to the relative major. Sometimes the two sections are related thematically, with the second section even beginning as a transposed version of the first, but continuing differently (Example 45).

The printed comic tunes from *Cupid and Psyche* are only of a slightly higher quality than those of *Orpheus*. Most of them are written in the same sort of binary form and rely on the same simple harmonic vocabulary. The *Cupid and Psyche* tunes, however, sometimes exhibit more harmonic, melodic, and rhythmic variety, with asymmetrical phrasing and less melodic repetition, and some of the *Cupid* tunes are more complex texturally as well, being printed with three voices rather than the traditional melody and bass lines.

Orchestration and Orchestral Accompaniment

Lampe came from a long line of fine orchestrators. Keiser's expressive and varied orchestrations were famous, and Telemann was every bit as careful an orchestrator. Handel's orchestration also was thoughtful and elaborate, employing in at least one of his operas almost every instrument then known. Although Lampe never had the monetary and instrumental resources of Handel or Keiser, with the means he had available, he often achieved considerable variety and expressiveness within apparent simplicity.

A great diversity of textures exists in Lampe's operas. In the early works, such as *Britannia* and *Dione,* the texture often is thick, with five or more independent instrumental voices in addition to the singer. In contrast, later operas like *The Sham Conjuror* and *Pyramus and Thisbe* usually have only three voices in their accompaniments. Lampe's orchestral texture often varies within an aria as well, with one section, usually the middle one of a da capo

---

[8] Ibid., 166.

aria, in a thinner texture. Sometimes the texture of that middle section is reduced to just the voice and continuo, as in "But to hear the children mutter" in *The Dragon*. A similar thinning of texture is common in many of the da capo arias of Handel, as in "Da' tuoi begl'occhi" in *Giustino* (1737), and it may be from Handel that Lampe learned the technique.

Lampe does not restrict his use of a thinner texture to the second section of an aria, however, and in "Aurora's beams dispelling night" in *Britannia,* for example, the second part of the main section of a da capo aria is scored for continuo accompaniment alone, while the middle section uses the full orchestra. In other *Britannia* arias short phrases for voice and continuo alone exist in additional places as well. *Britannia* and *Dione* provide an interesting study in orchestration with limited available resources, and the variety and different effects Lampe achieves are often astonishing. In "Royal daughter, only treasure," for example, only two actual voices exist during portions of the aria (Example 46), with the voice and the first violin in unison and the second violin and viola in unison. In another aria in the same manuscript, however, sections in five individual orchestral voices occur (Example 47). The strings can be treated in many other ways as well.

As with Handel, one can find in Lampe's orchestration elements of both concerto grosso techniques and thoroughbass principles. In many arias Lampe employs a full ripieno-like group during the opening and closing ritornellos, but a smaller group of instruments while the voice is singing. In such cases, the viola often is omitted during vocal sections, as in "Let my dearest be near me" in *The Dragon* or "Lovely fair" in *The Sham Conjuror*. Wind instruments also can participate in the ripieno alternation, as do the oboes in "Zeno, Plato, Aristotle" in *The Dragon*. In other instances the voice and orchestra appear to carry on a dialogue or conversation as equals. The accompaniment adds to, punctuates, and comments upon what the voice has said, but never overshadows it (Example 48), techniques that resemble Handel's writing much more than, for example, Bach's.

One particular accompaniment technique of Lampe seems related to the common thoroughbass notational and accompaniment practices of his day. In eighteenth-century England and Germany, songs and short instrumental pieces often were published either as broadsides or in collections, with only the vocal/melodic line and the continuo line printed. In performance the accompanist generally doubled the melody line, played his given thoroughbass line and, depending on his felicity, perhaps added a few other notes to create the impression of inner voices or supporting harmonies. But regardless of what was added, the emphasis clearly was on the two outer voices.

In some of Lampe's works, as in much of London's vernacular theater music of the time and in the serious operas of his contemporaries, one often finds pieces in which there are only two basic voices present: a thoroughbass line and a melody. The continuo line and vocal line can appear alone, but more often the upper strings and occasionally even the winds double the melody with few or no middle parts and a strong bass line, creating much contrapuntal tension and interest between the melody and bass (Example 49). Doubling the voice in this manner was not necessarily a slovenly practice, however, for it created a rich, sonorous effect, and Lampe seems to have employed it in specific circumstances, generally involving rustic or robust songs or characters. In *The Dragon,* for example, the technique is associated with the relationship of Moore and Mauxalinda, and occurs in numbers where they sing to or about one another.

Doubling the vocal line alone is closely related to the practice of doubling the voice by the first violins in somewhat thicker textures, a feature common in the accompaniments of Lampe, Handel, and many other opera composers. Yet Lampe did not invariably double the voice. Sometimes the first violin contains an ornamented version of the vocal line, as in the chorus "Fly, fly" in *The Dragon* or in the "Lion's song" in *Pyramus and Thisbe*

EXAMPLE 45. Tune No. 14, *Orpheus and Euridice.*

FIRST SECTION

SECOND SECTION

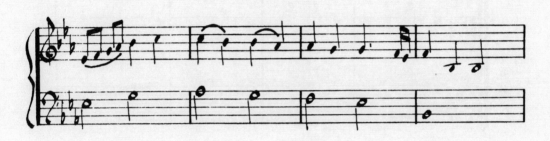

EXAMPLE 46. "Royal daughter, only treasure," *Britannia.*

Roy - al daughter on - ly trea - sure

EXAMPLE 47. "Virtue, Honour still attend me," *Britannia*.

EXAMPLE 48. "In ev'ry form," *The Sham Conjuror*.

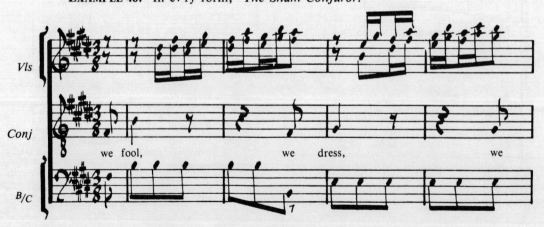

EXAMPLE 49. "By the beer as brown as berry," *The Dragon of Wantley.*

EXAMPLE 50. "Lion's song," *Pyramus and Thisbe.*

(Example 50). Often the first violin is independent, participating in its conversation with the voice even while the voice is singing (Example 51).

"Aurora's Beams," from *Britannia* is an example of a concerted type of aria, one with an accompaniment whose thematic substance is freely superimposed upon the vocal melody instead of following it. The concerted technique became popular in the late Baroque and reached such extremes that some of the arias of Bach seem almost like instrumental pieces

EXAMPLE 51. "Aurora's beams," *Britannia.*

with an added vocal part. It is fascinating, though, that Lampe should have written similarly complicated works as a young composer. In the *Britannia* arias the accompaniment's distinct thematic material often appears in the opening ritornello, which later may ingeniously appear along with the vocal melody during the course of the aria. In some cases (Example 51) the orchestral accompaniment of the voice is reproduced directly from one such opening ritornello.

The ritornello is an important element of Lampe's arias, ensembles, and choruses, and of their accompaniments. In the da capo structures the opening and closing ritornellos of the main section often are similar and sometimes are exactly the same, although they vary more in Lampe's later works. The ritornellos may include a motto beginning, and in some cases the motto may receive extensive treatment or development, as in the complete fugal exposition in the opening ritornello of "Thus distracted," from *Margery*. In other instances the melodies of the ritornellos differ much from the vocal melody (Example 51), and the latter is more typical in Lampe's earlier works, while motto beginnings are more common in the later operas. Even in *Pyramus and Thisbe,* however, ritornellos exist that are quite different from the vocal lines that they precede, as in "O wicked Wall."

Pyramus and Thisbe contains many good examples of Lampe's varied ritornello technique. The long ritornello in "O wicked Wall" helps to set the mood for the following aria, as do other of Lampe's ritornellos. In the "Lion's song" (part of which appears in Example 50 above), the opening ritornello is virtually identical with the accompaniment of the voice. One aria, "Approach ye Furies fell," begins with no ritornello at all, the orchestra echoing the voice after the first two measures. This aria is a rage aria, and Lampe employs the same technique with fine dramatic effect in similar instances where the emotions and anger of the character seem so great that words burst forth before the orchestra can begin (e.g., in the duets "O ungrateful to deceive me" and "Hear, oh! hear" in *Margery*). Even in some arias with opening ritornellos, Lampe will interrupt the voice shortly after it has begun, as in "Dragon, dragon" in *The Dragon,* another rage aria. Lampe possibly learned the techniques of beginning an aria without a ritornello and then interrupting the voice from Handel, who often used them to dramatic advantage (e.g., in "Barbaro! partirò" from *Radamisto,* 1720).

Lampe's ritornellos include another closely related practice that also is common in Handel (e.g., see Handel's *Tamerlano,* 1724): overlapping the ritornello and the voice. Lampe examples are especially prevalent in *Britannia* and *Dione*. In "Fly me love" (Example 52), the opening ritornello's final cadence overlaps the beginning of the voice, the cadence of the vocal phrase overlaps the beginning of the restatement of the ritornello, and the voice re-enters again before the ritornello is finished. (The bracketed section in Example 52 is quoted exactly from the opening ritornello.) An even more interesting use of ritornello material later within the aria is in "So Hercules of old" from *Margery,* where an elaborate twisting motive in the opening ritornello does not appear at all until the text speaks of a spinning wheel, more than twenty measures later, from which point the motive becomes virtually the only accompaniment for the rest of the aria.

Internal ritornellos are not at all standard ingredients in Lampe's work. When a ritornello does occur in the middle of an aria section it marks a major structural point, formally and tonally, although Lampe seems to get along just as well without these internal ritornellos as with them. The chief reason for their presence appears to be to help delineate and balance form and structure, and in general they have little dramatic significance.

Other interesting uses of both internal and framing ritornellos can be found in Lampe's unison arias, in which all instruments are in unison with the voice. Handel had employed the texture frequently with his often sinister basses, such as Emireno in *Ottone* (1732), Clito

EXAMPLE 52. "Fly me love," *Dione*.

Fly me love, thou headstrong boy,

Urchin fly this frozen breast thou never

150

in *Alessandro* (1726), the king in *Ariodante* (1735), Polidarte in *Giustino* (1737), Sergeste in *Arminio* (1737), Ariodante in *Serse* (1738), and many others. (Unison arias also were common in Venetian and Neapolitan operas, as well as those of Keiser.) Probably Lampe's choice of a unison setting for the dragon's one aria, "Oh, ho! Master Moore," derives from those practices of Handel and others, although Lampe's setting follows the voice somewhat more strictly than is usual with Handel.

In "Oh, ho! Master Moore" Lampe's instruments are in unison with the voice when it is present, but during the ritornellos his orchestra, like Handel's, plays in several parts. The violas do not play at all until the final ritornello (there is no opening one), a fact that supports earlier statements concerning the concerto-like nature of Lampe's accompaniments and the use of a larger group to play the opening and closing ritornellos.

Obbligato Instruments and Parts

Lampe often utilized wind instruments for dynamic purposes — to reinforce loud tutti passages, especially in ritornellos, or to support the musical texture with soft, sustained notes. Lampe's delight in wind instruments, particularly horns, probably can be traced to his German musical heritage. Winds had been important in German opera as early as Steffani, and Keiser's love of winds usually is credited with stimulating Handel's continued interest in them.

While Lampe often scores his winds in unison with strings or with the voice to provide changes in tone color, winds frequently appear as obbligato instruments. Lampe's obbligato parts are similar to Handel's, with the instrumental part designed to contrast with and complement the voice, but never cover it up. They are quite unlike Bach's generally elaborate obbligatos, which often come dangerously close to overshadowing the voice completely.

The oboes and bassoons, along with the strings and harpsichord, were basic members of the opera orchestra of Lampe's time, and whenever the oboes were present the bassoons generally doubled the bass line, whether indicated in the score or not. The oboes frequently followed the violin parts, but the practice was by no means automatic. Lampe is unusually careful in specifying where oboes double strings, where the oboes have separate parts, and where they do not play. Often his oboes play in ripieno or forte sections, such as the ritornellos, while only strings are used in soft passages or with the voice, and numerous examples exist, as "Zeno, Plato, Aristotle" and the overture of *The Dragon*. Oboes also can echo the voice, as in "Now I am dead" from *Pyramus and Thisbe*.

The oboes, and consequently the bassoons, are an important part of all Lampe's choral accompaniments, where they usually double the vocal lines, or the violins, when the chorus is not singing. In many cases, such as "Fly, fly" in *The Dragon,* the oboes double the chorus much more closely than the violins, which either have independent parts or an ornamented version of the vocal lines (Example 53). The bassoon part, when it is written out as in "Let's go to his dwelling" in *The Dragon,* also follows the vocal line more closely than does the bass/continuo part.

Solo oboe parts exist for three Lampe arias, "Gentle knight" in *The Dragon,* and "The Swain I adore" and "Cruel swain" in *Margery*. Of these three, only the aria in *The Dragon* has a true oboe obbligato, that is, a completely independent part participating and unfolding along with the voice. The two *Margery* arias include the oboe only in the ritornellos, except for a few brief punctuating figures along with the voice, and the oboe melody is either taken from the violins or the vocal line. As far as I have been able to determine, Lampe wrote no solo bassoon parts for his operas.

EXAMPLE 53. "Fly, fly," *The Dragon of Wantley.*

Oboe 1 and 2

Violin 1

Violin 2

Viola

Soprano

Fly, fly, fly, neighbours, fly, the dragon's nigh, save, save your lives, and fly, save, save your

Alto

Fly, fly, fly, neighbours, fly, the dragon's

Baritone

Bass continuo

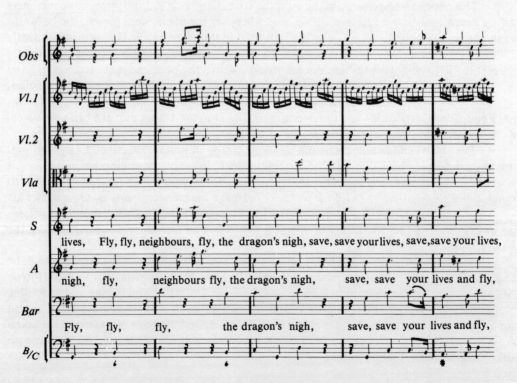

Obs

Vl.1

Vl.2

Vla

S

lives, Fly, fly, neighbours, fly, the dragon's nigh, save, save your lives, save, save your lives,

A

nigh, fly, neighbours fly, the dragon's nigh, save, save your lives and fly,

Bar

Fly, fly, fly, the dragon's nigh, save, save your lives and fly,

B/C

152

Transverse flutes were not as common in the opera orchestra as were oboes, and more often were employed as solo instruments than as part of the ripieno. Lampe flute parts exist in only three numbers, "Britannia heav'nly blest" in *Britannia,* "Pritty warblers" in *Dione,* and "O piercing anguish" in *Margery.* All three flute arias deal with grief or unhappiness, an association with the instrument frequent in Handel (e.g., in *Admeto,* 1727). The obbligato part in "Mars in vain" in *Britannia* also may be for flute, since the flute is the only obbligato or wind instrument mentioned in the entire manuscript. In two of the known flute numbers, "Britannia heav'nly blest" and "O piercing anguish," the flute mainly doubles the voice, as an addition in tone color. (The *Britannia* aria requires a pair of flutes.) In the other two arias, however, the flute is completely independent, and in "Pritty warblers" the obbligato is especially beautiful, at times imitating the "warblers" of the text. Lampe seems to have preferred the flute over the recorder, for there is no evidence of Lampe ever writing for the latter—quite in contrast to Handel.

German composers had enjoyed writing for the horn since before the beginning of the eighteenth century, so that one would expect to find horns figuring prominently in the operas of Handel and Lampe. In the Lampe operas the horn is the most common wind instrument after the oboes. It is found in most of the overtures and choruses, and pairs of horns also are added to some arias and duets, such as "Come follow brave boys" in *Margery*, "When you smile" in *The Sham Conjuror,* and "Thus folding, beholding" in *Pyramus and Thisbe.* The first is a typical hunting song of the period, and the horns play hunting-like flourishes and often echo the voice (Example 54). In the *Sham Conjuror* aria the horns frequently double the voice and violins, as is also true in the *Pyramus and Thisbe* duet.

In the overtures and choruses, the pair of horns frequently is assisted by a pair of trumpets. When both trumpets and horns are present, as in *The Dragon* and *Margery,* both sets of instruments are pitched in D, but in *The Sham Conjuror* and *Pyramus and Thisbe,* which have no trumpets, the horns are written in F. The trumpets and horns sometimes play together, as in the last two choruses of *The Dragon,* but at other times play on alternating phrases for a contrast in tone color and tessitura, as in the *Dragon* overture and the opening chorus of *Margery.* Only one instance exists of trumpets being used without horns—in the "Battle Piece" of *The Dragon.* In this latter case, as possibly in some of the others, the trumpets likely were supported by improvised kettle drum parts.

Although Lampe seems to have written for no wind instruments in his operas other than those mentioned above, he sometimes utilized strings as solo or obbligato instruments. Most such instances involve simple, thoroughbass-texture arias, such as "Lovely, fair" in *The Sham Conjuror.* In this aria the voice (a bass) and the continuo are in unison, while the violins play an elaborate countermelody in unison above them (Example 55). Sometimes the string solo is in the lowest voice rather than the highest. "Agree, agree" in *Margery* is accompanied only by a solo cello, and "O give me not up to the law" in *The Dragon,* a piece of similar character and texture, quite possibly is meant to be accompanied the same way. Also, other short passages for solo cello exist in *Margery, Pyramus and Thisbe,* and in additions to the *Dragon* manuscript score.

All in all, Lampe treated instruments quite creatively and inventively. His love of experimentation produced differing but satisfying and effective instrumental forms. His diversity in ritornello techniques adds to the interest of his arias, and his orchestration is an amazing study of the potentials for variety within very limited resources. The result is that his orchestra makes a positive contribution to the dramatic and musical success of his theater works, and his handling of it helps confirm a high opinion of his musical facility and craftsmanship.

EXAMPLE 54. "Come follow brave boys," *Margery*.

Come follow brave boys to the chace, for morning breaks on us a-pace, the

fogs and the mists dis-ap-pear, the dawn is de-light-ful-ly clear.

154

EXAMPLE 55. "Lovely, fair," *The Sham Conjuror.*

CHAPTER 10 EXTENDED ELEMENTS OF FORMAL ORGANIZATION

In Lampe's mature operas, as in many of Handel's works, the customary alternation of recitative and aria breaks down and more extended and often carefully organized structures occur. Sometimes only a cavatina/cabaletta pair of arias is involved, but in other cases a grand *scena* is created, including several arias, ariosos, instrumental numbers, choruses, etc., as in the final section of *The Dragon,* or the mad scene in Handel's *Orlando* (1733) or his death scene of Bajazet in *Tamerlano* (1724). Although such extended scenes were rare in opera seria, they sometimes occurred in the works of Hamburg composers (possibly through French influence), such as Mattheson's *Boris Goudenow* (1710), in which the finale includes a long combination of solos, duets, trios, and choruses. Also in *Boris Goudenow* instances exist of the chorus being combined with the soloist during an aria, an effect rare in Handel's operas but more common in the oratorios.

Lampe's operas contain one example of the chorus being combined with an aria like a refrain, in Gubbins's "Come follow brave boys" in *Margery.* Lampe breaks the recitative/aria rule as a matter of course on many occasions, but the grand *scena* that concludes *The Dragon* is perhaps his finest work of the sort. The alternation of recitatives and arias is not rigid during the early part of that opera, for the chorus is much too prominent. From Moore's aria "Dragon, dragon," however, the recitative/aria convention breaks down almost entirely throughout the balance of the opera. Following Moore's aria there is a recitative by Moore, a symphony that runs into a dragon recitative, the dragon's aria, a battle piece, an accompanied recitative for the dragon, a recitative by Moore and Margery, a duet, a Gubbins recitative, and the two final choruses. If the duet is removed, as it was later by Lampe in the extant manuscript score, there is, except for the opening recitative and aria, only one instance in the entire act where a recitative is followed with an aria by the same character. And in that sole occurrence, involving the dragon's aria, the recitative is approached quite indirectly, beginning while the final chord of the preceding symphony is still sounding. The *scena* also works with the inclusion of the duet, but is strengthened and the dramatic flow improved by its removal.

Lampe's ignoring the standard recitative/aria alternation convention is notable, for it emphasizes again his concern for dramatic values, far ahead of most opera seria composers of his time. Like Handel, Lampe modified the stereotyped and accepted forms, not for the fun of breaking conventions but to allow the drama to develop continuously instead of in a series of unrelated jerks. Thus the very conventions and expectations of opera seria contributed to the over-all effect, making Lampe's deviation from the norm even more dramatic and significant.

Tonality

More fascinating than Lampe's grand *scena* creations, however, is his use of tonality as a structural element to organize entire operas. Considerable study seems to indicate indisputably that many Handel operas are built with a careful and elaborate tonal plan.[1] The first act of *Amadigi* (1715), for example, is a symmetrical tonal structure. Like many of his operas, this work as a whole exhibits a preference for one key, establishing it at the beginning, returning to it somewhere in the second act, and confirming it strongly at the end of the third. Such close knit tonal organization does not seem to have been common in the operas of Schürmann, Scarlatti, Hasse, Rameau, and others, although isolated instances occur in Keiser (*Croesus,* 1711) and Purcell (*Dioclesian,* 1690). It is especially interesting, therefore, that all of Lampe's mature operas—*The Dragon, Margery, The Sham Conjuror,* and *Pyramus and Thisbe*—demonstrate a careful and deliberate tonal organization. Some of his earlier works may also have been so organized, but not enough survive to make a determination possible.

The Dragon (outlined in Table 12), is an example of an opera that, like some of Handel's mentioned above, establishes one key at the beginning, returns to it in the second act, and then confirms it in the finale. The key involved is D major, and especially noteworthy is the fact that although the overture is in D, the key appears nowhere else in the first act. Act II, however, states the main key twice, the second time ending the act. The third act begins with the dominant of D, the only instance in the opera where A functions as the tonal center of a number, and A likely occurs here to strengthen the preparation for the final return to D in the finale.

Lampe's use of D in the "Battle Piece" during the combat between Moore and the dragon may be inconsequential to the overall tonal form. The movement is not particularly substantial musically, and D could have been chosen because of the presence of the trumpets. On the other hand, the battle is the dramatic climax of the opera, so that the home key certainly is appropriate. The employment of D at dramatic high points also may account for the particular places of its appearance in Act II, since both the duet "Insulting gipsey," which possibly is analogous to the battle piece, and the final chorus are dramatically the most important numbers of the act.

It might be argued that Lampe wrote in D at the beginning and end of the opera because of the D trumpets and horns in those movements, although such reasoning does not account for the presence of the key in Act II. D was, in fact, a popular key for opera overtures, occurring in two out of the five extant Schürmann overtures, but its frequent appearance may have been because it was a good, bright key for the strings. The key is quite common in eighteenth-century string music; for example, ten of Mozart's forty-one symphonies are in D—but certainly not because of the many Mozart trumpet parts in them! Lampe's choice of D for *The Dragon* and *Margery* likely was influenced by the character assigned to the key in the so-called "doctrine of affections." Mattheson describes D major as being "by nature somewhat sharp and strong willed, but certainly more suitable for boisterous, amusing, military, and rousing subjects than is anything else".[2] Thus the key would have been particularly appropriate for both *The Dragon* and *Margery*.

---

[1] Hugo Leichtentritt, *Händel* (Stuttgart/Berlin: Deutsche Verlags-Anstalt, 1924), 643; Hugo Leichtentritt, *Music, History, and Ideas* (Cambridge, Mass.: Harvard University Press, 1938), 145; Rudolf Steglich, "Händels Opern," *Handbuch der Musikgeschichte,* ed. Guido Adler, 2nd ed., 2 vols. (Berlin/Wilmersdorf: H. Keller, 1930), 2: 663-67. See the examples given in Donald J. Grout, *A Short History of Opera,* 2nd ed. (New York: Columbia University Press, 1965), 162, n. 24, which include *Almira* (Bb), *Scipione* (G), *Alessandro* (D), and many others.

[2] "Von Natur *etwas scharf und eigensinnig;* zum Lermen, lustigen, kriegerischen, und auffmunternden Sachen wol am allerbequemsten." Johann Mattheson, *Das neu-eröffneten Orchestre* (Hamburg: Mattheson, 1713), 242.

TABLE 12

Tonal Organization of *The Dragon*

Act	Number	Title	Key
Act I/i	1	Overture	D
	2	"Fly, fly"	G
	3	Dragon's March	g
	5	"Poor children three"	E♭
	6	"Houses and churches"	F
	8	"But to hear the children mutter"	g
	10	"He's a man ev'ry inch"	g
	11	"Let's go to his dwelling"	F
Act I/ii	12	Symphony	B♭
	14	"Zeno, Plato, Aristotle"	G
	15	"O save us all"	C
	16	"Gentle knight"	F
	18	"If that's all you ask"	F
	20	"Let my dearest be near me"	d
	22	"By the beer"	g
	24	"Pigs shall not be"	G
Act II	25	"Sure my stays"	c
	27	"Insulting gipsey"	D
	29	"O give me not up"	a
	31	"O how easy is a woman"	G
	33	"Fill, fill, fill"	D
Act III	35	"Dragon, dragon"	A
	38	"Oh, ho! Master Moore"	b
	39	Battle Piece	D
	40	"Oh, oh"	f♯
	42	"My sweet honeysuckle"	G
	44	"Sing, sing, and rorio"	D
	45	"Huzza, huzza"	D

The key of the overture to *Margery* also cannot be explained as resulting from the presence of trumpets, since the movement is scored for strings alone. Interestingly enough, however, *Margery* possesses a tonal organization quite similar to that of *The Dragon*. D major is established strongly at the beginning of the opera, but never recurs in the first act. The end of Act II again emphasizes the key, with three numbers in D, two of which are accompanied by strings alone, and D major appears almost symmetrically at the beginning, middle, and end of Act III. The first two numbers of Act III possibly employ D because of their character and dramatic importance. "The lion in battle" is a martial simile aria, scored only for strings, and "Mauxalinda thus admiring" supplies the dramatic coup necessary for the *lieto fine*. The subsequent return to D at the end of the act provides the tonal unity within the opera.

The make-up of *Margery* was never as standardized as that of *The Dragon,* for Lampe and Carey often changed or added music to try to make the opera more successful.

TABLE 13
Tonal Organization of *Margery*

Act	Title	Key
Act I	Overture	D
	"Triumph, valor"	D
	"The swain I adore"	g
	"Thus the damsel"	G
	"Go cuckoldly cull"	G
	"Agree, agree"	b
	"You coxcomb"	A
	"So Hercules of old"	e
	"Oh sad, oh strange"	g
Act II	"Was ever man"	d
	"Cruel swain"	a
	"Around the wide world"	G
	"Come wet your whistle"	c
	"Wretched is a wife's condition"	b
	"No fate will conceal 'em"	g
	"Come follow, brave boys"	D
	"By these arms"	D
	"O ungrateful"	D
Act III	"The lion in battle"	D
	"O piercing anguish"	G
	"Hear, oh! hear"	c
	"Thus distracted"	g
	"Mauxalinda thus admiring"	D
	"Then come to my arms"	G
	"Never, never"	G
	"O happy transformation"	D
	"Strain your voices"	D

A common organization of the opera is shown above (Table 13), but one in which small details sometimes were altered, new numbers being inserted, and others omitted. It is significant, however, that the creators never tampered with any of the pieces in D major. Table 13 is sufficiently representative of the performances of *Margery* to demonstrate the opera's careful tonal organization and similarity to *The Dragon,* down to the final approach to D through the subdominant.

The tonal organization of Lampe's last two operas, *The Sham Conjuror* and *Pyramus and Thisbe*, is still more amazing than that of *The Dragon* and *Margery*. All the music of *Pyramus and Thisbe* except for the recitatives and a brief closing chorus survives, and although there is no available libretto with which to compare the printed full score of *The Sham Conjuror,* it appears to be complete or nearly so, excepting the recitatives. The extant music of *The Sham Conjuror* would be about the same length in

TABLE 14
Tonal Organization of *The Sham Conjuror*

Number		Key
1		F
2		C
3		e
4		a
5	—a third ↑ / —a third ↓	F
6		d
7		e
8		E
9		D
10	—a step ↑ / —a step ↓	C
11		B♭
12		F

performance as that of *Pyramus and Thisbe,* also a one-act opera, and the numbers that exist would work together, with the addition of intervening recitatives, to form a coherent whole.

The score of *The Sham Conjuror* again demonstrates Lampe's continuing concern for and careful treatment of tonality in his operas. Like *The Dragon* and *Margery, The Sham Conjuror* establishes one key at the beginning, comes back to it near the middle of the work, and confirms it at the end. But unlike the earlier operas, *The Sham Conjuror* also exhibits elements of tonal symmetry in its design (see Table 14). Lampe begins in F, arrives at F in the middle of the opera, and returns to it for the conclusion. The progression to the medial F proceeds through the tonal centers of C, E, and A. The tonal centers of C and E also occur, but in reverse order, in the progression from the middle of the work to the end. Although A does not appear in the progression from the middle F to the final one, D serves as its substitute; A is a third above F and D is a third below it. While three numbers, nos. 2, 3, and 4, are required to move from the initial F to its recurrence in the middle of the work, the symmetrical progression later is expanded, with twice as many numbers, nos. 6 through 11, needed to move from the middle F to the end. In the expanded form of the progression, E is used for two numbers together, one in minor as in no. 3, and one in major. The C

TABLE 15
Tonal Organization of *Pyramus and Thisbe*

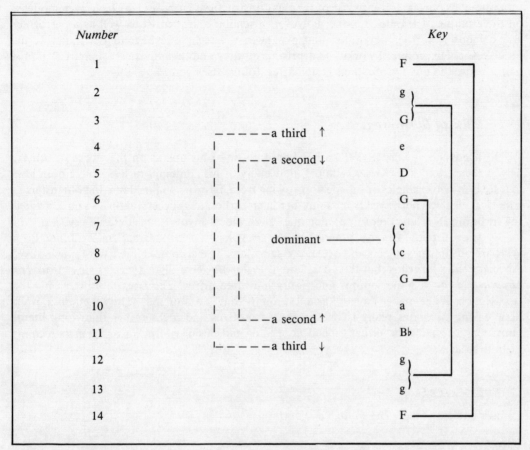

Number	Key
1	F
2	g
3	G
4	e
5	D
6	G
7	c
8	c
9	G
10	a
11	B♭
12	g
13	g
14	F

region also is expanded by adding two numbers around it, each a step away; this symmetrical second may be compared to the symmetrical third in nos. 3 to 5. In addition, the D fills in the interval between the structurally important tonal centers of E and C, while the B♭ provides a subdominant approach to the final statement of the tonic—the same approach found in the conclusions of both *The Dragon* and *Margery*.

The tonal symmetry of *Pyramus and Thisbe,* Lampe's last opera (see Table 15), is even more pronounced than that of *The Sham Conjuror*. Perhaps to avoid disturbing the symmetry, the return to the tonic in the middle of the opera is omitted and replaced by a pair of movements based on the dominant, so that the overall motion is from tonic to dominant to tonic. The two movements on the dominant are framed by a pair of movements, nos. 6 and 9, in the dominant's own dominant (G). G also is the tonal center of the two pairs of movements, nos. 2 and 3 and nos. 12 and 13, that are adjacent to the pair in F. The four remaining movements, nos. 4 and 5 and nos. 10 and 11, are related to the double pair of movements on G by a symmetrical series of thirds and seconds. The tonal symmetry of *Pyramus and Thisbe* thus exists on several levels. It testifies to a more pronounced and thoughtful organization through tonality than is the case in any of Lampe's other operas, or in the works of his contemporaries.

Given the above examples, it would seem that even the most incredulous critic must acknowledge that Lampe employed tonality deliberately and carefully as an organizational tool within his operas. His early use of tonality for structural purposes may have been modeled on the example of Handel. Lampe, however, a scholar and theorist as well as a performer and composer, further developed and expanded the technique beyond the limits of his predecessor. He produced works of surprising subtlety and inventiveness, such as *Pyramus and Thisbe,* the quality of which is not often found elsewhere.

Musical Borrowings

There is no evidence that Lampe based music of his operas on the works of others, as was the custom with Keiser, Handel, and many of his contemporaries. I have been able to trace only two examples of Lampe's borrowing from his own compositions. In both instances a musical idea was borrowed from a number in an earlier, less successful opera and reworked for inclusion in a later, more popular one. Both pieces involve considerable revision.

The source of "Dragon, dragon" in *The Dragon* is "Furies of Orcus" in *Britannia.* Both arias are on similar subjects and are in the same key. The accompaniments are much alike, especially the ritornellos, but the vocal line in *Britannia* generally is twice as slow as in *The Dragon* and the melodic contour and figuration often differ. *The Dragon* utilizes only the first section of the earlier da capo aria and omits long parts of that. Thus the relationship between the two arias really is one of shared motives and ideas rather than long literal quotations, excepting the virtually identical opening and closing ritornellos of the main sections of both arias.

EXAMPLE 56.

"Whilst endless tears," *The Fatal Falshood.*

Whilst end - less tears and sighs de - clare

"Was ever man," *Margery.*

Was ev - er man so much deceived

The only other occasion of borrowing within Lampe's works concerns "Whilst endless tears" in *The Fatal Falshood* and "Was ever man" in *Margery.* The connection between these two is even more tenuous than the one described above. Though the correlation between the first four measures of the melodies is close (see Example 56), it by no means involves an exact quotation, and after those initial four measures the resemblance between the two arias disappears entirely.

Musical Symbolism

Musical symbolism is an interesting but relatively unimportant element of Lampe's style. He understood the depiction of various moods and "affections" well, and wrote fine rage arias, laments, dance arias, petitions, hunting songs, sicilianos, drinking songs, comic numbers, and even a few simile arias. His tone painting generally serves either playful or dramatic purposes, but is never mystical or deeply symbolic as is the case in the works of J. S. Bach and some other composers.

Much of Lampe's symbolism is obvious and seems to have been included merely for fun. In the *Margery* duet "By these arms that round thee twine, like the ever circling vine," the melody twines around the tonic. Likewise, the word "wand'ring" is depicted pictorially in melismas in "Goddess propitious" in *Dione* (see a similar and familiar example in "All we like sheep" from *Messiah*), and long, almost interminable melismas occur on the word "ever" in "Britannia heav'nly blest" from *Britannia,* and elsewhere. An especially amusing example of Lampe's obvious tone painting is in "When to smile" from *The Sham Conjuror,* which opens with the following stanza of text:

> When to smile of me you deign,
> From my heart, my blood with fury,
> In a hurry, in a hurry,
> Then is running thro' each vein.

After a rather breathless but mostly syllabic beginning, the melody breaks into a furious, hurrying, running melisma on the "vein."

Lampe's tone painting can be dramatic and subtle, however, as well as simple and amusing. The tortured, twisting, and sighing vocal line in "Whilst endless tears" in *The Fatal Falshood* and "Ah, cruel, bloody fate" in *Theodosius* provide insight into the emotions of the character. Canons are used in "Insulting gipsey" in *The Dragon,* in "By these arms" in *Margery,* and elsewhere to symbolize characters sharing the same feelings. The *Margery* chorus "Oh sad, oh strange" is built over the age-old lament motive of a chromatically descending bass line. The spinning motive in "So Hercules of old" has been mentioned earlier. Even pauses are exploited for dramatic effect, especially in "Cease complaining" in *Dione,* and other similar examples could be cited.

Except for the simple and obvious use of flutes for bird calls, there is little evidence to indicate that Lampe attached particular symbolic significance to specific instruments as sometimes was the case with Telemann, Handel, and others. Rather, Lampe's choice of instruments seems to have been determined by what was available and by the dramatic effect desired. Lampe, however, like Handel, sometimes employs keys for symbolic purposes, probably because of doctrine of affections principles and his considerable consciousness of keys and tonality as structural elements, mentioned earlier. Both E minor and G minor especially seem to be keys of death and sadness for Lampe. G minor had been important as a pathetic key for Schürmann, although it served other functions for Handel, and both composers sometimes used E minor in cases of sorrow and death. Lampe also could change tonality and mode within an aria to reflect the changing emotions of a character, as in "Then come to my arms" in *Margery,* where a quick shift from G major to G minor occurs each time a sad thought (marrying an old man) crosses the singer's mind, but the mode shifts back when she thinks of more pleasant things (all of his money).

The musical symbolism mentioned above, although interesting, is not extraordinary. Such tone painting occurred frequently in the works of Handel and many other Baroque composers, and was a part of their general musical vocabulary. Often Lampe's symbolism, like Handel's, helps to intensify the dramatic mood and personality of a character or situation. But Lampe's works seem to lack either the exotic and mystical symbolism of the sort often claimed to exist in the music of Bach, or the overt and sometimes distracting tone painting of Haydn. Lampe had neither the situations nor the inclination for such extremes, and his music probably is the better because of it.

CONCLUSION

IN RETROSPECT, one wonders how John Frederick Lampe could have become so utterly forgotten. Such was not the case in the late eighteenth century, when a writer like Burney, usually quite critical of English vernacular music and composers, always described Lampe and his compositions in glowing terms. Even in the early nineteenth century, historians praised Lampe and his works highly in comparison with the compositions of his contemporaries. Hogarth, although he dismisses Arne's *Artaxerxes* as something that "cannot keep its place on the stage. There is nothing in it as drama to interest and attract,"[1] spends a half dozen pages describing *The Dragon,* calling the music "excellent . . . admirably adapted to the words. . . . The melodies are spirited and graceful; and the orchestral score . . . is clear and simple, yet very ingenious and full of charming effects."[2] He states that in Lampe's "attention to the emphasis and accent of English words, he may serve as a model even for our native musicians."[3]

It already was evident near the end of the eighteenth century, however, that Lampe and his music gradually were becoming mere memories to the general musical public, and sometimes distorted and uninteresting ones at that. His operas were out of fashion by the 1780s and ceased to be performed, and he and his works became confused with the person and music of his composer son. If Lampe had been spared his untimely death, perhaps he could have developed a style combining Gallant lyricism and Baroque solidity, and produced works at least equal in quality and appeal to the best of Arne and others. Lampe always was superior in musical and dramatic craftsmanship to Arne and most British composers writing in his day, and one finds Lampe's music of the late 1740s already moving toward a more modern idiom. The improving musical climate in London after the middle of the century almost surely would have inspired works of considerable value, perhaps leading to a new English opera revival that could have provided a firm musical and artistic foundation in London for the operas of Storace. Garrick, in fact, did lend some encouragement to all-sung vernacular opera in the 1750s and 1760s, which resulted in several new, but generally undistinguished, works by Arne, Boyce, Burney, and J. C. Smith. If the reliable, competent, and trustworthy Lampe had been available, Garrick's enthusiasm for opera might have been warmer. He certainly had enjoyed and frequently programmed *The Dragon* in the late 1740s.

Nevertheless, Lampe's and Carey's efforts at establishing a school of and appreciation for English vernacular opera may have been doomed from their beginnings in the 1730s. In the minds of both the eighteenth-century British theater public and management, opera never became a major art form but, along with theater music in general, remained secondary in interest and in emphasis to spoken drama, especially tragedy. And those musical connoisseurs

---

[1] George Hogarth, *Memoirs of the Musical Drama,* 2 vols. (London: Richard Bentley, 1838), 94.

[2] Ibid., 73-74.

[3] Ibid., 80.

(or snobs) who appreciated and were willing to support opera usually had a superior foreign (and hence exotically appealing) variety ready and available for immediate importation, so that little need or advantage could be seen in fostering a struggling, vernacular lyric theater. Against such attitudes, which held sway for centuries, one transplanted German and a few English musical zealots could have had little real chance of succeeding in a virtual revolution.

Thus one may be able to understand how, through changes or prejudices in style and taste, Lampe gradually could have been forgotten in the latter eighteenth century. Modern neglect of him and his music, however, is not so forgivable, for upon close examination he emerges as a person of considerable importance and influence, a composer of remarkable and enduring works of great dramatic and musical value, and hence an individual of significant historical interest. His numerous innovations and exceptional musical techniques and theoretical ideas are astonishing in their contrast to the usual practices of the time, their positive effect on the music of other composers, and their anticipation of later musical trends.

Lampe's song and hymn collections set high standards in his day, and became as popular and influential as his respected theory treatises. His breakdown of the aria/recitative convention and his omission of the da capo for dramatic purposes, as well as his dramatic representations of characters, is far more sophisticated than similar techniques in the works of any of his contemporaries, except occasionally in Handel. Lampe surpasses even Handel, however, in his writing for and in the frequency and dramatic use of the chorus. His emphasis on the cavatina in *Margery,* and perhaps even as early as *Amelia,* pushes back the previously accepted date of the initial flourishing of the form by twenty years. His writing of a vaudeville finale for *The Sham Conjuror* anticipates that form's previously stated earliest appearance by over ten years, as well as its considerable popularity in the latter half of the century. Lampe's pioneer work in the medley overture and his expansion of the minuet and trio form in the *Pyramus and Thisbe* overture also should be mentioned, as well as the striking organization of his operas by tonality, which surpassed anything similar to be found in the works of his contemporaries or in the generation of composers to follow.

Lampe's failure through lack of encouragement to establish a strong vernacular school of English opera is one of the great tragedies of eighteenth-century British music, as was his death while still in his forties. No composer of his experience, craftsmanship, and integrity existed to take his place. We may be grateful that some of his best music, especially his masterpiece *The Dragon of Wantley,* survives. *The Dragon* is more than an intriguing musical artifact. It is a work that can bridge the gap between the early eighteenth century and the present, and can become a delightful piece of music theater for today while providing a novel taste and improved understanding of some neglected elements of our musical heritage. One could ask little more of a composition — to be both enjoyable and instructive — or of a composer for that matter. If this present study has, as is hoped, helped to spark some interest in the rich and relatively unknown literature of eighteenth-century Britain and to have added a little to the general understanding of the music and musicians of the time, then it, like *The Dragon,* will at least to some extent have succeeded.

BIBLIOGRAPHY

Abraham, Gerald, ed. *Handel: A Symposium.* London: Oxford University Press, 1954.

Appleton, William W. *Charles Macklin.* Cambridge, Mass.: Harvard University Press, 1960.

Arnold, Frank T. *The Art of Accompaniment from a Thorough-Bass.* London: Oxford University Press, 1931. Reprint, with a new introduction by Denis Stevens, New York: Dover, 1965.

Arundell, Dennis. *The Story of Sadler's Wells.* New York: Theatre Arts Books, 1956.

Aurora's Nuptials. London: John Watts, 1734. (Libretto.)

Avery, Emmett L. "A Royal Wedding Royally Confounded." *The Western Humanities Review* 10 (1955-56): 153-64.

Avison, Charles. *An Essay on Musical Expression.* 2nd ed. London: C. Davis, 1753.

Baker, David Erskine. *Biographia Dramatica; or, A Companion to the Playhouse.* 3rd ed. 3 vols., ed. Isaac Reed and Stephen Jones. London: Longman, Hurst, Rees, Orme, Brown, 1812.

Baker, Frank. *Representative Verse of Charles Wesley.* London: Epworth Press, 1962.

Baughman, Ernest W. *Type and Motif-Index of the Folk-Tales of England and North America.* The Hague: Mouton, 1966.

Behse, Arthur. "Das Collegium musicum an der Helmstedter Universität." *Zeitschrift Alt-Helmstedt* 1:10 (1915).

Ben-Amos, Dan, ed. *Folklore Genres.* Austin: University of Texas Press, 1976.

Berger, Arthur V. *"The Beggar's Opera,* the Burlesque, and Italian Opera." *Music & Letters* 17 (April 1936): 93-105.

Blom, Eric. *Stepchildren of Music.* London: Dial Press, 1926.

Brenner, Rosamond. "Emotional Expression in Keiser's Operas." *Music Review* 32 (1972): 222-32.

Briggs, Katherine M. *A Dictionary of British Folk-Tales.* 2 parts. Bloomington: Indiana University Press, 1970.

The British Union-Catalogue of Early Music Printed before the Year 1801. Ed. Edith B. Schnapper. 2 vols. London: Butterworths Scientific Publications, 1957.

Broadbent, R. J. *A History of Pantomime.* London: Simpkin, Marshall, Hamilton, Kent, 1901.

Brockpähler, Renate. *Handbuch zur Geschichte der Barockoper in Deutschland.* Emsdetten: Lechte, 1964.

Brown, James Duff. *Biographical Dictionary of Musicians.* Paisley & London: A. Gardner, 1886.

Brown, John. *Letters on the Italian Opera.* 2nd ed. London: T. Cadell, 1791.

Bruford, Walter Horace. *Germany in the Eighteenth Century.* Cambridge: Cambridge University Press, 1935.

Burney, Charles. *An Account of the Musical Performances in Westminster-Abbey, and the Pantheon, May 26th, 27th, 29th; and June the 3d, and 5th, 1784. In Commemoration of Handel.* London: The Musical Fund, 1785.

————. *A General History of Music.* 4 vols. London, 1776-89. New ed. with critical and historical notes by Frank Mercer in 2 vols. New York: Dover, 1957.

Cannon, Beekman C. *Johann Mattheson, Spectator in Music.* New Haven: Yale University Press, 1947.

Carey, Henry. *The Dramatick Works of Henry Carey.* London: S. Gilbert, 1743.

————. *The Honest Yorkshireman. A Ballad Farce.* London: L. Gilliver, 1736. (Libretto.)

————. *Margery; or, A Worse Plague than the Dragon.* London: J. Shuckburgh, 1738. (Libretto.)

————. *The Musical Century.* 2 vols. London: Carey, 1737-40. Reprint ed., New York: Broude Bros., 1976.

————. *Poems on Several Occasions.* 3rd ed. London: E. Say, 1729.

Carse, Adam. *The Orchestra in the XVIIIth Century.* Cambridge: W. Heffer & Sons, 1940.

————. *A Short History of the Symphony in the Eighteenth Century.* London: Augener, 1951.

Cartwright, James J., ed. *The Wentworth Papers, 1705-1739.* London: Wyman & Sons, 1883.

Chancellor, Edwin Beresford. *The Pleasure Haunts of London.* Boston: Houghton Mifflin, 1925.

Chetwood, William Rufus. *The British Theatre.* London: R. Baldwin, 1752.

Clinton-Baddeley, Victor C. *The Burlesque Tradition in English Theatre after 1660.* London: Methuen, 1952.

A Collection of Old Ballads. [Ed. Ambrose Phillips?]. 3 vols. London: J. Butherton, 1723.

Cooke, William. *Memoirs of Charles Macklin, Comedian.* London: James Asperne, 1804.

Cox, William. *Anecdotes of George Frederick Handel, and John Christopher Smith.* London: W. Bulmer, 1799.

Cummings, William H. *Dr. Arne and Rule Britannia.* London: Novello, 1912.

Dane, Henry James. "The Life and Works of Henry Carey." Ph.D. dissertation, University of Pennsylvania, 1967.

Davies, Thomas. *Memoirs of the Life of David Garrick.* 2 vols. London: Thomas Davies, 1780.

Day, Cyrus Lawrence, and Eleanore Boswell Murrie. *English Song-Books 1651-1702.* London: The Bibliographical Society, 1940.

Dean, Winton. *Handel and the Opera Seria.* Berkeley & Los Angeles: University of California Press, 1969.

————. *Handel's Dramatic Oratorios and Masques.* London: Oxford University Press, 1959.

Deane, Basil. "Reinhard Keiser: An Interim Assessment." *Soundings* 4 (1974): 30-47.

Dent, Edward J. "Handel on the Stage." *Music & Letters* 16 (July 1935): 174-87.

————. "The Operas," in *Handel: A Symposium,* ed. Gerald Abraham. London: Oxford University Press, 1954.

Deutsch, Otto Erich. *Handel: A Documentary Biography.* New York: W. W. Norton, 1955.

Dibdin, Charles. *A Complete History of the Stage.* 5 vols. London: Charles Dibdin, 1800.

Dobrée, Bonamy. *English Literature in the Early Eighteenth Century, 1700-1740.* Oxford: Clarendon Press, 1955.

Dorris, George E. *Paolo Rolli and the Italian Circle in London, 1715-1744.* The Hague: Mouton, 1967.

Dürre, Hermann. *Geschichte der Stadt Braunschweig im Mittelalter.* Braunschweig: Grüneberg, 1861.

D'Urfey, Thomas, ed. *Wit and Mirth: or, Pills to Purge Melancholy.* 6 vols. London: W. Pearson & J. Tonson, 1719.

Egmont, John Percival. *Diary of Viscount Percival, Afterwards First Earl of Egmont.* 3 vols. London: H. M. Stationery Office, 1920-23.

"An Eighteenth-Century Directory of London Musicians." *Galpin Society Journal* 2 (1949): 27-31.

Eldredge, H. J. *The Stage Cyclopaedia.* London: "The Stage," 1909. Facsimile reprint, New York: Lenox Hill, 1970.

Elster, Richard, ed. *Gymnasium Martino-Katharineum Braunschweig: Festschrift zur 500-Jahr-feier am 17. und 18. März 1926.* Braunschweig: Friedr. Vieweg & Sohn, 1926.

Evans, J. Baird. "Henry Carey, John Wesley, and Namby Pamby." *London Quarterly and Holburn Review* 5 (1935): 40-51.

Farish, Stephen T., Jr. "The Vauxhall Songs of Thomas Augustine Arne." D.M.A. thesis, University of Illinois, 1962.

Farnscombe, Charles. "Arne and *Artaxerxes.*" *Opera* 13 (March 1962): 159-61.

Feind, Barthold, II. *Deutsche Gedichte.* Stade: H. Brummer, 1708.

Fielding, Henry. *The History of Tom Jones.* Wesleyan ed. of the *Works of Henry Fielding,* ed. Fredson Bowers, with introduction and commentary by Martin C. Battestein. Oxford: Clarendon Press, 1974.

Fiske, Roger. *English Theatre Music in the Eighteenth Century.* London: Oxford University Press, 1973.

————. "Lampe, Charles John Frederick," and "Lampe, John Frederick." *The New Grove Dictionary of Music and Musicians*, 10:419-21. 20 vols., ed. Stanley Sadie. London: Macmillan, 1980.

————. "Reviving England's 18th-Century Operas." *Opera* 22 (March 1971): 192-98.

Flögel, Bruno. "Studien zur Arientechnik in den Opern Händels." *Händel Jahrbuch* 2 (1929): 50-156.

Flood, William H. Grattan. *A History of Irish Music.* 4th ed. Dublin: Brown & Nolan, 1927.

Foss, Michael. *The Age of Patronage.* Ithaca, N.Y.: Cornell University Press, 1971.

Gagey, Edmond McAdoo. *Ballad Opera.* New York: Columbia University Press, 1937.

Genest, John. *Some Account of the English Stage.* 10 vols. Bath: H. E. Carrington, 1832.

Gill, Frederick C. *Charles Wesley, The First Methodist.* New York: Abington Press, 1964.

Grebe, Karl, ed. *Georg Philipp Telemann in Selbtzeugnissen und Bilddokumenten.* Reinbek bei Hamburg: Rowolte Taschenbuch, 1970.

Gregson, Matthew. *Portfolio of Fragments Relative to the History and Antiques, Topography and Geneologies of the County Palatine and Duchy of Lancashire.* 3rd ed., ed. John Harland. London: John Routledge & Sons, 1869.

Grout, Donald J. *A Short History of Opera.* 2nd ed. New York: Columbia University Press, 1965.

Harland, John, and T. T. Wilkinson. *Lancashire Legends.* London: John Heywood, 1882.

Harris, David Fraser. *Saint Cecilia's Hall in the Niddry Wynd.* Edinburgh & London: Oliphant, Anderson, & Ferrier, 1899.

Harris, Ellen T. *Handel and the Pastoral Tradition.* London: Oxford University Press, 1980.

Hawkins, Sir John. *A General History of the Science and Practice of Music.* 5 vols. London, 1776. Reprint of the 1853 Novello ed. in 2 vols., with a new introduction by Charles Cudworth, New York: Dover, 1963.

Heartz, Daniel. "From Garrick to Gluck: The Reform of Theatre and Opera in the Mid-Eighteenth Century." *Proceedings of the Royal Musical Association* 94 (1967-68): 111-27.

Herbage, Julian. "Arne: His Character and Environment." *Proceedings of the Royal Musical Association* 87 (1960-61): 15-29.

—————. "The Opera of Operas." *Monthly Musical Record,* May-June 1959, pp. 83-89.

—————. "The Vocal Style of Thomas Augustine Arne." *Proceedings of the Royal Musical Association* 78 (1951-52): 83-96.

Hervey, Lord John. *Some Material towards Memoirs of the Reign of King George II.* Ed. Romney Sedgwick. 3 vols. London: Eyre & Spottiswoode, 1931.

Hessenmüller, Carl. *Heinrich Lampe, der erste evangelische Prediger in der Stadt Braunschweig.* Braunschweig: Fr. Otto, 1852.

Highfill, Philip H., Jr., Kalman A. Burnim, and Edward A. Langhans, eds. *A Biographical Dictionary of Actors, Actresses, Musicians, Dancers, Managers & Other Stage Personnel in London, 1660-1800.* Carbondale: Southern Illinois University Press, 1973-.

Hill, Aaron, and William Popple. *The Prompter, a Theatrical Paper (1734-1736).* Selected and ed. William W. Appleton and Kalman A. Burnim. New York: Benjamin Blom, 1966.

Hogarth, George. *Memoirs of the Musical Drama.* 2 vols. London: Richard Bentley, 1838.

Hunter, Joseph. *South Yorkshire.* 2 vols. London: J. B. Nichols & Son, 1828-31.

Hutchings, Arthur. *The Baroque Concerto.* Rev. ed. New York: Charles Scribner's Sons, 1979.

Jewitt, Llewellynn. "The Dragon of Wantley & the Family of Moore." *The Reliquary* 18 (April 1878): 192-202.

Jöcher, Christian Gottlieb. *Allgemeines Gelehrten-Lexicon*. 6 vols. Leipzig: Johann Friedrich Gleditschen, 1784-87.

Kircher, Athanasius. *Musurgia universalis*. 2 vols. Rome, 1650.

Kirkman, James Thomas. *Memoirs of the Life of Charles Macklin*. 2 vols. London: Lackington, Allen, & Co., 1799.

Kleefeld, Wilhelm. "Das Orchester der Hamburg Oper 1678-1738." *Sammelbände der internationalen Musikgesellschaft* 1 (1899-1900): 219-89.

Klinger, Mary F. "Music and Theater in Hogarth." *Musical Quarterly* 57 (July 1971): 409-10.

Lang, Paul Henry. *George Frideric Handel*. New York: W. W. Norton, 1966.

—————. *Georg Friedrich Händel: Sein Leben, sein Stil und seine Stellung im Englischen Geistes- und Kulturleben*. Kassel: Bärenreiter, 1979.

Langley, Hubert. *Doctor Arne*. Cambridge: Cambridge University Press, 1938.

Lawrence, William John. "Early Irish Ballad and Comic Opera." *Musical Quarterly* 8 (July 1922): 397-412.

Lediard, Thomas. *Britannia, an English Opera*. London: J. Watts, 1732. (Libretto.)

—————. *Eine Collection curieuser Vorstellungen*. Hamburg: Philipp Ludwig Stromer, 1730.

Leichtentritt, Hugo. *Händel*. Stuttgart & Berlin: Deutsche Verlags-Anstalt, 1924.

—————. "Handel's Harmonic Art." *Musical Quarterly* 21 (April 1935): 208-23.

—————. *Music, History, and Ideas*. Cambridge, Mass.: Harvard University Press, 1938.

Lenanton, Carola Oman. *David Garrick*. Bunga, Suffolk: Hodder & Stoughton, 1956.

Lewis, Anthony. "Handel and the Aria." *Proceedings of the Royal Musical Association* 85 (1958-59): 95-107.

Lindner, Ernst Otto Timotheus. *Die erste stehende deutsche Oper*. 2 vols. Berlin: Schlesinger'sche Buch & Musikhandlung, 1855.

The London Stage, 1660-1800. 5 parts. Carbondale: Southern Illinois University Press, 1960-68.

Lord, Phillip. "The English-Italian Opera Companies 1732-3." *Music & Letters* 45 (July 1964): 239-51.

Love, James. *Scottish Church Music: Its Composers and Sources*. Edinburgh & London: William Blackwood & Sons, 1891.

Lowens, Irving. "*The Touch-Stone* (1728): A Neglected View of London Opera." *Musical Quarterly* 45 (July 1959): 325-42.

McClelland, Charles E. *State, Society, and University in Germany 1700-1914*. Cambridge: Cambridge University Press, 1980.

Macqueen-Pope, Walter James. *Theatre Royal, Drury Lane*. London: W. H. Allen, 1945.

Mainwaring, John. *Memoirs of the Life of the Late George Frederic Handel*. London: R. & J. Dodsley, 1760.

Marks, Jeanette A. *English Pastoral Drama*. London: Methuen, 1908.

Martin, Dennis R. "*Eine Collection curieuser Vorstellungen* (1730) and Thomas Lediard, an Early Eighteenth-Century Scenographer." *Current Musicology* 26 (1978): 83-98.

Mattheson, Johann. *Critica musica*. 2 vols. Hamburg: Mattheson, 1722-25.

————. *Grundlage einer Ehren-Pforte*. Hamburg: Mattheson, 1740.

————. *Das neu-eröffneten Orchestre*. Hamburg: Mattheson, 1713.

————. *Der vollkommene Capellmeister*. Hamburg: Christian Herold, 1739.

————. *Ehren-Pforte*. Hamburg: Mattheson, 1740.

Mayer, David, III. *Harlequin in His Element*. Cambridge, Mass.: Harvard University Press, 1969.

Mayer-Reinach, Albert. "Carl Heinrich Graun als Opernkomponist." *Sammelbände der internationalen Musikgesellschaft* 1 (1899-1900): 446-529.

McCredie, Andrew. "John Christopher Smith as a Dramatic Composer." *Music & Letters* 45 (January 1964): 22-38.

Millner, Frederick L. *The Operas of Johann Adolf Hasse*. Ann Arbor: UMI Research Press, 1979.

Moss, Harold Gene. "Popular Music and the Ballad Opera." *Journal of the American Musicological Society* 26 (Fall 1973): 365-82.

Moulin-Eckard, Richard Graf du. *Geschichte der deutschen Universitäten*. Stuttgart: Ferdinand Enke, 1929.

Mundhenke, Herbert, ed. *Die Matrikel der Universität Helmstedt 1685-1810*. Veröffentlichungen der Historische Kommission für Niedersachsen und Bremen, IX, Abt. 1, Bd. III. Hildesheim, 1979.

Murphy, Arthur. *The Life of David Garrick*. 2 vols. London: J. Wright, 1801.

Nagler, Alois M. *A Source Book in Theatrical History*. New York: Dover, 1959.

Nicoll, Allardyce. *A History of Early Eighteenth Century Drama*. Cambridge: Cambridge University Press, 1925.

————. *The World of Harlequin*. Cambridge: Cambridge University Press, 1963.

Oldfield, Edward Leonard. "The Achievement of Henry Carey (1687-1743)." Ph.D. dissertation, University of Washington, 1969.

Parke, William T. *Musical Memoirs*. 2 vols. London: H. Colburn & R. Bentley, 1830.

Parry, Edward Abbott. *Charles Macklin*. London: Kegan Paul, Trench, Trübner, 1891.

Parsons, Florence Mary. *Garrick and His Circle*. New York: G. Putnam's Sons, 1906.

Pedicord, Harry William. *The Theatrical Public in the Time of Garrick*. New York: King's Crown Press, 1954.

Percy, Thomas. *Reliques of Ancient English Poetry* (1765). 5th ed. 3 vols. London: F. C. & J. Riberton, 1812. Also, reprint of the 1886 ed., 3 vols., ed. Henry B. Wheatley. New York: Dover, 1966.

Petzold, Richard. *Georg Philipp Telemann, Leben und Werk*. Leipzig: VEB Deutscher Verlag für Musik, 1967.

Price, Richard B. "A Textual Dramatic and Musical Analysis of Two Burlesque Operas: *The Dragon of Wantley* and *Margery: or, A Worse Plague than the Dragon!*" Ph.D. dissertation, Literature, University of Texas at Austin, 1975.

Ralph, James. *The Touchstone*. London, 1728.

Rees, Abraham. *The Cyclopaedia; or, Universal Dictionary of Arts, Sciences and Literature . . . First American Edition*. 41 + 6 vols. Philadelphia: Robert Carr, 1810-17?

Rimbault, Edward F. *Musical Illustrations of Bishop Percy's Reliques of Ancient English Poetry*. London: Cramer, Beale, & Co., 1850.

Robinson, Michael F. "The Aria in Opera Seria, 1725-1780." *Proceedings of the Royal Musical Association* 88 (1961-62): 31-43.

Rosenfeld, Sybil. "The Career of Thomas Lediard." *Theatre Notebook* 2 (April-June 1948): 46-48.

————. *Foreign Theatrical Companies in Great Britain in the 17th and 18th Centuries*. London: Society for Theatre Research, 1955.

————. *Strolling Players & Drama in the Provinces.* Cambridge: Cambridge University Press, 1939.

————. *The Theatre of the London Fairs in the 18th Century.* Cambridge: Cambridge University Press, 1960.

Rosenthal, Harold. *Opera at Covent Garden: A Short History.* London: Victor Gollancz, 1967.

————. *Two Centuries of Opera at Covent Garden.* London: Putnam, 1958.

Ross, Frederick. *Legendary Yorkshire.* Hull: William Andrews, 1892.

Routley, Eric. *The Musical Wesleys.* New York: Oxford University Press, 1968.

Rubsamen, Walter H. "Ballad Burlesques and Extravaganzas." *Musical Quarterly* 36 (October 1950): 551-61.

Sand, Maurice. *The History of the Harlequinade.* 2 vols. Philadelphia: J. B. Lippincott, 1915.

Sands, Mollie. *Invitation to Ranelagh, 1742-1803.* London: John Westhouse, 1946.

————. "The Problem of *Teraminta.*" *Music & Letters* 33 (July 1952): 217-22.

————. "Some English Musical Clans." *Monthly Musical Record* 73 (October 1943): 179-83.

Schmidt, Gustav Friedrich. *Die frühdeutsche Oper und die musikdramatische Kunst Georg Caspar Schürmanns.* 2 vols. Regensburg: Gustav Bosse, 1933.

Scott, Hugh Arthur. "Sidelights on Thomas Arne." *Musical Quarterly* 21 (July 1935): 301-10.

Scott, Walter Sidney. *Green Retreats — The Story of Vauxhall Gardens, 1661-1859.* London: Oldham's Press, 1955.

————. *The Georgian Theatre.* London: Westinghouse, 1946.

Scouten, Arthur H. "The First Season of *The Honest Yorkshireman.*" *Modern Language Review* 40 (1945): 8-11.

Sheldon, Esther K. *Thomas Sheridan of Smock-Alley.* Princeton: Princeton University Press, 1967.

Simpson, Claude M. *The British Broadside Ballad.* New Brunswick, N.J.: Rutgers University Press, 1966.

Smith, Patrick J. *The Tenth Muse.* New York: Alfred A. Knopf, 1970.

Smith, William C. *Concerning Handel.* London: Cassel, 1948.

Smith, Winifred. *The Commedia dell'arte.* New York: Columbia University Press, 1912.

Southern, Richard. *Changeable Scenery: Its Origin and Development in the British Theatre.* London: Faber & Faber, 1952.

Southgate, Thomas Lea. "Music at the Pleasure Gardens of the Eighteenth Century." *Proceedings of the Royal Musical Association* 38 (1911-12): 143-60.

Spense, Lewis. *The Minor Traditions of British Mythology.* London: Rider, 1948.

Die Statuten der Universität Helmstedt 1685-1810. Ed. Peter Baumgart and Ernst Pitz. Göttingen: Vanderhoeck & Ruprecht, 1963.

Steglich, Rudolf. "Händels Opern," *Handbuch der Musikgeschichte.* Ed. Guido Adler. 2nd ed., 2 vols. Berlin/Wilmersdorf: H. Keller, 1930.

Streatfeild, Richard A. *Handel.* New York: John Lane, 1909.

————. "Handel, Rolli, and the Italian Opera in London in the Eighteenth Century." *Musical Quarterly* 3 (July 1917): 428-45.

Strohm, Reinhard. *Italienische Opernarien des frühen Settecento (1720-1730).* 2 vols. Cologne: Arno, 1976.

Taylor, George. "'The Just Delineation of the Passions': Theories of Acting in the Age of Garrick," in *Essays on the Eighteenth-Century Stage.* Ed. Kenneth Richards and Peter Thomson. London: Methuen, 1972.

Thompson, Stith. *Motif-Index of Folk-Literature.* Rev. and enl. ed. 6 vols. Bloomington: Indiana University Press, 1955-58.

Tosi, Pietro Francesco. *Observations on the Florid Song.* Trans. John Ernest Galliard. London: J. Wilcox, 1742.

Trevithick, Jack. "The Dramatic Work of Henry Carey." Ph.D. dissertation, Yale University, 1939.

Trowell, Brian. "Handel as a Man of the Theatre." *Proceedings of the Royal Musical Association* 88 (1961-62): 17-30.

Trussler, Simon, ed. *Burlesque Plays of the Eighteenth Century.* London: Oxford University Press, 1969.

Uffenbach, Zacharias Conrad von. *London in 1710.* Trans. and ed. W. H. Quarrell and Margaret Mare. London: Faber & Faber, 1934.

Victor, Benjamin. *The History of the Theatres of London and Dublin.* 3 vols. London: T. Davies, 1761.

Wakeley, Joseph Beaumont. *Anecdotes of the Wesleys.* New York: Carlton & Lanahan, 1869.

Walsh, T. J. *Opera in Dublin, 1705-1797: The Social Scene.* Dublin: Allen Figgis, 1973.

Weinstock, Herbert. *Handel.* New York: Alfred A. Knopf, 1946.

Wesley, Charles. *Representative Verse of Charles Wesley.* Selected and ed. Frank Baker. London: Epworth Press, 1912.

Wesley, John. *The Journal of the Rev. John Wesley.* Standard ed., ed. Nehemiah Curnock. 8 vols. London: Epworth Press, 1912.

————. *The Letters of the Rev. John Wesley.* Standard ed., ed. John Telfold. 8 vols. London: Epworth Press, 1931.

White, Eric Walter. *The Rise of English Opera.* New York: Philosophical Library, 1951.

Wilson, Albert Edward. *King Panto: The Story of Pantomime.* New York: E. P. Dutton, 1935.

Wolff, Hellmuth Christian. *Die Barockoper in Hamburg.* 2 vols. Wolfenbüttel: Möseler, 1957.

Wroth, Warwick, and Arthur Edgar Wroth. *The London Pleasure Gardens of the Eighteenth Century.* London: Macmillan, 1896.

Wyndham, Henry Saxe. *The Annals of Covent Garden Theatre.* 2 vols. London: Chatto & Windus, 1906.

York Ballad Operas and Yorkshiremen. Selected and arr. Walter H. Rubsamen. New York: Garland, 1974.

Young, Percy M. *Handel.* New York: E. P. Dutton, 1947.

————. *A History of British Music.* New York: W. W. Norton, 1967.

Zelm, Klaus. *Die Opern Reinhard Keisers: Studien zur Chronologie, Überlieferung und Stilentwicklung.* Musikwissenschaftliche Schriften, 8. Munich: E. Katzenbichler, 1975.

LAMPE'S BOOKS AND TREATISES, EXTANT OPERATIC MUSIC, AND SONG COLLECTIONS

Single songs and cantatas possibly sung in the theaters are omitted.

*Air by M*ʳ *Lampe in Pyramus and Thisbe,* "Fly swift good time". *GB* Lbm, Add. Ms. 31763, f. 30v. (Violin alone.)

The Art of Musick. London: C. Corbett, 1740.

British Melody; or, the Musical Magazine. Ed. John Frederick Lampe. London: Benjamin Cole, 1739. (Some copies with imprint J. Hodges & B. Cole, 1739.)

A Collection of All the Aires, Pastorells, Chacoons, Entre, Jiggs, Minuets, and Musette's in Columbine Courtezan. London: I. Walsh, [1734]. (Instrumental melody and continuo.)

A Collection of Hymns and Sacred Poems. Ed. John Frederick Lampe. Dublin, 1749. (Contains settings of Wesleyan hymns.)

The Comic Tunes in the Celebrated Entertainment, Call'd Orpheus and Euridice. London: I. Walsh, [1740?]. (Instrumental melody and continuo.)

The Dragon of Wantley. GB Lcm, Ms. 927. (A Ms. full score, including recitatives, lacking sections of some numbers.)

A Favourite Song in the Opera of Amelia [broadside caption-title], "Amelia wishes when she dies," [1732?]. (Violins, voice, and continuo).

From the Burlesque Opera the Dragon of Wantley, "But to hear the children mutter." *GB* Gu, Ms. Euing Coll., R.d.77⁵, ff. 13v-14r. (Voice only.)

The Grand Concerto, Favourite Song's, Dueto's, Trio & Chorus in the New Masque Call'd The Sham Conjuror. London: I. Simpson, [1741]. (Full score, lacking recitatives.)

Hymns on the Great Festivals, and Other Occasions. London: M. Cooper, 1746; 2nd ed., London: J. Cox, 1753. (Melody and figured bass; texts by Charles Wesley.)

De jure augustissimae et augustae domus Brunsvicensis in comitatum peinensem. Helmstedt: Hermann Daniel Hamm, 1720. (Lampe's Latin dissertation in law.)

The Ladies Amusement. Dublin: James Hoey, [1749]. (Includes music from *Theodosius.*)

Ladies don't fright ye. Song in Pyramus and Thisbe. US U, Musica de la theatro coll., Ms. 19. (Ms. instrumental partbooks of orchestral accompaniment.)

Lyra Britannia. London: John Simpson, [1740-45?]. (Includes one song from *Orpheus and Euridice.*)

Margery, or the Sequel to the Dragon of Wantley, in Score. 2 vols. London: J. Wilcox, 1739. (Full score, lacking recitatives; arias and duets in one volume, overture and choruses in the other.)

The Most Celebrated Aires in the Opera of Tom Thumb. London: Benjamin Cole, [1733]. (Voice and continuo; two songs may be by Arne.)

The Musical Entertainer. Ed. John Frederick Lampe. Engraved and selected by George Bickham. 2 vols. London: Charles Corbett, [1740]. Facsimile ed., New York: Broude Bros., 1965. (Includes arias from *The Dragon* and many single Lampe songs.)

Oh! ho! Master Moor. Song in the Dragon of Wantley. *US* U, Musica de la theatro coll., Ms. 20. (Ms. instrumental partbooks of orchestral accompaniment.)

[*The Overture, Choruses, and Trio of the Burlesque Opera, Call'd The Dragon of Wantley, in Score.* London: John Wilcox, 1738.] (Full score; all copies lack title-page, which has been reconstructed; apparently intended to be bound with the *Songs and Duetto's* volume below, as in *Margery,* above.)

The Parent Bird [from *Orpheus and Euridice*]. *GB* Lbm, Add. Ms. 37522, f. 26r. (Voice and continuo.)

Paternal Love [from *Orpheus and Euridice*], "The Parent Bird Whose Little Nest," in *The Universal Magazine* 1 (London, 1747), 184. (Voice and continuo; several other broadside editions exist.)

A Plain and Compendious Method of Teaching Thorough Bass. London: J. Wilcox, 1737. Facsimile ed., New York: Broude Bros., 1969.

Pyramus and Thisbe: A Mock-Opera. London: I. Walsh, [1745]. (Full score, lacking recitatives; some copies include an additional accompanied recitative.)

Set by Mr. Lampe from Shakespear[*e's Winter's Tale*] (broadside caption-title), "But shall I go mourn for that my dear," [1741-42?]. (Voice and continuo.)

A Song. But to hear the children mutter. *GB* Ouf, Ms. Mee e.1, f. 35r. (Voice only.)

A Song in Columbine Courtezan, "Who to win a woman's favour." *GB* Lbm, Add. Ms. 27932, f. 13r. (Voice and continuo.)

Song in Mr. Lampes Dragon of Wantley, "By the beer as brown as berry." *GB* Lbm, Add. Ms. 31763, f. 28r. (Violin only.)

A Song in Oroonoko [broadside caption-title], "Bright Cynthia's pow'r," [1749]. (Voice and continuo.)

A Song in Oroonoko [broadside caption-title], "A lass there lives upon the green," [1749]. (Voice and continuo.)

A Song in the New Tragedy of Fatal Falshood [broadside caption-title], "Whilst endless tears and sighs," [1734]. (Voice and continuo.)

A Song in the Opera of Amelia (broadside caption-title), "Ah traitress, wicked and impure," [1732?]. (Violins, voice, and continuo.)

The Songs and Duetto's in the Burlesque Opera, Call'd, The Dragon of Wantley. Adapted to the German Flute, Hautboy, or Violin, with Thorough Bass. London: John Wilcox, [1738]. (A solo instrument-continuo score.)

The Songs and Duetto's in the Burlesque Opera, Call'd The Dragon of Wantley, in Score. London: John Wilcox, 1738. (Full score; companion volume to the Overture/Choruses volume listed above.)

The Songs and Duetto's in the Burlesque Opera, Call'd The Dragon of Wantley, in Score. London: I. Walsh, [1746?]. (Re-issue of the above from the same plates, with a new title-page.)

Songs and Duetto's in the Burlesque Opera, Call'd Margery, Being a Sequel to The Dragon of Wantley. London: John Wilcox, 1739. (A single volume of the two-volume *Margery* full score listed above.)

The Songs, Duettos and Trio in the Burlesque Opera Call'd The Dragon of Wantley. London: John Cox, [1752]. (A posthumous continuo-vocal score, arranged by Lampe with the final editing done by Arne; some copies bear the imprint London: Wm. Smith.)

Songs in the Opera Britannia. *GB* Lbm, Add. Ms. 39816, ff. 1-45v. (A Ms. full score of some of the arias.)

Songs in the Opera Dione. *GB* Lbm, Add. Ms. 39816, ff. 46-79v. (A Ms. full score of some of the arias.)

Sung by Mr Salway in Columbine Courtezan [broadside caption-title], "Who to win a woman's favour," [1734?]. (Voice and continuo; at least three different prints exist.)

Wit Musically Embellished. London: Lampe, [1731]. (Lampe's earliest extant music.)

Zeno, Plato. A Song in y^e Dragon of Wantley. *GB* Lcm, Ms. 1064, ff. 31r-31v. (Voice and continuo.)

INDEX

DATE		